T0213746

Performance Analysis of Computer Networks

Matthew N.O. Sadiku • Sarhan M. Musa

Performance Analysis of Computer Networks

 Springer

Matthew N.O. Sadiku
Roy. G. Perry College of Engineering
Prairie View A&M University
Prairie View, TX, USA

Sarhan M. Musa
Roy. G. Perry College of Engineering
Prairie View A&M University
Prairie View, TX, USA

ISBN 978-3-319-37798-8   ISBN 978-3-319-01646-7 (eBook)
DOI 10.1007/978-3-319-01646-7
Springer Cham Heidelberg New York Dordrecht London

Printed on acid-free paper

Springer is part of Springer Science+Business Media (www.springer.com)

*To my late dad, Solomon, late mom, Ayisat,
and my wife, Kikelomo.*

*To my late father, Mahmoud,
mother, Fatmeh, and my wife, Lama.*

Preface

Modeling and performance analysis play an important role in the design of computer communication systems. Models are tools for designers to study a system before it is actually implemented. Performance evaluation of models of computer networks during the architecture design, development, and implementation stages provides means to assess critical issues and components. It gives the designer the freedom and flexibility to adjust various parameters of the network in the planning rather than in the operational phase.

The major goal of the book is to present a concise introduction to the performance evaluation of computer communication networks. The book begins by providing the necessary background in probability theory, random variables, and stochastic processes. It introduces queueing theory and simulation as the major tools analysts have at their disposal. It presents performance analysis on local, metropolitan, and wide area networks as well as on wireless networks. It concludes with a brief introduction to self-similarity.

The book is designed for a one-semester course for senior-year undergraduate and graduate engineering students. The prerequisite for taking the course is a background knowledge of probability theory and data communication in general. The book can be used in giving short seminars on performance evaluation. It may also serve as a fingertip reference for engineers developing communication networks, managers involved in systems planning, and researchers and instructors of computer communication networks.

We owe a debt of appreciation to Prairie View A&M University for providing the environment to develop our ideas. We would like to acknowledge the support of the departmental head, Dr. John O. Attia, and college dean, Dr. Kendall Harris. Special thanks are due to Dr. Sadiku's graduate student, Nana Ampah, for carefully going through the entire manuscript. (Nana has graduated now with his doctoral degree.) Dr. Sadiku would like to thank his daughter, Ann, for helping in many ways especially with the figures. Without the constant support and prayers of our families, this project would not have been possible.

Prairie View, TX, USA   Matthew N.O. Sadiku
Prairie View, TX, USA   Sarhan M. Musa

Contents

Chapter 1
Performance Measures

Education is a companion which no misfortune can depress,
no crime can destroy, no enemy can alienate, no despotism
can enslave...

—Joseph Addison

Modeling and performance analysis of computer networks play an important role in the design of computer communication networks. Models are tools for designers to study a system before it is actually implemented. Performance evaluation of models of computer networks gives the designer the freedom and flexibility to adjust various parameters of the network in the planning rather than the operational phase.

This book provides the basic performance analysis background necessary to analyze complex scenarios commonly encountered in today's computer network design. It covers the mathematical techniques and computer simulation—the two methods for investigating network traffic performance.

Two most often asked questions when assessing network performance are [1]:

1. What is the delay (or latency) for a packet to traverse the network?
2. What is the end-to-end throughput expected when transmitting a large data file across the network?

Network design engineers ought to be able to answer these questions.

In this chapter, we present a brief introduction into computer networks and the common measures used in evaluating their performance.

1.1 Computer Communication Networks

It is becoming apparent that the world is matching towards a digital revolution where communication networks mediate every aspect of life. Communication networks are becoming commonplace and are helping to change the face of

M.N.O. Sadiku and S.M. Musa, *Performance Analysis of Computer Networks*,
DOI 10.1007/978-3-319-01646-7_1, © Springer International Publishing Switzerland 2013

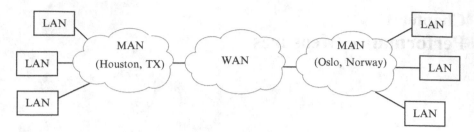

Fig. 1.1 Interconnection of LANs, MANs, and WANs

education, research, development, production, and business. Their advantages include: (1) the ease of communication between users, (2) being able to share expensive resources, (3) the convenient use of data that are located remotely, and (4) the increase in reliability that results from not being dependent on any single piece of computing hardware. The major objective of a communication network is to provide services to users connected to the network. The services may include information transport, signaling, and billing.

One may characterize computer communication networks according to their size as local area networks (LANs), metropolitan area networks (MANs), and wide area networks (WANs).

The local area networks (LANs) are often used to connect devices owned and operated by the same organization over relatively short distances, say 1 km. Examples include the Ethernet, token ring, and star networks.

The metropolitan area networks (MANs) are extensions of LANs over a city or metro area, within a radius of 1–50 km. A MAN is a high-speed network used to interconnect a number of LANs. Examples include fiber distributed data interface (FDDI), IEEE 803.6 or switched multisegment data service (SMDS), and Gigabit Ethernet.

The wide area networks (WANs) provide long-haul communication services to various points within a large geographical area e.g. North America, a continent. Examples of such networks include the Internet, frame relay, and broadband integrated services digital network (BISDN), and ATM.

The interconnection of these networks is shown in Fig. 1.1. These networks differ in geographic scope, type of organization using them, types of services provided, and transmission techniques. For example, the size of the network has implications for the underlying technology. Our goal in this book is to cover those techniques that are mainly used for analyzing these networks.

1.2   Techniques for Performance Analysis

Scientists or engineers only have three basic techniques at their disposal for performance evaluation of a network [2]: (1) measurement, (2) analytic modeling, and (3) simulation.

Measurement is the most fundamental approach. This may be done in hardware, software or in a hybrid manner. However, a measurement experiment could be rather involved, expensive and time-consuming.

Analytic modeling involves developing a mathematical model of the network at the desired level of detail and then solving it. As we will see later in this book, analytic modeling requires a high degree of ingenuity, skill, and effort and only a narrow range of practical problems can be investigated.

Simulation involves designing a model that resembles a real system in certain important aspects. It has the advantage of being general and flexible. Almost any behavior can be easily simulated. It is a cost-effective way of solving engineering problems.

Of the three methods, we focus on analytic modeling and simulation in this book.

1.3 Performance Measures

We will be examining the long run performance of systems. Therefore, we will regard the system to be in statistical equilibrium or steady state. This implies that the system has settled down and the probability of the system being in a particular state is not changing with time.

The performance measures of interest usually depend on the system under consideration. They are used to indicate the predicted performance under certain conditions. Here are some common performance measures [3]:

1. *Capacity*: This is a measure of the quantity of traffic with which the system can cope. Capacity is typically measured in Erlangs, bits/s or packets/s.
2. *Throughput*: This is a measure of how much traffic is successfully received at the intended destination. Hence, the maximum throughput is equivalent to the system capacity, assuming that the channel is error free. For LAN, for example, both channel capacity and throughput are measured in Mbps. In most cases, throughput is normalized.
3. *Delay*: This consists of the time required to transmit the traffic. Delay D is the sum of the service time S , the time W spent waiting to transmit all messages queued ahead of it, and the actual propagation delay T, i.e.

$$D = W + S + T \qquad (1.1)$$

4. *Loss Probability*: This is a measure of the chance that traffic is lost. A packet may be lost because the buffer is full, due to collision, etc. The value of the loss probability obtained depends on the traffic intensity and its distribution. For example, cell loss probability is used to assess an ATM network.
5. *Queue length*: This is a parameter used in some cases because there are waiting facilities in a communication network queue. This measure may be used to estimate the required length of a buffer.

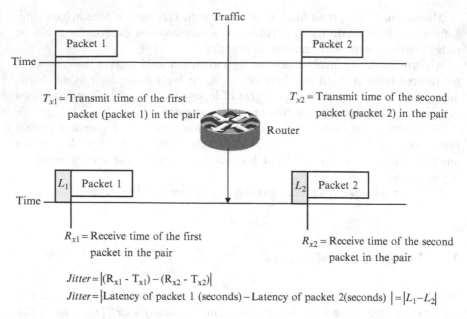

Fig. 1.2 Jitter calculations of two successive packets 1 and 2

6. *Jitter*: This is the measure of variation in packet delivery timing. In fact, it is the change in latency from packet to packet. Jitter reduces call quality in Internet telephony systems. Note that, when the jitter is low the network performance becomes better. There are three common methods of measuring jitter [4]:

1. inter-arrival time method,
2. capture and post-process method,
3. and the true real-time jitter measurement method.

Jitter can be defined as the absolute value of the difference between the forwarding delay of two consecutive received packets belonging to the same stream as in Fig. 1.2.

References

1. R. G. Cole and R. Ramaswamy, *Wide-Area Data Network Performance Engineering*. Boston, MA: Artech House, 2000, pp. 55–56.
2. K. Kant, *Introduction to Computer System Performance Evaluation*. New York: McGraw-Hill, 199, pp. 6–9.
3. G. N. Higginbottom, *Performance Evaluation of Communication Networks*. Boston, MA: Artech House, 1998, pp. 2–6.
4. http://www.spirent.com/

Chapter 2
Probability and Random Variables

Philosophy is a game with objectives and no rules.
Mathematics is a game with rules and no objectives.

—Anonymous

Most signals we deal with in practice are random (unpredictable or erratic) and not deterministic. Random signals are encountered in one form or another in every practical communication system. They occur in communication both as information-conveying signal and as unwanted noise signal.

A **random quantity** is one having values which are regulated in some probabilistic way.

Thus, our work with random quantities must begin with the theory of probability, which is the mathematical discipline that deals with the statistical characterization of random signals and random processes. Although the reader is expected to have had at least one course on probability theory and random variables, this chapter provides a cursory review of the basic concepts needed throughout this book. The concepts include probabilities, random variables, statistical averages or mean values, and probability models. A reader already versed in these concepts may skip this chapter.

2.1 Probability Fundamentals

A fundamental concept in the probability theory is the idea of an *experiment*. An experiment (or trial) is the performance of an operation that leads to results called *outcomes*. In other words, an outcome is a result of performing the experiment once. An *event* is one or more outcomes of an experiment. The relationship between outcomes and events is shown in the Venn diagram of Fig. 2.1.

M.N.O. Sadiku and S.M. Musa, *Performance Analysis of Computer Networks*,
DOI 10.1007/978-3-319-01646-7_2, © Springer International Publishing Switzerland 2013

Fig. 2.1 Sample space
illustrating the relationship
between outcomes (*points*)
and events (*circles*)

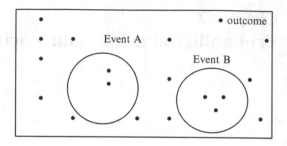

Thus,

> An **experiment** consists of making a measurement or observation.
> An **outcome** is a possible result of the experiment.
> An **event** is a collection of outcomes.

An experiment is said to be *random* if its outcome cannot be predicted. Thus a random experiment is one that can be repeated a number of times but yields unpredictable outcome at each trial. Examples of random experiments are tossing a coin, rolling a die, observing the number of cars arriving at a toll booth, and keeping track of the number of telephone calls at your home. If we consider the experiment of rolling a die and regard event A as the appearance of the number 4. That event may or may not occur for every experiment.

2.1.1 Simple Probability

We now define the probability of an event. The probability of event A is the number of ways event A can occur divided by the total number of possible outcomes. Suppose we perform n trials of an experiment and we observe that outcomes satisfying event A occur n_A times. We define the probability P(A) of event A occurring as

$$P(A) = \lim_{n \to \infty} \frac{n_A}{n} \tag{2.1}$$

This is known as the *relative frequency* of event A. Two key points should be noted from Eq. (2.1). First, we note that the probability P of an event is always a positive number and that

$$0 \le P \le 1 \tag{2.2}$$

where P = 0 when an event is not possible (never occurs) and P = 1 when the event is sure (always occurs). Second, observe that for the probability to have meaning, the number of trials n must be large.

Fig. 2.2 Mutually
exclusive or disjoint events

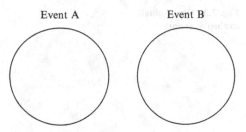

If events A and B are disjoint or mutually exclusive, it follows that the two events cannot occur simultaneously or that the two events have no outcomes in common, as shown in Fig. 2.2.

In this case, the probability that either event A or B occurs is equal to the sum of their probabilities, i.e.

$$P(A \text{ or } B) = P(A) + P(B) \tag{2.3}$$

To prove this, suppose in an experiments with n trials, event A occurs n_A times, while event B occurs n_B times. Then event A or event B occurs $n_A + n_B$ times and

$$P(A \text{ or } B) = \frac{n_A + n_B}{n} = \frac{n_A}{n} + \frac{n_B}{n} = P(A) + P(B) \tag{2.4}$$

This result can be extended to the case when all possible events in an experiment are A, B, C, ..., Z. If the experiment is performed n times and event A occurs n_A times, event B occurs n_B times, etc. Since some event must occur at each trial,

$$n_A + n_B + n_C + \cdots + n_Z = n$$

Dividing by n and assuming n is very large, we obtain

$$P(A) + P(B) + P(C) + \cdots + P(Z) = 1 \tag{2.5}$$

which indicates that the probabilities of mutually exclusive events must add up to unity. A special case of this is when two events are complimentary, i.e. if event A occurs, B must not occur and vice versa. In this case,

$$P(A) + P(B) = 1 \tag{2.6}$$

or

$$P(A) = 1 - P(B) \tag{2.7}$$

For example, in tossing a coin, the event of a head appearing is complementary to that of tail appearing. Since the probability of either event is ½, their probabilities add up to 1.

Fig. 2.3 Non-mutually
exclusive events

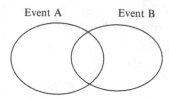

Event A   Event B

2.1.2 Joint Probability

Next, we consider when events A and B are not mutually exclusive. Two events are non-mutually exclusive if they have one or more outcomes in common, as illustrated in Fig. 2.3.

The probability of the union event A or B (or A + B) is

$$P(A + B) = P(A) + P(B) - P(AB)$$ (2.8)

where P(AB) is called the *joint probability* of events A and B, i.e. the probability of the intersection or joint event AB.

2.1.3 Conditional Probability

Sometimes we are confronted with a situation in which the outcome of one event depends on another event. The dependence of event B on event A is measured by the *conditional probability* P(B|A) given by

$$P(B|A) = \frac{P(AB)}{P(A)}$$ (2.9)

where P(AB) is the joint probability of events A and B. The notation B|A stands "B given A." In case events A and B are mutually exclusive, the joint probability P(AB) = 0 so that the conditional probability P(B|A) = 0. Similarly, the conditional probability of A given B is

$$\boxed{P(A|B) = \frac{P(AB)}{P(B)}}$$ (2.10)

From Eqs. (2.9) and (2.10), we obtain

$$P(AB) = P(B|A)P(A) = P(A|B)P(B)$$ (2.11)

Eliminating P(AB) gives

$$P(B|A) = \frac{P(B)P(A|B)}{P(A)} \tag{2.12}$$

which is a form of *Bayes' theorem*.

2.1.4 Statistical Independence

Lastly, suppose events A and B do not depend on each other. In this case, events A and B are said to be *statistically independent*. Since B has no influence of A or vice versa,

$$P(A|B) = P(A), \qquad P(B|A) = P(B) \tag{2.13}$$

From Eqs. (2.11) and (2.13), we obtain

$$P(AB) = P(A)P(B) \tag{2.14}$$

indicating that the joint probability of statistically independent events is the product of the individual event probabilities. This can be extended to three or more statistically independent events

$$P(ABC\dots) = P(A)P(B)P(C)\dots \tag{2.15}$$

Example 2.1 Three coins are tossed simultaneously. Find: (a) the probability of getting exactly two heads, (b) the probability of getting at least one tail.

Solution

If we denote HTH as a head on the first coin, a tail on the second coin, and a head on the third coin, the $2^3 = 8$ possible outcomes of tossing three coins simultaneously are the following:

$$HHH, HTH, HHT, HTT, THH, TTH, THT, TTT$$

The problem can be solved in several ways

Method 1: (Intuitive approach)

(a) Let event A correspond to having exactly two heads, then

$$\text{Event } A = \{HHT, HTH, THH\}$$

Since we have eight outcomes in total and three of them are in event A, then

$$P(A) = 3/8 = 0.375$$

Table 2.1 For Example 2.2; number of capacitors with given values and voltage ratings

	Voltage rating			
Capacitance	10 V	50 V	100 V	Total
4 pF	9	11	13	33
12 pF	12	16	8	36
20 pF	10	14	7	31
Total	31	41	28	100

(b) Let B denote having at least one tail,

$$\text{Event } B = \{HTH, HHT, HTT, THH, TTH, THT, TTT\}$$

Hence,

$$P(B) = 7/8 = 0.875$$

Method 2: (Analytic approach) Since the outcome of each separate coin is statistically independent, with head and tail equally likely,

$$P(H) = P(T) = \tfrac{1}{2}$$

(a) Event consists of mutually exclusive outcomes. Hence,

$$P(A) = P(HHT, HTH, THH) = \left(\frac{1}{2}\right)\left(\frac{1}{2}\right)\left(\frac{1}{2}\right) + \left(\frac{1}{2}\right)\left(\frac{1}{2}\right)\left(\frac{1}{2}\right) + \left(\frac{1}{2}\right)\left(\frac{1}{2}\right)\left(\frac{1}{2}\right)$$

$$= \frac{3}{8} = 0.375$$

(b) Similarly,

$$P(B) = (HTH, HHT, HTT, THH, TTH, THT, TTT)$$

$$= \left(\frac{1}{2}\right)\left(\frac{1}{2}\right)\left(\frac{1}{2}\right) + \text{in seven places} = \frac{7}{8} = 0.875$$

Example 2.2 In a lab, there are 100 capacitors of three values and three voltage ratings as shown in Table 2.1. Let event A be drawing 12 pF capacitor and event B be drawing a 50 V capacitor. Determine: (a) P(A) and P(B), (b) P(AB), (c) P(A|B), (d) P(B|A).

Solution

(a) From Table 2.1,

$$P(A) = P(12 \text{ pF}) = 36/100 = 0.36$$

and

$$P(B) = P(50 \text{ V}) = 41/100 = 0.41$$

(b) From the table,

$$P(AB) = P(12 \text{ pF}, 50 \text{ V}) = 16/100 = 0.16$$

(c) From the table

$$P(A|B) = P(12 \text{ pF}|50 \text{ V}) = 16/41 = 0.3902$$

Check: From Eq. (2.10),

$$P(A|B) = \frac{P(AB)}{P(B)} = \frac{16/100}{41/100} = 0.3902$$

(d) From the table,

$$P(B|A) = P(50 \text{ V}|12 \text{ pF}) = 16/36 = 0.4444$$

Check: From Eq. (2.9),

$$P(B|A) = \frac{P(AB)}{P(A)} = \frac{16/100}{36/100} = 0.4444$$

2.2 Random Variables

Random variables are used in probability theory for at least two reasons [1, 2]. First, the way we have defined probabilities earlier in terms of events is awkward. We cannot use that approach in describing sets of objects such as cars, apples, and houses. It is preferable to have numerical values for all outcomes. Second, mathematicians and communication engineers in particular deal with random processes that generate numerical outcomes. Such processes are handled using random variables.

The term "random variable" is a misnomer; a random variable is neither random nor a variable. Rather, it is a function or rule that produces numbers from the outcome of a random experiment. In other words, for every possible outcome of an experiment, a real number is assigned to the outcome. This outcome becomes the value of the random variable. We usually represent a random variable by an uppercase letters such as X, Y, and Z, while the value of a random variable (which is fixed) is represented by a lowercase letter such as x, y, and z. Thus, X is a function that maps elements of the sample space S to the real line $-\infty \leq x \leq \infty$, as illustrated in Fig. 2.4.

A **random variable** X is a single-valued real function that assigns a real value X(x) to every point x in the sample space.

Random variable X may be either discrete or continuous. X is said to be discrete random variable if it can take only discrete values. It is said to be continuous if it

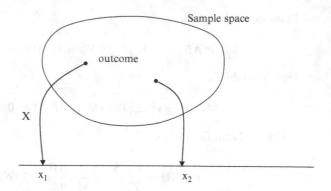

Fig. 2.4 Random variable
X maps elements of the
sample space to the real line

takes continuous values. An example of a discrete random variable is the outcome
of rolling a die. An example of continuous random variable is one that is Gaussian
distributed, to be discussed later.

2.2.1 Cumulative Distribution Function

Whether X is discrete or continuous, we need a probabilistic description of it in
order to work with it. All random variables (discrete and continuous) have a
cumulative distribution function (CDF).

> The **cumulative distribution function** (CDF) is a function given by the probability that the
> random variable X is less than or equal to x, for every value x.

Let us denote the probability of the event $X \leq x$, where x is given, as $P(X \leq x)$.
The *cumulative distribution function* (CDF) of X is given by

$$F_X(x) = P(X \leq x), \quad -\infty \leq x \leq \infty \tag{2.16}$$

for a continuous random variable X. Note that $F_X(x)$ does not depend on the random
variable X, but on the assigned value of X. $F_X(x)$ has the following five properties:

1. $$F_X(-\infty) = 0 \tag{2.17a}$$

2. $$F_X(\infty) = 1 \tag{2.17b}$$

3. $$0 \leq F_X(x) \leq 1 \tag{2.17c}$$

4. $$F_X(x_1) \leq F_X(x_2), \quad \text{if } x_1 < x_2 \tag{2.17d}$$

5. $$P(x_1 < X \leq x_2) = F_X(x_2) - F_X(x_1) \tag{2.17e}$$

The first and second properties show that the $F_X(-\infty)$ includes no possible
events and $F_X(\infty)$ includes all possible events. The third property follows from the
fact that $F_X(x)$ is a probability. The fourth property indicates that $F_X(x)$ is a
nondecreasing function. And the last property is easy to prove since

$$P(X \le x_2) = P(X \le x_1) + P(x_1 < X \le x_2)$$

or

$$P(x_1 < X \le x_2) = P(X \le x_2) - P(X \le x_1) = F_X(x_2) - F_X(x_1) \qquad (2.18)$$

If X is discrete, then

$$F_X(x) = \sum_{i=0}^{N} P(x_i) \qquad (2.19)$$

where $P(x_i) = P(X = x_i)$ is the probability of obtaining event x_i, and N is the largest integer such that $x_N \le x$ and $N \le M$, and M is the total number of points in the discrete distribution. It is assumed that $x_1 < x_2 < x_3 < \cdots < x_M$.

2.2.2   Probability Density Function

It is sometimes convenient to use the derivative of $F_X(x)$, which is given by

$$f_X(x) = \frac{dF_x(x)}{dx} \qquad (2.20a)$$

or

$$F_X(x) = \int_{-\infty}^{x} f_X(x) dx \qquad (2.20b)$$

where $f_X(x)$ is known as the *probability density function* (PDF). Note that $f_X(x)$ has the following properties:

1. $$f_X(x) \ge 0 \qquad (2.21a)$$

2. $$\int_{-\infty}^{\infty} f_X(x) dx = 1 \qquad (2.21b)$$

3. $$P(x_1 \le x \le x_2) = \int_{x_1}^{x_2} f_X(x) dx \qquad (2.21c)$$

Properties 1 and 2 follows from the fact that $F_X(-\infty) = 0$ and $F_X(\infty) = 1$

Fig. 2.5 A typical PDF

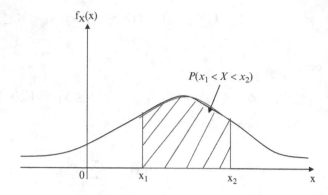

respectively. As mentioned earlier, since $F_X(x)$ must be nondecreasing, its derivative $f_X(x)$ must always be nonnegative, as stated by Property 1. Property 3 is easy to prove. From Eq. (2.18),

$$P(x_1 < X \le x_2) = F_X(x_2) - F_X(x_1)$$

$$= \int_{-\infty}^{x_2} f_X(x)dx - \int_{-\infty}^{x_1} f_X(x)dx = \int_{x_1}^{x_2} f_X(x)dx \qquad (2.22)$$

which is typically illustrated in Fig. 2.5 for a continuous random variable.

For discrete X,

$$f_X(x) = \sum_{i=1}^{M} P(x_i)\delta(x - x_i) \qquad (2.23)$$

where M is the total number of discrete events, $P(x_i) = P(x = x_i)$, and $\delta(x)$ is the impulse function. Thus,

The **probability density function** (PDF) of a continuous (or discrete) random variable is a function which can be integrated (or summed) to obtain the probability that the random variable takes a value in a given interval.

2.2.3 Joint Distribution

We have focused on cases when a single random variable is involved. Sometimes several random variables are required to describe the outcome of an experiment. Here we consider situations involving two random variables X and Y; this may be extended to any number of random variables. The *joint cumulative distribution function* (joint cdf) of X and Y is the function

$$F_{XY}(x, y) = P(X \le x, Y \le y) \qquad (2.24)$$

where $-\infty < x < \infty$, $-\infty < y < \infty$. If $F_{XY}(x,y)$ is continuous, the *joint probability density function* (joint PDF) of X and Y is given by

$$f_{XY}(x,y) = \frac{\partial^2 F_{XY}(x,y)}{\partial x \partial y} \qquad (2.25)$$

where $f_{XY}(x,y) \geq 0$. Just as we did for a single variable, the probability of event $x_1 < X \leq x_2$ and $y_1 < Y \leq y_2$ is

$$P(x_1 < X \leq x_2, y_1 < Y \leq y_2) = F_{XY}(x,y) = \int_{x_1}^{x_2}\int_{y_1}^{y_2} f_{XY}(x,y)dxdy \qquad (2.26)$$

From this, we obtain the case where the entire sample space is included as

$$F_{XY}(\infty,\infty) = \int_{-\infty}^{\infty}\int_{-\infty}^{\infty} f_{XY}(x,y)dxdy = 1 \qquad (2.27)$$

since the total probability must be unity.

Given the joint CDF of X and Y, we can obtain the individual CDFs of the random variables X and Y. For X,

$$F_X(x) = P(X \leq x, -\infty < Y < \infty) = F_{XY}(x,\infty) = \int_{-\infty}^{x}\int_{-\infty}^{\infty} f_{XY}(x,y)dxdy \qquad (2.28)$$

and for Y,

$$F_Y(y) = P(-\infty < x < \infty, y \leq Y) = F_{XY}(\infty,y)$$
$$= \int_{-\infty}^{\infty}\int_{-\infty}^{y} f_{XY}(x,y)dxdy \qquad (2.29)$$

$F_X(x)$ and $F_Y(y)$ are known as the *marginal cumulative distribution functions* (marginal CDFs).

Similarly, the individual PDFs of the random variables X and Y can be obtained from their joint PDF. For X,

$$f_X(x) = \frac{dF_X(x)}{dx} = \int_{-\infty}^{\infty} f_{XY}(x,y)dy \qquad (2.30)$$

and for Y,

$$f_Y(y) = \frac{dF_Y(y)}{dy} = \int_{-\infty}^{\infty} f_{XY}(x,y)dx \qquad (2.31)$$

$f_X(x)$ and $f_Y(y)$ are known as the *marginal probability density functions* (marginal PDFs).

As mentioned earlier, two random variables are independent if the values taken by one do not affect the other. As a result,

$$P(X \le x, Y \le y) = P(X \le x)P(Y \le y) \tag{2.32}$$

or

$$F_{XY}(x, y) = F_X(x)F_Y(y) \tag{2.33}$$

This condition is equivalent to

$$f_{XY}(x, y) = f_X(x)f_Y(y) \tag{2.34}$$

Thus, two random variables are independent when their joint distribution (or density) is the product of their individual marginal distributions (or densities).

Finally, we may extend the concept of conditional probabilities to the case of continuous random variables. The conditional probability density function (conditional PDF) of X given the event $Y = y$ is

$$f_X(x|Y = y) = \frac{f_{XY}(x, y)}{f_Y(y)} \tag{2.35}$$

where $f_Y(y)$ is the marginal PDF of Y. Note that $f_X(x|Y = y)$ is a function of x with y fixed. Similarly, the conditional PFD of Y given $X = x$ is

$$f_Y(y|X = x) = \frac{f_{XY}(x, y)}{f_X(x)} \tag{2.36}$$

where $f_X(x)$ is the marginal PDF of X. By combining Eqs. (2.34) and (2.36), we get

$$f_Y(y|X = x) = \frac{f_X(x|Y = y)f_Y(y)}{f_X(x)} \tag{2.37}$$

which is Bayes' theorem for continuous random variables. If X and Y are independent, combining Eqs. (2.34)–(2.36) gives

$$f_X(x|Y = y) = f_X(x) \tag{2.38a}$$

$$f_Y(y|X = x) = f_Y(y) \tag{2.38b}$$

indicating that one random variable has no effect on the other.

Example 2.3 An analog-to-digital converter is an eight-level quantizer with the output of 0, 1, 2, 3, 4, 5, 6, 7. Each level has the probability given by

$$P(X = x) = 1/8, \quad x = 0, 1, 2, \ldots 7$$

(a) Sketch $F_X(x)$ and $f_X(x)$. (b) Find $P(X \leq 1)$, $P(X > 3)$, (c) Determine $P(2 \leq X \leq 5)$.

Solution

(a) The random variable is discrete. Since the values of x are limited to $0 \leq x \leq 7$,

$$F_X(-1) = P(X < -1) = 0$$

$$F_X(0) = P(X \leq 0) = 1/8$$

$$F_X(1) = P(X \leq 1) = P(X = 0) + P(X = 1) = 2/8$$

$$F_X(2) = P(X \leq 2) = P(X = 0) + P(X = 1) + P(X = 2) = 3/8$$

Thus, in general

$$F_X(i) = \begin{cases} (i+1)/8, & 2 \leq i \leq 7 \\ 1, & i > 7 \end{cases} \tag{2.3.1}$$

The distribution function is sketched in Fig. 2.6a. Its derivative produces the PDF, which is given by

$$f_X(x) = \sum_{i=0}^{7} \delta(x - i)/8 \tag{2.3.2}$$

and sketched in Fig. 2.6b.

(b) We already found $P(X \leq 1)$ as

$$P(X \leq 1) = P(X = 0) + P(X = 1) = 1/4$$

$$P(X > 3) = 1 - P(X \leq 3) = 1 - F_X(3)$$

But

$$F_X(3) = P(X \leq 3) = P(X = 0) + P(X = 1) + P(X = 2) + P(X = 3) = 4/8$$

We can also obtain this from Eq. (2.3.1). Hence,

$$P(X > 3) = 1 - 4/8 = \frac{1}{2}.$$

(c) For $P(2 \leq X \leq 5)$, using Eq. (2.3.1)

$$P(2 \leq X \leq 5) = F_X(5) - F_X(2) = 5/8 - 2/8 = 3/8.$$

Fig. 2.6 For Example 2.3:
(a) distribution function
of X, (b) probability density
function of X

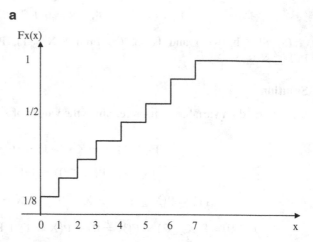

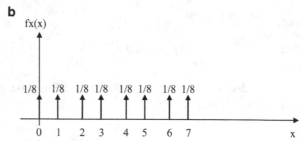

Example 2.4 The CDF of a random variable is given by

$$F_X(x) = \begin{cases} 0, & x < 1 \\ \dfrac{x-1}{8}, & 1 \le x < 9 \\ 1, & x \ge 9 \end{cases}$$

(a) Sketch $F_X(x)$ and $f_X(x)$. (b) Find $P(X \le 4)$ and $P(2 < X \le 7)$.

Solution

(a) In this case, X is a continuous random variable. $F_X(x)$ is sketched in Fig. 2.7a.
We obtain the PDF of X by taking the derivative of $F_X(x)$, i.e.

$$f_X(x) = \begin{cases} 0, & x < 1 \\ \dfrac{1}{8}, & 1 \le x < 9 \\ 0, & x \ge 9 \end{cases}$$

which is sketched in Fig. 2.7b. Notice that $f_X(x)$ satisfies the requirement of a
probability because the area under the curve in Fig. 2.7b is unity. A random
number having a PDF such as shown in Fig. 2.7b is said to be *uniformly
distributed* because $f_X(x)$ is constant within 1 and 9.

Fig. 2.7 For Example 2.4: (a) CDF, (b) PDF

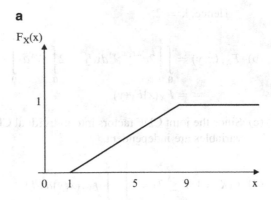

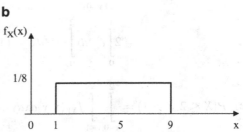

(b) $P(X \le 4) = F_X(4) = 3/8$

$P(2 < x \le 7) = F_X(7) - F_X(2) = 6/8 - 1/8 = 5/8$

Example 2.5 Given that two random variables have the joint PDF

$$f_{XY}(x,y) = \begin{cases} ke^{-(x+2y)}, & 0 \le x \le \infty, 0 \le y \le \infty \\ 0, & \text{otherwise} \end{cases}$$

(a) Evaluate k such that the PDF is a valid one. (b) Determine $F_{XY}(x,y)$. (c) Are X and Y independent random variables? (d) Find the probabilities that $X \le 1$ and $Y \le 2$. (e) Find the probability that $X \le 2$ and $Y > 1$.

Solution

(a) In order for the given PDF to be valid, Eq. (2.27) must be satisfied, i.e.

$$\int_{-\infty}^{\infty} \int_{-\infty}^{\infty} f_{XY}(x,y)dxdy = 1$$

so that

$$1 = \int_{0}^{\infty}\int_{0}^{\infty} ke^{-(x+2y)}dxdy = k\int_{0}^{\infty} e^{-x}dx \int_{0}^{\infty} e^{-2y}dy = k(1)\left(\frac{1}{2}\right)$$

Hence, k = 2.

(b) $F_{XY}(x, y) = \int\limits_0^x \int\limits_0^y 2e^{-(x+2y)} dx dy = 2\int\limits_0^x e^{-x} dx \int\limits_0^y e^{-2y} dy = (e^{-x} - 1)(e^{-2y} - 1)$

$\qquad = F_X(x)F_Y(y)$

(c) Since the joint CDF factors into individual CDFs, we conclude that the random variables are independent.

(d) $P(X \le 1, Y \le 2) = \int\limits_{x=0}^{1} \int\limits_{y=0}^{2} f_{XY}(x, y) dx dy$

$\qquad\qquad\qquad\quad = 2\int\limits_0^1 e^{-x} dx \int\limits_0^2 e^{-2y} dy = (1 - e^{-1})(1 - e^{-4}) = 0.6205$

(e) $P(X \le 2, Y > 1) = \int\limits_{x=0}^{2} \int\limits_{y=1}^{\infty} f_{XY}(x, y) dx dy$

$\qquad\qquad\qquad\quad = 2\int\limits_0^2 e^{-x} dx \int\limits_1^{\infty} e - 2y dy = (e^{-2} - 1)(e^{-2}) = 0.117$

2.3   Operations on Random Variables

There are several operations that can be performed on random variables. These include the expected value, moments, variance, covariance, correlation, and transformation of the random variables. The operations are very important in our study of computer communications systems. We will consider some of them in this section, while others will be covered in later sections. We begin with the mean or average values of a random variable.

2.3.1   Expectations and Moments

Let X be a discrete random variable which takes on M values $x_1, x_2, x_3, \cdots, x_M$ that respectively occur $n_1, n_2, n_3, \cdots, n_M$ in n trials, where n is very large. The statistical average (mean or expectation) of X is given by

$$\overline{X} = \frac{n_1 x_1 + n_2 x_2 + n_3 x_3 + \cdots + n_M x_M}{n} = \sum_{i=1}^{M} x_i \frac{n_i}{n} \qquad (2.39)$$

But by the relative-frequency definition of probability in Eq. (2.1), $n_i/n = P(x_i)$. Hence, the mean or expected value of the discrete random variable X is

$$\boxed{\overline{X} = E[X] = \sum_{i=0}^{\infty} x_i P(x_i)} \qquad (2.40)$$

where E stands for the expectation operator.

If X is a continuous random variable, we apply a similar argument. Rather than doing that, we can replace the summation in Eq. (2.40) with integration and obtain

$$\boxed{\overline{X} = E[X] = \int_{-\infty}^{\infty} x f_X(x) dx} \qquad (2.41)$$

where $f_X(x)$ is the PDF of X.

In addition to the expected value of X, we are also interested in the expected value of functions of X. In general, the expected value of a function g(X) of the random variable X is given by

$$\overline{g(X)} = E[g(X)] = \int_{-\infty}^{\infty} g(x) f_X(x) dx \qquad (2.42)$$

for continuous random variable X. If X is discrete, we replace the integration with summation and obtain

$$\overline{g(X)} = E[g(X)] = \sum_{i=1}^{M} g(x_i) P(x_i) \qquad (2.43)$$

Consider the special case when $g(x) = X^n$. Equation (2.42) becomes

$$\overline{X^n} = E[X^n] = \int_{-\infty}^{\infty} x^n f_X(x) dx \qquad (2.44)$$

$E(X^n)$ is known as the *nth moment* of the random variable X. When n = 1, we have the first moment $\overline{X}$ as in Eq. (2.42). When n = 2, we have the second moment $\overline{X^2}$ and so on.

2.3.2 Variance

The moments defined in Eq. (2.44) may be regarded as moments about the origin,
We may also define central moments, which are moments about the mean value
$m_X = E(X)$ of X. If X is a continuous random variable,

$$E[(X - m_X)^n\} = \int_{-\infty}^{\infty} (x - m_X)^n f_X(x) dx \qquad (2.45)$$

It is evident that the central moment is zero when n = 1. When n = 2, the
second central moment is known as the *variance* σ_X^2 of X, i.e.

$$\text{Var}(X) = \sigma_X^2 = E\left[(X - m_X)^2\} = \int_{-\infty}^{\infty} (x - m_X)^2 f_X(x) dx \qquad (2.46)$$

If X is discrete,

$$\text{Var}(X) = \sigma_X^2 = E\left[(X - m_x)^2\right] = \sum_{i=0}^{\infty} (x_i - m_X)^2 P(x_i) \qquad (2.47)$$

The square root of the variance (i.e. σ_X) is called the *standard deviation* of
X. By expansion,

$$\begin{aligned} \sigma_X^2 &= E\left[(X - m_X)^2\right] = E[X^2 - 2m_X X + m_X^2] = E[X^2] - 2m_X E[X] + m_X^2 \\ &= E[X^2] - m_X^2 \end{aligned} \qquad (2.48)$$

or

$$\boxed{\sigma_X^2 = E[X^2] - m_X^2} \qquad (2.49)$$

Note that from Eq. (2.48) that if the mean $m_X = 0$, the variance is equal to the
second moment $E[X^2]$.

2.3.3 Multivariate Expectations

We can extend what we have discussed so far for one random variable to two or
more random variables. If g(X,Y) is a function of random variables X and Y, its
expected value is

$$\overline{g(X,Y)} = E[g(X,Y)] = \int_{-\infty}^{\infty}\int_{-\infty}^{\infty} g(x,y) f_{XY}(x,y) dx\, dy \qquad (2.50)$$

Consider a special case in which g(X,Y) = X + Y, where X and Y need not be independent, then

$$\overline{X + Y} = \overline{X} + \overline{Y} = m_X + m_Y \tag{2.51}$$

indicating the mean of the sum of two random variables is equal to the sum of their individual means. This may be extended to any number of random variables.

Next, consider the case in which g(X,Y) = XY, then

$$\overline{XY} = E[XY] = \int_{-\infty}^{\infty} \int_{-\infty}^{\infty} xy f_{XY}(x) dx\, dy \tag{2.52}$$

If X and Y are independent,

$$\overline{XY} = \int_{-\infty}^{\infty} \int_{-\infty}^{\infty} xy f_X(x) f_Y(y) dx\, dy = \int_{-\infty}^{\infty} x f_X(x) dx \int_{-\infty}^{\infty} y f_Y(y) dy = m_X m_Y \tag{2.53}$$

implying that the mean of the product of two independent random variables is equal to the product of their individual means.

2.3.4 Covariance and Correlation

If we let $g(X,Y) = X^n Y^k$, the generalized moments are defined as

$$E[X^n Y^k] = \int_{-\infty}^{\infty} \int_{-\infty}^{\infty} x^n y^k f_{XY}(x) dx\, dy \tag{2.54}$$

We notice that Eq. (2.50) is a special case of Eq. (2.54). The joint moments in Eqs. (2.52) and (2.54) are about the origin. The generalized central moments are defined by

$$E\left[(X - m_X)^n (Y - m_Y)^k\right] = \int_{-\infty}^{\infty} \int_{-\infty}^{\infty} (x - m_X)^n (y - m_Y)^k f_{XY}(x) dx\, dy \tag{2.55}$$

The sum of n and k is the order of the moment. Of particular importance is the second central moment (when n = k = 1) and it is called *covariance* of X and Y, i.e.

$$\mathrm{Cov}(X, Y) = E[(X - m_X)(Y - m_Y)] = \int_{-\infty}^{\infty} \int_{-\infty}^{\infty} (x - m_X)(y - m_Y) f_{XY}(x) dx\, dy$$

or

Table 2.2 For Example 2.6

No. of failures	0	1	2	3	4	5
Probability	0.2	0.33	0.25	0.15	0.05	0.02

$$\boxed{\text{Cov}(X,Y) = E(XY) - m_X m_Y} \tag{2.56}$$

Their *correlation coefficient* ρ_{XY} is given by

$$\boxed{\rho_{XY} = \frac{\text{Cov}(X,Y)}{\sigma_X \sigma_Y}} \tag{2.57}$$

where $-1 \leq \rho_{XY} \leq 1$. Both covariance and correlation coefficient serve as measures of the interdependence of X and Y. $\rho_{XY} = 1$ when $Y = X$ and $\rho_{XY} = -1$ when $Y = -X$. Two random variables X and Y are said to be *uncorrelated* if

$$\text{Cov}(X,Y) = 0 \rightarrow E[XY] = E[X]E[Y] \tag{2.58}$$

and they are *orthogonal* if

$$E[XY] = 0 \tag{2.59}$$

If X and Y are independent, we can readily show that $\text{Cov}(X,Y) = 0 = \rho_{XY}$. This indicates that when two random variables are independent, they are also uncorrelated.

Example 2.6 A complex communication system is checked on regular basis. The number of failures of the system in a month of operation has the probability distribution given in Table 2.2. (a) Find the average number and variance of failures in a month. (b) If X denotes the number of failures, determine mean and variance of $Y = X + 1$.

Solution

(a) Using Eq. (2.40)

$$\overline{X} = m_X = \sum_{i=1}^{M} x_i P(x_i)$$
$$= 0(0.2) + 1(0.33) + 2(0.25) + 3(0.15) + 4(0.05) + 5(0.02)$$
$$= 1.58$$

To get the variance, we need the second moment.

$$\overline{X^2} = E(X^2) = \sum_{i=1}^{M} x_i^2 P(x_i)$$
$$= 0^2(0.2) + 1^2(0.33) + 2^2(0.25) + 3^2(0.15) + 4^2(0.05) + 5^2(0.02)$$
$$= 3.98$$

$$\text{Var}(X) = \sigma_X^2 = E[X^2] - m_X^2 = 3.98 - 1.58^2 = 1.4836$$

(b) If Y = X + 1, then

$$\overline{Y} = m_Y = \sum_{i=1}^{M}(x_i + 1)P(x_i)$$
$$= 1(0.2) + 2(0.33) + 3(0.25) + 4(0.15) + 5(0.05) + 6(0.02)$$
$$= 2.58$$

Similarly,

$$\overline{Y^2} = E(Y^2) = \sum_{i=1}^{M}(x_i + 1)^2 P(x_i)$$
$$= 1^2(0.2) + 2^2(0.33) + 3^2(0.25) + 4^2(0.15) + 5^2(0.05) + 6^2(0.02)$$
$$= 8.14$$

$$\text{Var}(Y) = \sigma_y^2 = E[Y^2] - m_Y^2 = 8.14 - 2.58^2 = 1.4836$$

which is the same as Var(X). This should be expected because adding a constant value of 1 to X does not change its randomness.

Example 2.7 Given a continuous random variable X with PDF

$$f_X(x) = 2e^{-2x}u(x)$$

(a) Determine E(X) and E(X^2). (b) Assuming that Y = 3X + 1, calculate E(Y) and Var(Y).

Solution

(a) Using Eq. (2.41),

$$E(X) = \int_{-\infty}^{\infty} x f_X(x)dx = \int_{0}^{\infty} x(2e^{-2x})dx$$
$$= 2\left[\frac{e^{-2x}}{4}(-2x - 1)\right]_{0}^{\infty} = \frac{1}{2}$$

$$E(X^2) = \int_{-\infty}^{\infty} x^2 f_X(x)dx = \int_{0}^{\infty} x^2(2e^{-2x})dx$$
$$= 2\left[\frac{e^{-2x}}{-8}(4x^2 + 4x + 2)\right]_{0}^{\infty} = \frac{1}{2}$$

$$\text{Var}(X) = E(X^2) - [E(X)]^2 = \frac{1}{2} - \frac{1}{4} = \frac{1}{4}$$

(b) Rather than carrying out a similar complex integration, we can use common sense or intuitive argument to obtain E(Y) and E(Y²). Since Y is linearly dependent on X and the mean value of 1 is 1,

$$E(Y) = E(3X + 1) = 3E(X) + E(1) = 3/2 + 1 = 5/2.$$

Since the 1 in Y = 3X + 1 is constant, it does not affect the Var(Y). And because a square factor is involved in the calculation of variance,

$$\mathrm{Var}(Y) = 3^2 \mathrm{Var}(X) = 9/4.$$

We would have got the same thing if we have carried the integration in Eq. (2.45). To be sure this is the case,

$$E(Y^2) = \int_{-\infty}^{\infty} (3x+1)^2 f_X(x)dx = \int_{-\infty}^{\infty} (9x^2 + 6x + 1)f_X(x)dx$$

$$= 9E(X^2) + 6E(X) + E(1) = \frac{9}{2} + \frac{6}{2} + 1 = \frac{17}{2}$$

$$\mathrm{Var}(Y) = E(Y^2) - E^2(Y) = \frac{17}{2} - \frac{25}{4} = \frac{9}{4}$$

confirming our intuitive approach.

Example 2.8 X and Y are two random variables with joint PDF given by

$$f_{XY}(x,y) = \begin{cases} x+y, & 0 \le x \le 1, 0 \le y \le 1 \\ 0, & \text{elsewhere} \end{cases}$$

(a) Find E(X + Y) and E(XY). (b) Compute Cov(X,Y) and ρ_{XY}. (c) Determine whether X and Y are uncorrelated and/or orthogonal.

Solution

(a)

$$\overline{X+Y} = E[X+Y] = \int_{-\infty}^{\infty}\int_{-\infty}^{\infty} (x+y)f_{XY}(x)dxdy = \int_0^1\int_0^1 (x+y)(x+y)dxdy$$

$$= \int_0^1\int_0^1 (x^2 + 2xy + y^2)dxdy = \int_0^1 \left[\frac{x^3}{3} + x^2 y + xy^2\right]_{x=0}^{x=1} dy = \int_0^1 \left(\frac{1}{3} + y + y^2\right)dy$$

$$= \left[\frac{1}{3}y + \frac{y^2}{2} + \frac{y^3}{3}\right]_0^1 = \frac{7}{6}$$

An indirect way of obtaining this result is using Eq. (2.51) but that will require that we first find the marginal PDFs $f_X(x)$ and $f_Y(y)$.

Similarly,

$$\overline{XY} = E[XY] = \int_{-\infty}^{\infty}\int_{-\infty}^{\infty} xy f_{XY}(x)dxdy = \int_0^1\int_0^1 xy(x+y)dxdy$$

$$= \int_0^1\int_0^1 (x^2y + xy^2)dxdy = \int_0^1 \left[\frac{x^3}{3}y + \frac{x^2}{2}y^2\right]_{x=0}^{x=1} dy = \int_0^1 \left(\frac{1}{3}y + \frac{1}{2}y^2\right) dy$$

$$= \left[\frac{y^2}{6} + \frac{y^3}{6}\right]_0^1 = \frac{1}{3}$$

(b) To find Cov(X,Y), we need the marginal PDFs.

$$f_X(x) = \int_{-\infty}^{\infty} f_{XY}(x,y)dy = \begin{cases} \int_0^1 (x+y)dy = \left[xy + \frac{y^2}{2}\right]_0^1 = x + \frac{1}{2} \\ 0, \quad \text{otherwise} \end{cases}$$

$$m_X = \int_0^1 x f_X(x)dx = \int_0^1 x\left(x + \frac{1}{2}\right)dx = \left[\frac{x^3}{3} + \frac{x^2}{4}\right]_0^1 = \frac{7}{12}$$

Due to the symmetry of the joint PDF, $m_Y = 7/12$.

$$E[X^2] = \int_0^1 x^2\left(x + \frac{1}{2}\right)dx = \left[\frac{x^4}{4} + \frac{x^6}{6}\right]_0^1 = \frac{5}{12}$$

$$\sigma_X^2 = E[X^2] - m_X^2 = \frac{5}{12} - \frac{49}{144} = \frac{11}{144}$$

$$\text{Cov}(X,Y) = E(XY) - m_X m_Y = \frac{1}{3} - \frac{49}{144} = -\frac{1}{144}$$

Similarly, $\sigma_Y^2 = \frac{11}{144}$. Thus,

$$\rho_{XY} = \frac{\text{Cov}(X,Y)}{\sigma_X \sigma_Y} = \frac{\frac{-1}{144}}{\frac{11}{144}} = -\frac{1}{11}$$

(c) Since $E[XY] = \frac{1}{3} \neq m_X m_Y$, X and Y are correlated. Also, since $E[XY] \neq 0$, they are not orthogonal.

2.4   Discrete Probability Models

Based on experience and usage, several probability distributions have been developed by engineers and scientists as models of physical phenomena. These distributions often arise in communication problems and deserve special attention. It is needless to say that each of these distributions satisfies the axioms of probability covered in Sect. 2.1. In this section, we discuss four discrete probability distributions; continuous probability distributions will be covered in the next section. In fact, some of these distributions have already been considered earlier in the chapter. In this and the next section, we will briefly consider their CDF, PDF, and their parameters such as mean and variance [3–5].

2.4.1   Bernoulli Distribution

A Bernoulli trial is an experiment that has two possible outcomes. Examples are tossing a coin with the two outcomes (heads and tails) and the output of half-wave rectifier which is 0 or 1. Let us denote the outcome of ith trial as 0 (failure) or 1 (success) and let X be a Bernoulli random variable with $P(X = 1) = p$ and $P(X = 0) = 1 - p$. Then the probability mass function (PMF) of X is given by

$$P(x) = \begin{cases} p, & x = 1 \\ 1 - p, & x = 0 \\ 0, & \text{otherwise} \end{cases} \qquad (2.60)$$

which is illustrated in Fig. 2.8.

The parameters of the Bernoulli distribution are easily obtained as

$$E[X] = p \qquad (2.61a)$$

$$E[X^2] = p \qquad (2.61b)$$

$$Var(X) = p(1 - p) \qquad (2.61c)$$

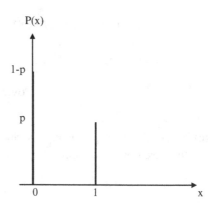

Fig. 2.8 Probability mass function of the Bernoulli distribution

Fig. 2.9 PDF for binomial distribution with n = 5 and p = 0.6

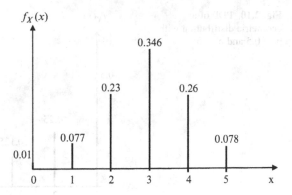

2.4.2 Binomial Distribution

This is an extension of Bernoulli distribution. A random variable follows a Binomial distribution when: (1) n Bernoulli trials are involved, (2) the n trials are independent of each other, and (3) the probabilities of the outcome remain constant as p for success and q = 1 − p for failure. The random variable X for Binomial distribution represents the number of successes in n Bernoulli trials.

In order to find the probability of k successes in n trials, we first define different ways of combining k out of n things, which is

$$^nC_k = \binom{n}{k} = \frac{n!}{k!(n-k)!} \tag{2.62}$$

Note that $\binom{n}{k} = \binom{n}{n-k}$. Hence, the probability of having k successes in n trials is

$$P(k) = \binom{n}{k} p^k (1-p)^{n-k} \tag{2.63}$$

since there are k successes each with probability p and n − k failures each with probability q = 1 − p and all the trials are independent of each other. If we let x = k, where k = 0, 1, 2, . . ., n, the PDF of the Binomial random variable X is

$$f_X(x) = \sum_{k=0}^{n} P(k)\delta(x-k) \tag{2.64}$$

which is illustrated in Fig. 2.9 for n = 5 and p = 0.6.

From $f_X(x)$, we can obtain the mean and variance for X as

$$E(X) = np \tag{2.65a}$$

$$\text{Var}(X) = npq = np(1-p) \tag{2.65b}$$

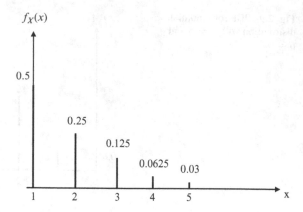

Fig. 2.10 PDF of a geometric distribution with p = 0.5 and n = 5

2.4.3 Geometric Distribution

The geometric distribution is related to Bernoulli trials. A geometric random variable represents the number of Bernoulli trials required to achieve the first success. Thus, a random variable X has a geometric distribution if it takes the values of 1, 2, 3, ... with probability

$$P(k) = pq^{k-1}, \quad k = 1, 2, 3, \ldots \tag{2.66}$$

where p = probability of success (0 < p < 1) and q = 1 − p = probability of failure. This forms a geometric sequence so that

$$\sum_{k=1}^{\infty} pq^{k-1} = \frac{p}{1-q} = 1 \tag{2.67}$$

Figure 2.10 shows the PDF of the geometric random variable for p = 0.5 and x = k = 1, 2, ... 5.

The mean and variance of the geometric distribution are

$$E(X) = \frac{1}{p} \tag{2.68a}$$

$$\mathrm{Var}(X) = \frac{q}{p^2} \tag{2.68b}$$

The geometric distribution is somehow related to binomial distribution. They are both based on independent Bernoulli trials with equal probability of success p. However, a geometric random variable is the number of trials required to achieve the first success, whereas a binomial random variable is the number of successes in n trials.

2.4.4 Poisson Distribution

The Poisson distribution is perhaps the most important discrete probability distribution in engineering. It can be obtained as a special case of Binomial distribution when n is very large and p is very small. Poisson distribution is commonly used in engineering to model problems such as queueing (birth-and-death process or waiting on line), radioactive experiments, the telephone calls received at an office, the emission of electrons from a cathode, and natural hazards (earthquakes, hurricanes, or tornados). A random variable X has a Poisson distribution with parameter λ if it takes the values 0, 1, 2, ... with

$$P(k) = \frac{\lambda^k}{k!} e^{-\lambda}, \quad k = 0, 1, 2, \cdots \qquad (2.69)$$

The corresponding PDF is

$$f_X(x) = \sum_{k=0}^{\infty} P(k)\delta(x - k) \qquad (2.70)$$

which is shown in Fig. 2.11 for $\lambda = 2$.

The mean and variance of X are

$$E[X] = \lambda \qquad (2.71a)$$

$$\mathrm{Var}(X) = \lambda \qquad (2.71b)$$

Note from Eq. (2.71a) that the parameter λ represents the average rate of occurrence of X. A summary of the properties of the four discrete probability distributions is provided in Table 2.3.

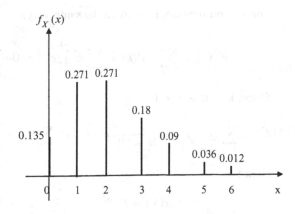

Fig. 2.11 PDF for Poisson distribution with $\lambda = 2$

Table 2.3 Properties of discrete probability distributions

Name	P(k)	PDF	Mean	Variance
Bernoulli	$P(x) = \begin{cases} p, & x = 1 \\ 1-p, & x = 0 \\ 0, & \text{otherwise} \end{cases}$	$f_X(x) = \sum_{k=0}^{1} P(k)\delta(x-k)$	p	p(1 − p)
Binomial	$P(k) = \binom{n}{k} p^k (1-p)^{n-k}$	$f_X(x) = \sum_{k=0}^{n} P(k)\delta(x-k)$	np	np(1 − p)
Geometric	$P(k) = pq^{k-1}$	$f_X(x) = \sum_{k=0}^{n} P(k)\delta(x-k)$	1/p	q/p^2
Poisson	$P(k) = \dfrac{\lambda^k}{k!} e^{-\lambda}$	$f_X(x) = \sum_{k=0}^{\infty} P(k)\delta(x-k)$	λ	λ

Example 2.9 Verify Eq. (2.71).

Solution

First, we notice that

$$\sum_{k=0}^{\infty} P(k) = \sum_{k=0}^{\infty} \frac{\lambda^k}{k!} e^{-\lambda} = e^{-\lambda} \sum_{k=0}^{\infty} \frac{\lambda^k}{k!} = e^{-\lambda}(e^{\lambda}) = 1$$

We obtain the mean value of X as

$$E[X] = \sum_{k=0}^{\infty} kP(k) = \sum_{k=0}^{\infty} k\frac{\lambda^k}{k!} e^{-\lambda} = 0 + \sum_{k=1}^{\infty} \frac{\lambda^{k-1}}{(k-1)!} \lambda e^{-\lambda}$$

If we let n = k − 1, we get

$$E[X] = \lambda e^{-\lambda} \sum_{n=0}^{\infty} \frac{\lambda^n}{n!} = \lambda e^{-\lambda}(e^{\lambda}) = \lambda$$

The second moment is handled the same way.

$$E[X^2] = \sum_{k=0}^{\infty} k^2 P(k) = \sum_{k=0}^{\infty} k^2 \frac{\lambda^k}{k!} e^{-\lambda} = 0 + \sum_{k=1}^{\infty} k\frac{\lambda^{k-1}}{(k-1)!} \lambda e^{-\lambda}$$

Since, k = k − 1 + 1

$$E[X^2] = \sum_{k=1}^{\infty} (k-1+1)\frac{\lambda^{k-1}}{(k-1)!} \lambda e^{-\lambda} = \lambda^2 e^{-\lambda} \sum_{k=1}^{\infty} \frac{\lambda^{k-2}}{(k-2)!} + \lambda e^{-\lambda} \sum_{k=1}^{\infty} \frac{\lambda^{k-1}}{(k-1)!} = \lambda^2 + \lambda$$

Hence

$$\text{Var}(X) = E[X^2] - E^2[X] = \lambda^2 + \lambda - \lambda^2 = \lambda$$

as expected.

2.5 Continuous Probability Models

In this section, we consider five continuous probability distributions: uniform, exponential, Erlang, hyperexponential, and Gaussian distributions [3–5].

2.5.1 Uniform Distribution

This distribution, also known as *rectangular distribution*, is very important for performing pseudo random number generation used in simulation. It is also useful for describing quantizing noise that is generated in pulse-code modulation. It is a distribution in which the density is constant. It models random events in which every value between a minimum and maximum value is equally likely. A random variable X has a uniform distribution if its PDF is given by

$$f_X(x) = \begin{cases} \dfrac{1}{b-a}, & a \leq x \leq b \\ 0, & \text{otherwise} \end{cases} \tag{2.72}$$

which is shown in Fig. 2.12.

The mean and variance are given by

$$E(X) = \frac{b+a}{2} \tag{2.73a}$$

$$\text{Var}(X) = \frac{(b-a)^2}{12} \tag{2.73b}$$

A special uniform distribution for which a = 0, b = 1, called the standard uniform distribution, is very useful in generating random samples from any probability distribution function. Also, if Y = Asin X, where X is a uniformly distributed random variable, the distribution of Y is said to be *sinusoidal distribution*.

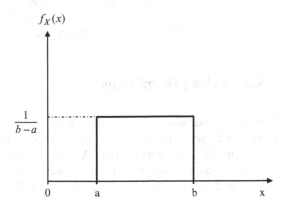

Fig. 2.12 PDF for a uniform random variable

Fig. 2.13 PDF for an
exponential random
variable

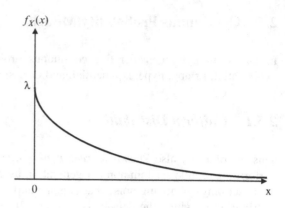

2.5.2 Exponential Distribution

This distribution, also known as *negative exponential distribution*, is important
because of its relationship to the Poisson distribution. It is frequently used in
simulation of queueing systems to describe the interarrival or interdeparture times
of customers at a server. Its frequent use is due to the lack of conditioning of
remaining time on past time expended. This peculiar characteristic is known
variably as Markov, *forgetfulness* or *lack of memory* property. For a given Poisson
process, the time interval X between occurrence of events has an exponential
distribution with the following PDF

$$f_X(x) = \lambda e^{-\lambda x} u(x) \tag{2.74}$$

which is portrayed in Fig. 2.13.

The mean and the variance of X are

$$E(X) = \frac{1}{\lambda} \tag{2.75a}$$

$$\mathrm{Var}(X) = \frac{1}{\lambda^2} \tag{2.75b}$$

2.5.3 Erlang Distribution

This is an extension of the exponential distribution. It is commonly used in
queueing theory to model an activity that occurs in phases, with each phase being
exponentially distributed. Let $X_1, X_2, \cdots, X_n$ be independent, identically
distributed random variables having exponential distribution with mean $1/\lambda$. Then
their sum $X = X_1 + X_2 + \cdots X_n$ has n-stage Erlang distribution. The PDF of X is

$$f_X(x) = \frac{\lambda^k x^{k-1}}{(n-1)!} e^{-\lambda x} \qquad (2.76)$$

with mean

$$E(X) = \frac{n}{\lambda} \qquad (2.77a)$$

and variance

$$\mathrm{Var}(X) = \frac{n}{\lambda^2} \qquad (2.77b)$$

2.5.4 Hyperexponential Distribution

This is another extension of the exponential distribution. Suppose X_1 and X_2 are two exponentially distributed random variables with means $1/\lambda_1$ and $1/\lambda_2$ respectively. If the random variable X assumes the value X_1 with probability p, and the value of X_2 with probability $q = 1 - p$, then the PFD of X is

$$f_X(x) = p\lambda_1 e^{-\lambda_1 x} + q\lambda_2 e^{-\lambda_2 x} \qquad (2.78)$$

This is known as a two-stage hyperexponential distribution. Its mean and variance are given by

$$E(X) = \frac{p}{\lambda_1} + \frac{q}{\lambda_2} \qquad (2.79)$$

$$\mathrm{Var}(X) = \frac{p(2-p)}{\lambda_1^2} + \frac{1-p^2}{\lambda_2^2} - \frac{2p(1-p)}{\lambda_1\lambda_2} \qquad (2.80)$$

2.5.5 Gaussian Distribution

This distribution, also known as *normal* distribution, is the most important probability distribution in engineering. It is used to describe phenomena with symmetric variations above and below the mean μ. A random variable X with Gaussian distribution has its PDF of the form

$$f_X(x) = \frac{1}{\sigma\sqrt{2\pi}} \exp\left[-\frac{1}{2}\left(\frac{x-\mu}{\sigma}\right)^2\right], \qquad -\infty < x < \infty \qquad (2.81)$$

where the mean

Fig. 2.14 PDF for an
Gaussian random variable

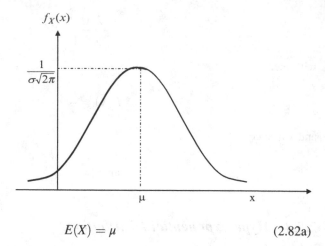

$$E(X) = \mu \qquad\qquad (2.82a)$$

and the variance

$$\mathrm{Var}(X) = \sigma^2 \qquad\qquad (2.82b)$$

are themselves incorporated in the PDF. Figure 2.14 shows the Gaussian PDF.

It is a common practice to use the notation $X \approx N(\mu, \sigma^2)$ to denote a normal random variable X with mean μ and variance σ^2. When $\mu = 0$ and $\sigma = 1$, we have $X = N(0,1)$, and the *normalized* or *standard normal* distribution function with

$$f_X(x) = \frac{1}{\sqrt{2\pi}} e^{-x^2/2} \qquad\qquad (2.83)$$

which is widely tabulated.

It is important that we note the following points about the normal distribution which make the distribution the most prominent in probability and statistics and also in communication.

1. The binomial probability function with parameters n and p is approximated by a Gaussian PDF with $\mu = np$ and $\sigma^2 = np(1 - p)$ for large n and finite p.
2. The Poisson probability function with parameter λ can be approximated by a normal distribution with $\mu = \sigma^2 = \lambda$ for large λ.
3. The normal distribution is useful in characterizing the uncertainty associated with the estimated values. In other words, it is used in performing statistical analysis on simulation output.
4. The justification for the use of normal distribution comes from the *central limit theorem*.

   The **central limit theorem** states that the distribution of the sum of n independent random variables from any distribution approaches a normal distribution as n becomes large.

(We will elaborate on the theorem a little later.) Thus the normal distribution is used to model the cumulative effect of many small disturbances each of which contributes to the stochastic variable X. It has the advantage of being mathematically tractable. Consequently, many statistical analysis such as those of regression and variance have been derived assuming a normal density function. In several communication applications, we assume that noise is Gaussian distributed in view of the central limit theorem because noise is due to the sum of several random parameters. A summary of the properties of the five continuous probability distributions is provided in Table 2.4.

Example 2.10 Let X be a Gaussian random variable. (a) Find E[X], E[X^2], and Var(X). (b) Calculate P(a < X < b).

Solution

(a) By definition,

$$E[X] = \int_{-\infty}^{\infty} x f_X(x)dx = \int_{-\infty}^{\infty} x \frac{1}{\sigma\sqrt{2\pi}} e^{-(x-\mu)^2/2\sigma^2} dx \tag{2.10.1}$$

Let y = (x − μ)/σ so that

$$E[X] = \frac{1}{\sqrt{2\pi}} \int_{-\infty}^{\infty} (\sigma y + \mu)e^{-y^2/2}dy = \frac{\sigma}{\sqrt{2\pi}} \int_{-\infty}^{\infty} ye^{-y^2/2}dy + \frac{\mu}{\sqrt{2\pi}} \int_{-\infty}^{\infty} e^{-y^2/2}dy$$

$$= 0 + \mu$$

$$\tag{2.10.2}$$

Notice the first integral on the right-hand side is zero since the integrand is an odd function and the second integral gives μ since it represents the PDF of a Gaussian random variable N(0,1). Hence,

$$E[X] = \mu \tag{2.10.3}$$

Similarly,

$$E[X^2] = \int_{-\infty}^{\infty} x^2 \frac{1}{\sigma\sqrt{2\pi}} e^{-(x-\mu)^2/2\sigma^2} dx$$

Again, we let y = (x − μ)/σ so that

$$E[X^2] = \frac{1}{\sqrt{2\pi}} \int_{-\infty}^{\infty} (\sigma y + \mu)^2 e^{-y^2/2}dy = \frac{1}{\sqrt{2\pi}} \int_{-\infty}^{\infty} \sigma^2 y^2 e^{-y^2/2}dy + \frac{1}{\sqrt{2\pi}} \int_{-\infty}^{\infty} 2\sigma\mu ye^{-y^2/2}dy$$

$$+ \frac{1}{\sqrt{2\pi}} \int_{-\infty}^{\infty} \mu^2 e^{-y^2/2}dy$$

$$\tag{2.10.4}$$

We can evaluate the first integral on the right-hand side by parts. The second integral is zero because the integrand is an odd function of y. The third integral yields μ^2 since it represents the PDF of a Gaussian random variable N(0,1). Thus,

Table 2.4 Properties of continuous probability distributions

Name	PDF	CDF	Mean	Variance
Uniform	$f_X(x) = \dfrac{1}{b-a}$	$F_X(x) = \dfrac{x-a}{b-a}$	$\dfrac{b+a}{2}$	$\dfrac{(b-a)^2}{12}$
Exponential	$f_X(x) = \lambda e^{-\lambda x} u(x)$	$F_X(x) = 1 - e^{-\lambda x}$	$\dfrac{1}{\lambda}$	$\dfrac{1}{\lambda^2}$
Erlang	$f_X(x) = \dfrac{\lambda^k x^{k-1}}{(n-1)!} e^{-\lambda x}$	$F_X(x) = 1 - e^{-\lambda x} \displaystyle\sum_{k=0}^{n-1} \dfrac{(\lambda x)^k}{k!}$	$\dfrac{n}{\lambda}$	$\dfrac{n}{\lambda^2}$
Hyperexponential	$f_X(x) = p\lambda_1 e^{-\lambda_1 x} + q\lambda_2 e^{-\lambda_2 x}$	$\dfrac{p}{\lambda_1} + \dfrac{q}{\lambda_2}$	$F_X(x) = p\left(1 - e^{-\lambda_1 t}\right) + q\left(1 - e^{-\lambda_2 t}\right)$	$\dfrac{p(2-p)}{\lambda_1^2} + \dfrac{1-p^2}{\lambda_2^2} - \dfrac{2p(1-p)}{\lambda_1 \lambda_2}$
Gaussian	$f_X(x) = \dfrac{1}{\sigma\sqrt{2\pi}} \exp\left[-\dfrac{1}{2}\left(\dfrac{x-\mu}{\sigma}\right)^2\right]$	$F_X(x) = \dfrac{1}{2}\left[1 + \mathrm{erf}\left(\dfrac{x-\mu}{\sigma\sqrt{2}}\right)\right]$	μ	σ^2

Where erf(.) is the error function to be discussed in Example 2.10.

$$E[X^2] = \frac{\sigma^2}{\sqrt{2\pi}} \left[y e^{-y^2/2} \Big|_{-\infty}^{\infty} + \int_{-\infty}^{\infty} e^{-y^2/2} dy \right] + 2\sigma\mu(0) + \mu^2 = \sigma^2 + \mu^2 \quad (2.10.5)$$

and

$$\text{Var}(X) = E[X^2] - E^2[X] = \sigma^2 + \mu^2 - \mu^2 = \sigma^2$$

We have established that for any real and finite number a and b, the following three integrals hold.

$$\int_{-\infty}^{\infty} \frac{1}{b\sqrt{2\pi}} \exp\left[-\frac{(x-a)^2}{2b^2} \right] dx = 1 \qquad (2.10.6a)$$

$$\int_{-\infty}^{\infty} \frac{x}{b\sqrt{2\pi}} \exp\left[-\frac{(x-a)^2}{2b^2} \right] dx = a \qquad (2.10.6b)$$

$$\int_{-\infty}^{\infty} \frac{x^2}{b\sqrt{2\pi}} \exp\left[-\frac{(x-a)^2}{2b^2} \right] dx = a^2 + b^2 \qquad (2.10.6c)$$

(b) To determine the Gaussian probability, we need the CDF of the Gaussian random variable X.

$$F_X(x) = \int_{-\infty}^{x} f_X(x) dx = \int_{-\infty}^{x} \frac{1}{\sigma\sqrt{2\pi}} e^{-(x-\mu)^2/2\sigma^2} dx$$

$$= \int_{-\infty}^{\infty} \frac{1}{\sigma\sqrt{2\pi}} e^{-(x-\mu)^2/2\sigma^2} dx - \int_{x}^{\infty} \frac{1}{\sigma\sqrt{2\pi}} e^{-(x-\mu)^2/2\sigma^2} dx$$

The value of the first integral is 1 since we are integrating the Gaussian PDF over its entire domain. For the second integral, we substitute

$$z = \frac{(x-\mu)}{\sigma\sqrt{2}}, \quad dz = \frac{dx}{\sigma\sqrt{2}}$$

and obtain

$$F_X(x) = 1 - \int_{x}^{\infty} \frac{1}{\sqrt{\pi}} e^{-z^2} dz \qquad (2.10.7)$$

We define *error function* as

$$\text{erf}(x) = \frac{2}{\sqrt{\pi}} \int_0^x e^{-t^2} dt \qquad (2.10.8)$$

and the complimentary error function as

$$erfc(x) = 1 - erf(x) = \frac{2}{\sqrt{\pi}} \int_x^\infty e^{-z^2} dz \qquad (2.10.9)$$

Hence, from Eqs. (2.10.7)–(2.10.9),

$$F_X(x) = \frac{1}{2}\left[1 + \text{erf}\left(\frac{x - \mu}{\sigma\sqrt{2}}\right)\right] \qquad (2.10.10)$$

and

$$P(a < x < b) = F_X(b) - F_X(a) = \frac{1}{2}\text{erf}\left(\frac{b - \mu}{\sigma\sqrt{2}}\right) - \frac{1}{2}\text{erf}\left(\frac{a - \mu}{\sigma\sqrt{2}}\right) \qquad (2.10.11)$$

Note that the definition of erf(x) varies from one book to another. Based on its definition in Eq. (2.10.8), some tabulated values are presented in Table 2.5. For example, given a Gaussian distribution with mean 0 and variance 2, we use the table to obtain

$$P(1 < x < 2) = \frac{1}{2}\text{erf}(1) - \frac{1}{2}\text{erf}(0.5) = 0.1611$$

2.6 Transformation of a Random Variable

It is sometimes required in system analysis that we obtain the PDF $f_Y(y)$ of the output random variable Y given that the PDF $f_X(x)$ for the input random variable X is known and the input-output transformation function

$$Y = g(X) \qquad (2.84)$$

is provided. If we assume that g(X) is continuous or piecewise continuous, then Y will be a random variable. Our goal is to get $f_Y(y)$. We begin with the distribution of Y.

$$F_Y(y) = P[Y \le y] = P[g(X) \le y] = P\left[X \le g^{-1}(y)\right] = F_X\left(g^{-1}(y)\right)$$

Hence

Table 2.5 Error function

x	erf(x)	x	erf(x)
0.00	0.00000	1.10	0.88021
0.05	0.05637	1.15	0.89612
0.10	0.11246	1.20	0.91031
0.15	0.16800	1.25	0.92290
0.20	0.22270	1.30	0.93401
0.25	0.27633	1.35	0.94376
0.30	0.32863	1.40	0.95229
0.35	0.37938	1.45	0.95970
0.40	0.42839	1.50	0.96611
0.45	0.47548	1.55	0.97162
0.50	0.52050	1.60	0.97635
0.55	0.56332	1.65	0.98038
0.60	0.60386	1.70	0.98379
0.65	0.64203	1.75	0.98667
0.70	0.67780	1.80	0.98909
0.75	0.71116	1.85	0.99111
0.80	0.74210	1.90	0.99279
0.85	0.77067	1.95	0.99418
0.90	0.79691	2.00	0.99532
0.95	0.82089	2.50	0.99959
1.00	0.84270	3.00	0.99998
1.05	0.86244	3.30	1.0

$$f_Y(y) = \frac{d}{dy} F_X\big(g^{-1}(y)\big) = \frac{d}{dx} F_X\big(g^{-1}(y)\big) \frac{dx}{dy}$$

or

$$f_Y(y) = \frac{f_X(x)}{\left|\dfrac{dy}{dx}\right|} \qquad (2.85)$$

where $x = g^{-1}(y)$. In case $Y = g(X)$ has a finite number of roots $X_1, X_2, \ldots, X_n$ such that

$$Y = g(X_1) = g(X_2) = \cdots = g(X_n)$$

then the PDF of y becomes

$$f_X(y) = \frac{f_X(x_1)}{\left|\dfrac{dy}{dx_1}\right|} + \frac{f_X(x_2)}{\left|\dfrac{dy}{dx_2}\right|} + \cdots + \frac{f_X(x_n)}{\left|\dfrac{dy}{dx_n}\right|} \qquad (2.86)$$

Once the PDF of Y is determined, we can find its mean and variance using the regular approach.

Example 2.11 Suppose that X is a Gaussian random variable with mean 3 and variance 4 and $Y = 3X - 1$. Find the PDF of Y and its mean and variance.

Solution

With $\mu = 3$ and $\sigma^2 = 4$, the PDF of X is obtained using Eq. (2.81) as

$$f_X(x) = \frac{1}{2\sqrt{2\pi}} \exp\left[-\frac{1}{2}\left(\frac{x-3}{2}\right)^2\right]$$

Since $Y = g(X) = 3X - 1$, $X = (Y + 1)/3$ and

$$\frac{dy}{dx} = 3$$

Hence,

$$f_Y(y) = \frac{f_X(x)}{3} = \frac{1}{3}f_X\left(\frac{y+1}{3}\right) = \frac{1}{6\sqrt{2\pi}}\exp\left[-\frac{1}{2}\left(\frac{\frac{y+1}{3}-3}{2}\right)^2\right]$$

or

$$f_Y(y) = \frac{1}{6\sqrt{2\pi}}\exp\left[-\frac{1}{2}\left(\frac{y-8}{6}\right)^2\right]$$

Comparing this with Eq. (2.81) indicates that Y has a Gaussian distribution with mean 8 and variance $6^2 = 36$. We can easily check this.

$$E[Y] = E[3X - 1] = 3E[X] - 1 = 3 \times 3 - 1 = 8$$

$$Var(Y) = 3^2 Var(X) = 9 \times 4 = 36.$$

2.7   Generating Functions

It is sometimes more convenient to work with generating functions. A probability generating function, often called the *z-transform*, is a tool for manipulating infinite series. Generating functions are important for at least two reasons. First, they may have a closed form. Second, they may be used to generate probability distribution and the moments of the distributions.

If $p_0, p_1, p_2, \cdots$ form a probability distribution, the probability generating function is

$$G(z) = E[z^i] = \sum_{i=0}^{\infty} z^i p_i \tag{2.87}$$

Notice that $G(1) = 1$ since the probabilities must sum up to 1. The generating function $G(z)$ contains all the information that the individual probabilities have. We can find the individual probabilities from $G(z)$ by repeated differentiation as

$$p_n = \frac{1}{n!} \frac{d^n G(z)}{dz^n}\Big|_{z=0} \tag{2.88}$$

The moments of the random variable can be obtained from $G(z)$. For example, for the first moment,

$$E[X] = \sum_{i=0}^{\infty} i p_i = \sum_{i=0}^{\infty} i p_i z^{i-1}\Big|_{z=1} = \frac{d}{dz} \sum_{i=0}^{\infty} p_i z^i\Big|_{z=1} = G'(1) \tag{2.89}$$

For the second moment,

$$\begin{aligned}
E[X^2] &= \sum_{i=0}^{\infty} i^2 p_i = \sum_{i=0}^{\infty} i(i-1)p_i + \sum_{i=0}^{\infty} i p_i \\
&= \sum_{i=0}^{\infty} i(i-1)p_i z^{i-2}\Big|_{z=1} + \sum_{i=0}^{\infty} i p_i z^{i-1}\Big|_{z=1} \\
&= G''(1) + G'(1)
\end{aligned} \tag{2.90}$$

Example 2.12 Find the generating function for geometric distribution.

Solution

For geometric distribution, $q = 1 - p$ and $p_i = pq^{i-1}$. Hence,

$$G(z) = \sum_{i=1}^{\infty} pq^{i-1} z^i = pz \sum_{i=1}^{\infty} (qz)^{i-1} = \frac{pz}{1 - qz}$$

For $n \geq 1$,

$$\frac{d^n G(z)}{dz^n} = \frac{n! pq^{n-1}}{(1 - qz)^{n+1}}$$

Thus,

$$E[X] = G'(1) = \frac{p}{(1-q)^2} = \frac{1}{p}$$

and

$$E[X^2] = G'(1) + G''(1) = \frac{1}{p} + \frac{2q}{p^2} = \frac{1+q}{p^2}$$

so that variance is

$$\text{Var}(X) = E[X^2] - E^2[X] = \frac{q}{p^2}$$

2.8 Central Limit Theorem

This is a fundamental result in probability theory. The theorem explains why many random variables encountered in nature have distributions close to the Gaussian distribution. To derive the theorem, consider the binomial function

$$B(M) = \frac{N!}{M!(N-M)!} p^M q^{N-M} \tag{2.91}$$

which is the probability of M successes in N independent trials. If M and $N - M$ are large, we may use Stirling's formula

$$n! \cong n^n e^{-n} \sqrt{2n\pi} \tag{2.92}$$

Hence,

$$B(M) = f(x) = \frac{1}{\sigma\sqrt{2\pi}} \exp\left[-\frac{(x-\mu)^2}{2\sigma^2}\right] \tag{2.93}$$

which is a normal distribution, $\mu = Np$ and $\sigma = \sqrt{Npq}$. Thus, as $N \to \infty$, the sum of a large number of random variables tends to be normally distributed. This is known as the *central limit theorem*.

> The **central limit theorem** states that the PDF of the sum of a large number of individual random variables approaches a Gaussian (normal) distribution regardless of whether or not the distribution of the individual variables are normal.

Although the derivation above is based on binomial distribution, the central limit theorem is true for all distributions. A simple consequence of the theorem is that any random variable which is the sum of n independent identical random variables approximates a normal random variable as n becomes large.

Fig. 2.15 (a) PDF of
uniform random variable X,
(b) PDF of $Y = X_1 + X_2$,
(c) PDF of
$Z = X_1 + X_2 + X_3$

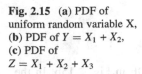
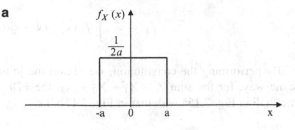
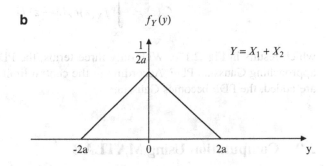
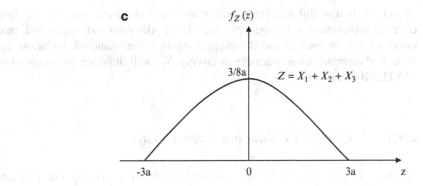

Example 2.13 This example illustrates the central limit theorem. If $X_1, X_2, X_3, \ldots X_n$ are n dependent random variables and $c_1, c_2, c_3, \ldots, c_n$ are constants, then

$$X = c_1X_1 + c_2X_2 + c_3X_3 + \ldots + c_nX_n$$

is a Gaussian random variable as n becomes large.

Solution

To make things simple, let use assume that $X_1, X_2, X_3, \ldots X_n$ are identical uniform variable with one of them as shown in Fig. 2.15a. For the sum $Y = X_1 + X_2$, the PDF of y is a convolution of the PDF in Fig. 2.15a with itself, i.e.

$$f_Y(y) = \int\limits_{-\infty}^{\infty} f_X(x) f_X(y-x) dx$$

By performing the convolution, we obtain the joint PDF in Fig. 2.15b. In the same way, for the sum $Z = X_1 + X_2 + X_3$, the PDF of Z is the convolution of the PDF in Fig. 2.15a with that in Fig. 2.15b, i.e.

$$f_Z(z) = \int\limits_{-\infty}^{\infty} f_X(\lambda) f_Y(\lambda - z) d\lambda$$

which results in Fig. 2.15c. With only three terms, the PDF of the sum is already approaching Gaussian PDF. According to the central limit theorem, as more terms are added, the PDF becomes Gaussian.

2.9   Computation Using MATLAB

MATLAB is a useful tool for handling and demonstrating some of the concepts covered in this chapter. For example, the MATLAB commands **mean**, **std**, **cov**, and **corrcoef** can be used to find the average/mean value, standard deviation, covariance, and correlation coefficient respectively. We will illustrate with examples how MATLAB can be used.

2.9.1   Performing a Random Experiment

Suppose we want to carry out the random experiment of tossing a die, we can use the MATLAB command **unidrnd** to generate as many trials as possible, with each trial yield randomly 1, 2, . . .6.

We use this command to generate a 12 × 12 matrix with numbers that are uniformly distributed between 1 and 6 as follows.

```
>> x = unidrnd(6,12,12)
x =
    5    3    5    4    6    3    5    6    4    3    1    5
    3    4    1    2    5    3    4    5    1    3    4    1
    1    2    6    6    5    6    5    3    2    2    5    3
    4    4    6    3    5    4    1    4    4    3    2    4
    3    1    4    5    5    2    3    6    2    2    2    5
    1    4    2    1    2    3    3    4    4    3    5    4
    4    5    6    3    2    4    1    2    2    4    5    3
```

```
        5   6   4   3   4   1   5   3   4   5   6   3
        5   5   5   3   4   5   6   2   4   2   3   1
        6   5   3   4   1   6   3   3   3   1   6   3
        6   3   6   4   1   4   6   3   4   3   3   3
        1   4   1   1   2   1   1   3   6   3   5   2
>> x1 = mean(x)
x1 =
  Columns 1 through 10
    3.6667   3.8333   4.0833   3.2500   3.5000   3.5000   3.5833
3.6667   3.3333   2.8333
  Columns 11 through 12
    3.9167   3.0833
>> x2 = mean(x1)
x2 =
    3.5208
>> y1 = std(x)
y1 =
  Columns 1 through 10
    1.8749   1.4035   1.9287   1.4848   1.7838   1.6787   1.8809
1.3707   1.3707   1.0299
  Columns 11 through 12
    1.6765   1.3114
>> y2 = std(y1)
y2 =
    0.2796
```

From 144 outcomes above, we tabulate the results as shown in Table 2.6. We expect $P(x_i) = 1/6 = 0.1667$ for all $i = 1, 2, \ldots 6$ but it is not quite so because the number of trials is not large enough. We have chosen 144 to make the result manageable. If higher number of trials is selected, the results would be more accurate. We also find the mean value to be 3.5208 instead of 3.5 and the standard deviation to be 0.2796.

2.9.2 Plotting PDF

MATLAB can also be used in plotting the cumulative distribution functions (CDF) or probability density function (PDF) of a random variable. The MATLAB commands for the CDF and PDF for various types of random variables we considered in Sects. 2.4 and 2.5 are provided in Table 2.7. One may use the **help** command to get assistance on how to use any of these commands.

For example, we will use MATLAB code to plot PDF or $P(x)$ for Binomial distribution for cases (1) $p = 0.6$, $n = 20$, (2) $p = 0.6$, $n = 100$ by using the command **binopdf**. The MATLAB commands are:

Table 2.6 Outcomes of the experiment of tossing a die

Number (i)	1	2	3	4	5	6
No. of occurrence	20	18	34	29	25	18
$P(x_i)$	0.1389	0.1250	0.2361	0.2014	0.1736	0.1250

Table 2.7 MATLAB commands for commom CDFs and PDFs

Name	CDF	PDF
Binomial	**binocdf**	**binopdf**
Poisson	**poisscdf**	**poisspdf**
Geometric	**geocdf**	**geopdf**
Uniform (discrete)	**unidcdf**	**unidpdf**
Uniform (continuous)	**unifcdf**	**unifpdf**
Exponential	**expcdf**	**exppdf**
Gaussian (Normal)	**normcdf**	**normpdf**
Rayleigh	**raylcdf**	**raylpdf**

```
>> n = 20; % later change n to 100
>> p = 0.6;
>> x = 1:n;
>> y = binopdf(x,n,p);
>> stem(x,y); %plots the discrete distribution
```

The two cases are shown in Fig. 2.16. Notice that as n increases, the distribution approaches Gaussian distribution, as expected.

MATLAB can also be used to plot the CDF or PDF when there is no MATLAB command. For example, suppose we are given a joint PDF for random variables X and Y as

$$f_{XY}(x, y) = \frac{1}{2\pi} \exp\left[-\left(x^2 + y^2\right)/2\right], \quad -\infty < x < \infty, \quad -\infty < y < \infty \quad (2.94)$$

Since the computer cannot possibly cover the entire domain of the PDF, we may restrict x and y to $[-4,4]$. The following MATLAB code can be used to plot the PDF in Eq. (2.94) as shown in Fig. 2.17.

```
[x,y] = meshgrid(-4:0.2:4,-4:0.2:4); % defines grid
f = exp(-(x.^2 + y.^2)/2)/(2*pi); % pdf to be plotted
surf(x,y,f) % creates 3-D plot
xlabel('x'); ylabel('y'); zlabel('pdf');
```

2.9.3 Gaussian Function

As mentioned earlier, the Gaussian distribution is the most important PDF in communications. We can use MATLAB commands **normpdf** and **normcdf** to

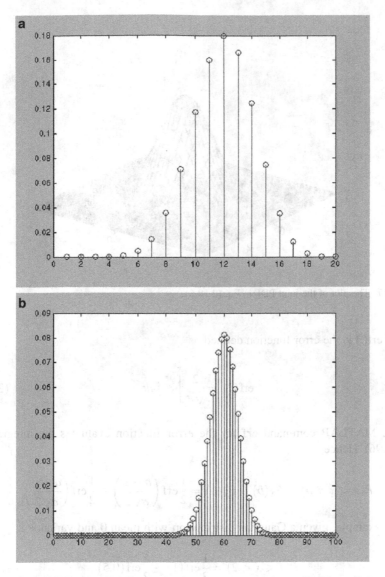

Fig. 2.16   Plot PDF for Binomial distribution for cases (**a**) p = 0.6, n = 20, (**b**) p = 0.6, n = 100

plot the PDF and CDF of the Gaussian distribution. In Sect. 2.5, we defined CDF of the Gaussian random variable X as

$$F_X(x) = \frac{1}{2} + \frac{1}{2}\mathrm{erf}\left(\frac{x-\mu}{\sigma\sqrt{2}}\right) \qquad (2.95)$$

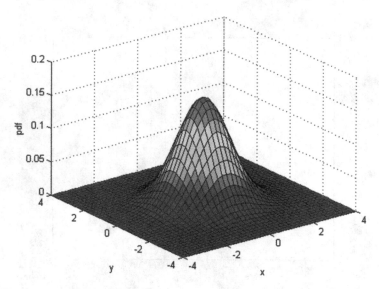

Fig. 2.17 The plot of the joint PDF in Eq. (2.10.5)

where erf(.) is the error function defined as

$$\mathrm{erf}(x) = \frac{2}{\sqrt{\pi}} \int\limits_0^x e^{-t^2} dt \tag{2.96}$$

The MATLAB command **erf** for the error function evaluates the integral in Eq. (2.96). Hence

$$P(a < x < b) = F_X(b) - F_X(a) = \frac{1}{2}\mathrm{erf}\left(\frac{b-\mu}{\sigma\sqrt{2}}\right) - \frac{1}{2}\mathrm{erf}\left(\frac{a-\mu}{\sigma\sqrt{2}}\right)$$

For example, given a Gaussian distribution with mean 0 and variance 2

$$P(1 < x < 2) = \frac{1}{2}\mathrm{erf}(1) - \frac{1}{2}\mathrm{erf}(0.5)$$

Rather than using Table 2.5 to figure this out, we can use MATLAB.

```
> > P = 0.5*(erf(1) - erf(0.5))
P =
0.1611
```

i.e. P(1 < x < 2) = 0.1611, in agreement with what we got in Example 2.10. MATLAB becomes indispensable when the value of erf(x) is not tabulated.

2.10 Summary

1. The probability of an event is the measure of how likely the event will occur as a result of a random experiment. A random experiment is one in which all the outcomes solely depend on *chance*, i.e., each outcome is equally likely to happen.
2. The relative-frequency definition of the probability of an event A assumes that if an experiment is repeated for a large number of times n and event A occurs n_A times,

$$P(A) = \frac{n_A}{n}$$

3. A random variable is a real-value function defined over a sample space. A discrete random variable is one which may take on only a countable number of distinct values such as 0, 1, 2, 3, ...

   A continuous random variable is one which takes an infinite number of possible values.
4. The cumulative distribution function (CDF) $F_X(x)$ of a random variable X is defined as the probability $P(X \leq x)$ and $F_X(x)$ lies between 0 and 1.
5. The probability density function (PDF) $f_X(x)$ of a random variable X is the derivative of the CDF $F_X(x)$, i.e.

$$f_X(x) = \frac{dF_X(x)}{dx} \longleftrightarrow F_X(x) = \int_{-\infty}^{x} f_X(x)dx$$

   Note that $f_X(x)dx$ is the probability of a random variable X lying within dx of x.
6. The joint CDF $F_{XY}(x,y)$ of two random variables X and Y is the probability $P(X \leq x, Y \leq y)$, while the joint PDF $f_{XY}(x,y)$ is the second partial derivative of the joint CDF with respect to x and y. The PDF of X alone (the marginal PDF) is obtained by integrating the joint PDF $f_{XY}(x,y)$ over all y. The joint CDF or PDF of two independent random variables are factors.
7. The mean value of a random variable X is

$$E(X) = \int_{-\infty}^{\infty} xf_X(x)dx \text{ if X is continuous}$$

   or

$$E(X) = \sum_{i=1}^{M} x_i P(x_i) \text{ if X is discrete}$$

8. The variance of random variable X is

$$\mathrm{Var(x)} = \sigma_X^2 = E\left[X^2\right] - E^2(X)$$

where σ_X is the standard deviation of the random variable; σ_X is a measure of the width of its PDF.

9. Table 2.3 summarizes the P(k), PDF, mean, and variance of common discrete probability distributions: Bernoulli, binomial, geometric, and Poisson.

10. Table 2.4 summarizes the CDF, PDF, mean, and variance of common continuous probability distributions: uniform, exponential, Erlang, hyperexponential, and Gaussian.

11. The central limit theorem is the usual justification for using the Gaussian distribution for modeling. It states that the sum of independent samples from any distribution approaches the Gaussian distribution as the sample size becomes large.

12. MATLAB can be used to plot or generate CDF and PDF, perform random experiments, and determine mean and standard deviation of a given random variable.

For more information on the material covered in this chapter, see [6, 7].

Problems

2.1 An experiment consists of throwing two dice simultaneously. (a) Calculate the probability of having a 2 and a 5 appearing together. (b) What is the probability of the sum being 8.

2.2 A circle is split into ten equal sectors which are numbered 1–10. When the circle is rotated about its center, a pointer indicates where it stops (like a wheel of fortune). Determine the probability: (a) of stopping at number 8, (b) of stopping at an odd number, (c) of stopping at numbers 1, 4, or 6, (d) of stopping at a number greater than 4.

2.3 A jar initially contains four white marbles, three green marbles, and two red marbles. Two marbles are drawn randomly one after the other without replacement. (a) Find the probability that the two marbles are red. (b) Calculate the probability that the two marbles have marching colors.

2.4 The telephone numbers are selected randomly from a telephone directory and the first digit (k) is observed. The result of the observation for 100 telephone numbers is shown below.

k	0	1	2	3	4	5	6	7	8	9
N_k	0	2	18	11	20	13	19	15	1	1

What is the probability that a phone number: (a) starts with 6? (b) begins with an odd number?

2.5 A class has 50 students. Suppose 20 of them are Chinese and 4 of the Chinese students are female. Let event A denote "student is Chinese" and event B denote "student is female." Find: (a) P(A), (b) P(AB), (c) P(B|A).

2.6 In a particular city, voters registration follows the tabulated statistics below. What is the probability that a person selected at random will be a male given that the person is also a Republican?

	Male (%)	Female (%)
Democrat	26	28
Republican	20	13
Independent	12	12

2.7 For three events A, B, and C, show that

$$P(A + B + C) = P(A) + P(B) + P(C) - P(AB) - P(AC) - P(BC) + P(ABC)$$

2.8 A continuous random variable X has the following PDF

$$f_X(x) = \begin{cases} kx, & 1 < x < 4 \\ 0, & \text{otherwise} \end{cases}$$

(a) Find the value of constant k.
(b) Obtain $F_X(x)$.
(c) Evaluate $P(X \le 2.5)$.

2.9 A random variable has a PDF given by

$$f_X(x) = \begin{cases} \dfrac{1}{2\sqrt{x}}, & 0 < x < 1 \\ 0, & \text{otherwise} \end{cases}$$

Find the corresponding $F_X(x)$ and P(0.5 < x < 0.75).

2.10 A Cauchy random variable X has PDF

$$f_X(x) = \frac{1}{\pi(1 + x^2)}, \quad -\infty < x < \infty$$

Find the corresponding CDF.

2.11 A joint PDF is given by

$$f_{XY}(x, y) = ke^{-(2x+3y)/6}u(x)u(y)$$

(a) Determine the value of the constant k such that the PDF is valid.
(b) Obtain the corresponding CDF $F_{XY}(x,y)$.
(c) Calculate the marginal PDFs $f_X(x)$ and $f_Y(y)$.
(d) Find $P(X \le 3, Y > 2)$ and P(0 < X < 1, 1 < Y < 3).

2.12 X and Y are random variables which assume values 0 and 1 according to the probabilities in the table below. Find Cov(X,Y).

		X		
		0	1	Total
Y	0	0.3	0.4	0.7
	1	0.1	0.2	0.3
	Total	0.4	0.6	1.0

2.13 The random variables X and Y have joint PDF as

$$f_{XY}(x,y) = \begin{cases} \dfrac{1}{4}, & 0 < x < 2, \quad 0 < y < 2 \\ 0, & \text{otherwise} \end{cases}$$

Find: (a) E[X + Y], (b) E[XY].

2.14 Given that a is a constant, show that

(a) $\text{Var}(aX) = a^2 \text{Vax}(X)$
(b) $\text{Var}(X + a) = \text{Var}(X)$

2.15 If X and Y are two independent random variables with mean μ_X and μ_Y and variances σ_X^2 and σ_y^2 respectively, show that

$$\text{Var}[XY] = \sigma_X^2 \sigma_y^2 + \sigma_X^2 \mu_y^2 + \mu_X^2 \sigma_y^2$$

2.16 Let $f(x) = \begin{cases} e^{-ax}(\beta x + \gamma), & x > 0 \\ 0, & \text{otherwise} \end{cases}$

Find the conditions for α, β, and γ so that f(x) is a probability density function.

2.17 Given the joint PDF of random variables X and Y as

$$f_{XY}(x,y) = \begin{cases} \dfrac{1}{2}(x + 3y), & 0 < x < 1, \quad 0 < y < 1 \\ 0, & \text{otherwise} \end{cases}$$

(a) Find E[X + Y] and E[XY].
(b) Calculate Cov(X,Y) and ρ_{XY}.
(c) Are X and Y uncorrelated? Are they orthogonal?

2.18 The joint PDF of two random variables X and Y is

$$f_{XY}(x, y) = ye^{-y(x+1)}u(x)u(y)$$

(a) Find the marginal PDFs $f_X(x)$ and $f_Y(y)$.
(b) Are X and Y independent?
(c) Calculate the mean and variance of X.
(d) Determine $P(X < Y)$.

2.19 Given the joint PDF

$$f_{XY}(x, y) = \begin{cases} k(x + xy), & 0 < x < 2, \quad 0 < y < 2 \\ 0, & \text{otherwise} \end{cases}$$

(a) Evaluate k.
(b) Determine $P(X < 1, y > 1)$.
(c) Find $F_{XY}(0.5, 1.5)$.
(d) Obtain $F_Y(y|X = x)$.
(e) Calculate $\text{Cov}(X, Y)$.

2.20 The *skew* is defined as the third moment taken about the mean, i.e.

$$\text{skew}(X) = E\left[(X - m_x)^3\right] = \int_{-\infty}^{\infty} (x - m_x)^3 f_X(x) dx$$

Given that a random variable X has a PDF

$$f_X(x) = \begin{cases} \frac{1}{6}(8 - x), & 4 < x < 10 \\ 0, & \text{otherwise} \end{cases}$$

find skew(X).

2.21 Refer to the previous problem for the definition of skewness. Calculate skew(X), where X is a random variable with the following distributions:

(a) Binomial with parameters n and p
(b) Poisson with parameter λ.
(c) Uniform on the interval (a,b).
(d) Exponential with parameter α.

2.22 There are four resistors in a circuit and the circuit will fail if two or more resistors are defective. If the probability of a resistor being defective is 0.005, calculate the probability that the circuit does not fail.

Fig. 2.18 For Prob. 2.27

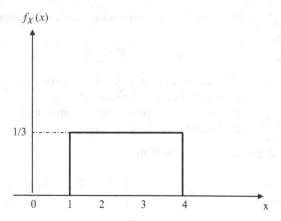

2.23 Let X be a binomial random variable with p = 0.5 and n = 20. Find
$P(4 \leq X \leq 7)$.

   Hint: $P(4 \leq X \leq 7) = P(X = 4) + P(4 < X \leq 7)$.

2.24 The occurrence of earthquakes can be modeled by a Poisson process. If the
annual rate of occurrence of earthquakes in a particular area is 0.02, calculate
the probability of having exactly one earthquake in 2 years.

2.25 The number of cars arriving at a toll booth during any time interval T
(in minutes) follows Poisson distribution with parameter T/2. Calculate the
probability that it takes more than 2 min for the first car to arrive at the booth.

2.26 A uniform random variable X has $E[X] = 1$ and $Var(X) = 1/2$. Find its PDF
and determine $P(X > 1)$.

2.27 Two independent random variables are uniformly distributed, each having the
PDF shown in Fig. 2.18. (a) Calculate the mean and variance of each.
(b) Determine the PDF of the sum of the two random variables.

2.28 A continuous random variable X may take any value with equal probability
within the interval range 0 to α. Find $E[X]$, $E[X^2]$, and $Var(X)$.

2.29 A random variable X with mean 3 follows an exponential distribution.
(a) Calculate $P(X < 1)$ and $P(X > 1.5)$. (b) Determine λ such that
$P(X < \lambda) = 0.2$.

2.30 A zero-mean Gaussian random variable has a variance of 9. Find a such that
$P(|X| > a) < 0.01$.

2.31 A random variable T represents the lifetime of an electronic component.
Its PDF is given by

$$f_T(t) = \frac{t}{\alpha^2} \exp\left[-\frac{t^2}{\alpha^2}\right] u(t)$$

where $\alpha = 10^3$. Find $E[T]$ and $Var(T)$.

Fig. 2.19 For Prob. 2.33

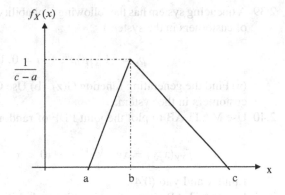

Fig. 2.20 PDF of a
Rayleigh random variable
for Prob. 2.37

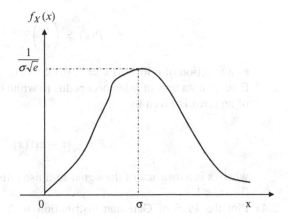

2.32 A measurement of a noise voltage produces a Gaussian random signal with zero mean and variance 2×10^{-11} V^2. Find the probability that a sample measurement exceeds 4 µV.

2.33 A random variable has triangular PDF as shown Fig. 2.19. Find E[X] and Var(X).

2.34 A transformation between X and Y is defined by $Y = e^{-3X}$. Obtain the PDF of Y if:

(a) X is uniformly distributed between -1 and 1, (b) $f_X(x) = e^{-x}u(x)$.

2.35 If $f_X(x) = ae^{-ax}$, $0 < x < \infty$ and $Y = 1/X$, find $f_Y(y)$.

2.36 Let X be a Gaussian random variable with mean µ and variance σ^2. (a) Find the PDF of $Y = e^X$. (b) Determine the PDF of $Y = X^2$.

2.37 If X and Y are two independent Gaussian random variables each with zero mean and the same variance σ, show that random variable $R = \sqrt{X^2 + Y^2}$ has a Rayleigh distribution as shown Fig. 2.20. Hint: The joint PDF is $f_{XY}(x,y)$
$= f_X(x)f_Y(y)$ and $f_R(r) = \dfrac{r}{\sigma^2}e^{-r^2/2\sigma^2}u(r)$.

2.38 Obtain the generating function for Poisson distribution.

2.39 A queueing system has the following probability of being in state n (n = number of customers in the system)

$$p_n = (1 - \rho)\rho^n, \quad n = 0, 1, 2, \cdots$$

(a) Find the generating function G(z). (b) Use G(z) to find the mean number of customers in the system.

2.40 Use MATLAB to plot the joint PDF of random variables X and Y given by

$$f_{XY}(x, y) = xye^{-(x^2+y^2)}, \quad 0 < x < \infty, 0 < y < \infty$$

Limit x and y to (0,4).

2.41 Use MATLAB to plot the binomial probabilities

$$P(k) = \binom{k}{n} 2^{-k}$$

as a function of n for: (a) k = 5, (b) k = 10.

2.42 Error in data transmission occurs due to white Gaussian noise. The probability of an error is given by

$$P = \frac{1}{2}[1 - \mathrm{erf}(x)]$$

where x is a measure of the signal-to-noise ratio. Use MATLAB to plot P over 0 < x < 1.

2.43 Plot the PDF of Gaussian distribution with mean 2 and variance 4 using MATLAB.

2.44 Using the MATLAB command **rand**, one can generate random numbers uniformly distributed on the interval (0,1). Generate 10,000 such numbers and compute the mean and variance. Compare your result with that obtained using E[X] = (a + b)/2 and Var(X) = (b − a)^2/12.

References

1. G. R. Grimmett and D.R. Stirzaker, *Probability and Random Processes*. Oxford: Oxford University Press, 2001, pp. 26–45.
2. X. R. Li, Probability, *Random Signals, and Statistics*. Boca Raton, FL: CRC Press, 1999, pp. 65–143.
3. R. Jain, *The Art of Computer Systems Performance Analysis*. New York: John Wiley & Sons, 1991, pp. 483–501.
4. R. Nelson, *Probability, Stochastic Processes, and Queueing Theory*. New York: Springer-Verlag, 1995, pp. 101–165.

5. P. G. Harrison and N. M. Patel, *Performance Modelling of Communication Networks and Computer Architecture.* Wokingham, UK: Addison-Wesley, 1992, pp. 19–48.
6. R. Goodman, *Introduction to Stochastic Models.* Mineola, NY: Dover Publications, 2nd ed., 2006.
7. O. C. Ibe, *Markov Processes for Stochastic Modeling.* Burlington, MA: Elsevier Academic Press, 2009.

Chapter 3
Stochastic Processes

For me problem-solving is the most interesting thing in life.
To be handed something that's a complete mess and
straighten it out. To organize where there is no organization.
To give form to a medium that has no form.

—Sylvester Weaver

This chapter is an extension of the previous chapter. In the previous chapter, we focused essentially on random variables. In this chapter, we introduce the concept of *random* (or *stochastic*) *process* as a generalization of a random variable to include another dimension—time. While a random variable depends on the outcome of a random experiment, a random process depends on both the outcome of a random experiment and time. In other words, if a random variable X is time-dependent, X(t) is known as a *random process*. Thus, a random process may be regarded as any process that changes with time and controlled by some probabilistic law. For example, the number of customers N in a queueing system varies with time; hence N(t) is a random process

Figure 3.1 portrays typical *realizations* or *sample functions* of a random process. From this figure, we notice that a random process is a mapping from the sample space into an ensemble (family, set, collection) of time functions known as sample functions. Here $X(t,s_k)$ denotes the sample function or a realization of the random process for the s_k experimental outcome. It is customary to drop the s variable and use X(t) to denote a random process. For a fixed time t_1, $X(t_1) = X_1$ is a random variable. Thus,

A **random (or stochastic) process** is a family of random variables X(t), indexed by the parameter t and defined on a common probability space.

It should be note that the parameter t does not have to always represent time; it can represent any other variable such as space.

M.N.O. Sadiku and S.M. Musa, *Performance Analysis of Computer Networks*, 61
DOI 10.1007/978-3-319-01646-7_3, © Springer International Publishing Switzerland 2013

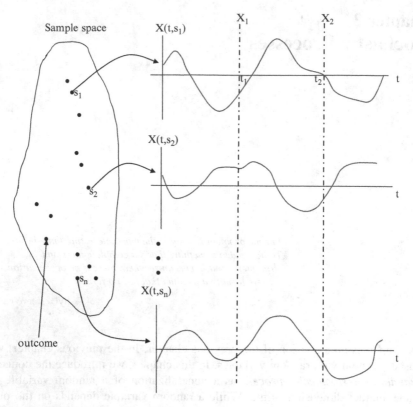

Fig. 3.1 Realizations of a random process

In this chapter, we discuss random processes, their properties, and the basic tools used for their mathematical analysis. Specifically, we will discuss random walks, Markov processes, birth-death processes, Poisson processes, and renewal processes. We will also consider how the concepts developed can be demonstrated using MATLAB.

3.1   Classification of Random Processes

It is expedient to begin our discussion of random processes by developing the terminology for describing random processes [1–3]. An appropriate way of achieving this is to consider the various types of random processes. Random processes may be classified as:

- Continuous or discrete
- Deterministic or nondeterministic
- Stationary or nonstationary
- Ergodic or nonergodic

3.1.1   Continuous Versus Discrete Random Process

A *continuous-time random process* is one that has both a continuous random variable and continuous time. Noise in transistors and wind velocity are examples of continuous random processes. So are Wiener process and Brownian motion. A *discrete-time random process* is one in which the random variables are discrete, i.e. it is a sequence of random variables. For example, a voltage that assumes a value of either 0 or 12 V because of switching operation is a sample function from a discrete random process. The binomial counting and random walk processes are discrete processes. It is also possible to have a mixed or hybrid random process which is partly continuous and partly discrete.

3.1.2   Deterministic Versus Nondeterministic Random Process

A *deterministic random process* is one for which the future value of any sample function can be predicted from a knowledge of the past values. For example, consider a random process described by

$$X(t) = A \cos(\omega t + \Phi) \qquad (3.1)$$

where A and ω are constants and Φ is a random variable with a known probability distribution. Although X(t) is a random process, one can predict its future values and hence X(t) is deterministic. For a *nondeterministic random process*, each sample function is a random function of time and its future values cannot be predicted from the past values.

3.1.3   Stationary Versus Nonstationary Random Process

A *stationary random process* is one in which the probability density function of the random variable does not change with time. In other words, a random process is stationary when its statistical characteristics are time-invariant, i.e. not affected by a shift in time origin. Thus, the random process is stationary if all marginal and joint density functions of the process are not affected by the choice of time origin. A *nonstationary random process* is one in which the probability density function of the random variable is a function of time.

Fig. 3.2 Relationship
between stationary and
ergodic random processes

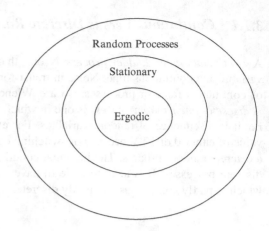

3.1.4   *Ergodic Versus Nonergodic Random Process*

An ergodic random process is one in which every member of the ensemble possesses the same statistical behavior as the entire ensemble. Thus, for ergodic processes, it is possible to determine the statistical characteristic by examining only one typical sample function, i.e. the average value and moments can be determined by time averages as well as by ensemble averages. For example, the nth moment is given by

$$\overline{X^n} = \int_{-\infty}^{\infty} x^n f_X(x)dx = \lim_{T \to \infty} \frac{1}{2T} \int_{-T}^{T} X^n(t)dt \tag{3.2}$$

This condition will only be satisfied if the process is stationary. This implies that ergodic processes are stationary as well. A nonergodic process does not satisfy the condition in Eq. (3.2). All non-stationary processes are nonergodic but a stationary process could also be nonergodic. Figure 3.2 shows the relationship between stationary and ergodic processes. These terms will become clearer as we move along in the chapter.

Example 3.1 Consider the random process

$$X(t) = \cos\left(2\pi t + \Theta\right)$$

where Θ is a random variable uniformly distributed on the interval $[0,2\pi]$.

Solution

We are given an analytic expression for the random process and it is evident that it is a continuous-time and deterministic random process. Figure 3.3 displays some sample functions or realizations of the process.

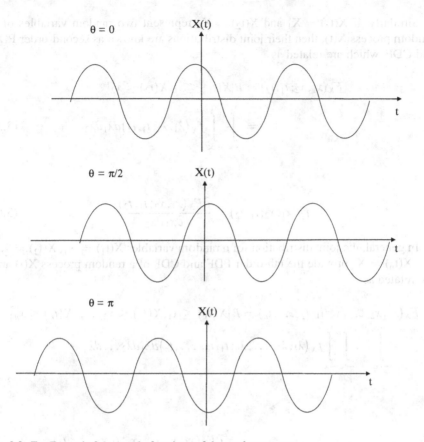

Fig. 3.3 For Example 3.1; sample functions of the random process

3.2 Statistics of Random Processes and Stationarity

Since a random process specifies a random variable at any given time, we can find the statistical averages for the process through the statistical averages of the corresponding random variables. For example, the first-order probability density function (PDF) for a random process X(t) is $f_X(x;t)$, while the corresponding first-order cumulative distribution function (CDF) of X(t) is

$$F_X(x;t) = P[X(t) \leq x] = \int_{-\infty}^{x} f_X(\lambda;t)d\lambda \tag{3.3}$$

or

$$f_X(x;t) = \frac{\partial F_X(x;t)}{\partial x} \tag{3.4}$$

Similarly, if $X(t_1) = X_1$ and $X(t_2) = X_2$ represent two random variables of a random process $X(t)$, then their joint distributions are known as second-order PDF and CDF, which are related as

$$F_X(x_1, x_2; t_1, t_2) = P[X(t_1) \leq x_1, X(t_2) \leq x_2]$$

$$= \int\limits_{-\infty}^{x_2} \int\limits_{-\infty}^{x_1} f_X(\lambda_1, \lambda_2; t_1, t_2) d\lambda_1 d\lambda_2 \tag{3.5}$$

or

$$f_X(x_1, x_2; t_1, t_2) = \frac{\partial F_X(x_1, x_2; t_1, t_2)}{\partial x_1 \partial x_2} \tag{3.6}$$

In general, the joint distributions of n random variables $X(t_1) = X_1$, $X(t_2) = X_2$, ..., $X(t_n) = X_n$ provide the nth-order PDF and CDF of a random process $X(t)$ and are related as

$$F_X(x_1, x_2, \ldots, x_n; t_1, t_2, \ldots, t_n) = P[X(t_1) \leq x_1, X(t_2) \leq x_2, \ldots, X(t_n) \leq x_n]$$

$$= \int\limits_{-\infty}^{x_n} \cdots \int\limits_{-\infty}^{x_2} \int\limits_{-\infty}^{x_1} f_X(\lambda_1, \lambda_2, \ldots, \lambda_n; t_1, t_2, \ldots, t_n) d\lambda_1 d\lambda_2 \ldots d\lambda_n$$

$$\tag{3.7}$$

or

$$f_X(x_1, x_2, \ldots, x_n; t_1, t_2, \ldots, t_n) = \frac{\partial F_X(x_1, x_2, \ldots, x_n; t_1, t_2, \ldots, t_n)}{\partial x_1 \partial x_2 \ldots \partial x_n} \tag{3.8}$$

A random process $X(t)$ is said to be *strictly stationary of order n* if its nth-order PDF and CDF are time-invariant, i.e.

$$F_X(x_1, x_2, \ldots, x; t_1 + \tau, t_2 + \tau, \ldots, t_n + \tau)$$

$$= F_X(x_1, x_2, \ldots, x; t_1, t_2, \ldots, t_n) \tag{3.9}$$

i.e. the CDF depends only on the relative location of $t_1, t_2, \ldots, t_n$ and not on their direct values.

We say that $\{X_k\}$, $k = 0, 1, 2, \cdots, n$ is an independent process if and only if

$$F_X(x_0, x_1, \cdots, x_n; t_0, t_1, \cdots, t_n) = F_{X_0}(x_0; t_0) F_{X_1}(x_1; t_1) \cdots F_{X_n}(x_n; t_n)$$

In addition, if all random variables are drawn from the same distribution, the process is characterized by a single CDF, $F_{X_k}(x_k; t_k)$, $k = 0, 1, 2, \cdots, n$. In this case, we call $\{X_k\}$ a sequence of independent and identically distributed (IID) random variables.

Having defined the CDF and PDF for a random process X(t), we are now prepared to define the statistical (or ensemble) averages—the mean, variance, autocorrelation, and autocovariance of X(t). As in the case of random variables, these statistics play an important role in practical applications.

The *mean* or *expected value* of the random process X(t) is

$$m_X(t) = \overline{X(t)} = E[X(t)] = \int_{-\infty}^{-\infty} x f_X(x;t)dx \qquad (3.10)$$

where $E[\bullet]$ denotes ensemble average, $f_X(x;t)$ is the PDF of X(t) and X(t) is regarded as a random variable for a fixed value of t. In general, the mean $m_X(t)$ is a function of time.

The *variance* of a random process X(t) is given by

$$\text{Var}(X) = \sigma_X^2 = E\left[(X(t) - m_X(t))^2\right] = E\left[X^2\right] - m_X^2 \qquad (3.11)$$

The *autocorrelation* of a random process X(t) is the joint moment of $X(t_1)$ and $X(t_2)$, i.e.

$$\boxed{R_X(t_1,t_2) = E[X(t_1)X(t_2)] = \int_{-\infty}^{\infty}\int_{-\infty}^{\infty} x_1 x_2 f_X(x_1,x_2;t_1,t_2)dx_1 dx_2} \qquad (3.12)$$

where $f_X(x_1,x_2;t_1,t_2)$ is the second-order PDF of X(t). In general, $R_X(t_1,t_2)$ is a deterministic function of two variables t_1 and t_2. The autocorrection function is important because it describes the power-spectral density of a random process.

The *covariance* or *autocovariance* of a random process X(t) is the covariance of $X(t_1)$ and $X(t_2)$, i.e.

$$\text{Cov}[X(t_1),X(t_2)] = C_X(t_1,t_2) = E[\{X(t_1) - m_X(t_1)\}\{X(t_2) - m_X(t_2)\}] \qquad (3.13a)$$

Or

$$\boxed{\text{Cov}[X(t_1),X(t_2)] = R_X(t_1,t_2) - m_X(t_1)m_X(t_2)} \qquad (3.13b)$$

indicating that the autocovariance can be expressed in terms of the autocorrelation and the means. Note that the variance of X(t) can be expressed in terms of its autocovariance, i.e.

$$\text{Var}(X(t)) = C_X(t,t) \qquad (3.14)$$

The *correlation coefficient* of a random process X(t) is the correlation coefficient of $X(t_1)$ and $X(t_2)$, i.e.

$$\rho_X(t_1, t_2) = \frac{C_X(t_1, t_2)}{\sqrt{C_X(t_1, t_1)C_X(t_2, t_2)}} \qquad (3.15)$$

where $|\rho_X(t_1, t_2)| \leq 1$.

Finally, we define the *nth joint moment* of X(t) as

$$E[X(t_1)X(t_2)\ldots X(t_n)]$$

$$= \int\limits_{-\infty}^{\infty} \ldots \int\limits_{-\infty}^{\infty} \int\limits_{-\infty}^{\infty} x_1 x_2 \ldots x_n f_X(x_1, x_2, \ldots, x_n; t_1, t_2, \ldots, t_n) dx_1 dx_2 \ldots dx_n \qquad (3.16)$$

We should keep in mind that the mean, variance, autocorrelation, autocovariance, and nth joint moment are good indicators of the behavior of a random process but only partial characterizations of the process.

In terms of these statistics, a random process may be classified as follows.

1. A random process is *wide-sense stationary* (WSS) or weakly stationary if its mean is constant, i.e.

$$E[X(t)] = E[X(t_1)] = E[X(t_2)] = m_x = \text{constant} \qquad (3.17)$$

and its autocorrelation depends only on the absolute time difference $\tau = |t_1 - t_2|$, i.e.

$$E[X(t)X(t+\tau)] = R_X(\tau) \qquad (3.18)$$

Note that the autocovariance of a WSS process depends only on the time difference τ

$$C_X(\tau) = R_X(\tau) - m_x^2 \qquad (3.19)$$

and that by setting $\tau = 0$ in Eq. (3.18), we get

$$E[X^2(t)] = R_X(0) \qquad (3.20)$$

indicating that the mean power of a WSS process X(t) does not depend on t. The autocorrelation function has its maximum value when $\tau = 0$ so that we can write

$$-R_X(0) \leq R_X(\tau) \leq R_X(0) \qquad (3.21)$$

2. A random process is said to be *strict-sense stationary* (SSS) if its statistics are invariant to shift in the time axis. Hence,

$$F_X(x_1, x_2, \ldots, x_n; t_1 + \tau, t_2 + \tau, \ldots, t_n + \tau)$$
$$= F_X(x_1, x_2, \ldots, x_n; t_1, t_2, \ldots, t_n) \qquad (3.22)$$

An SSS random process is also WSS but the converse is not generally true.

In general terms, a random process is **stationary** if all its statistical properties do not vary with time.

Example 3.2 A random process is given by

$$X(t) = A \cos{(\omega t + \Theta)}$$

where A and ω are constants and Θ is uniformly distributed over (0,2π). (a) Find E [X(t)] , E[X^2(t)] and E[X(t)X(t+τ)]. (b) Is X(t) WSS?

Solution

(a) Since Θ has a uniform distribution, its PDF is given by

$$f_\Theta(\theta) = \begin{cases} \dfrac{1}{2\pi}, & 0 \le \theta \le 2\pi \\ 0, & \text{otherwise} \end{cases}$$

Hence,

$$E[X(t)] = \int_{-\infty}^{\infty} x f_\Theta(\theta) d\theta = A \int_0^{2\pi} \cos{(\omega t + \theta)} \frac{1}{2\pi} d\theta = 0$$

$$E[X^2(t)] = \int_{-\infty}^{\infty} x^2 f_\Theta(\theta) d\theta = A^2 \int_0^{2\pi} \cos^2{(\omega t + \theta)} \frac{1}{2\pi} d\theta$$

$$= A^2 \int_0^{2\pi} \frac{1}{2}[1 + \cos{2(\omega t + \theta)}] \frac{1}{2\pi} d\theta = \frac{A^2}{2}$$

where the trigonometric identity $\cos^2{\alpha} = \frac{1}{2}[1 + \cos{2\alpha}]$ and the fact that $\omega = 2\pi/T$ have been applied.

$$E[X(t)X(t + \tau)] = \int_0^{2\pi} A \cos{(\omega t + \theta)} A \cos{[\omega(t + \tau) + \theta]} \frac{1}{2\pi} d\theta$$

$$= \frac{A^2}{2\pi} \int_0^{2\pi} \frac{1}{2}[\cos{(\omega \tau + 2\omega t + 2\theta)} + \cos{\omega \tau}] d\theta = \frac{A^2}{2} \cos{\omega \tau}$$

where we have used the trigonometric identity $\cos{A} \cos{B} = \frac{1}{2}[\cos{(A + B)} + \cos{(A - B)}]$.

(b) Since the mean of X(t) is constant and its autocorrelation is a function of τ only, X(t) is a WSS random process.

Example 3.3 Let $X(t) = A \sin(\pi t/2)$, where A is a Gaussian or normal random variable with mean μ and variance σ^2, i.e. $A = N(\mu,\sigma)$. (a) Determine the mean, autocorrelation, and autocovariance of $X(t)$. (b) Find the density functions for $X(1)$ and $X(3)$. (c) Is $X(t)$ stationary in any sense?

Solution

Given that $E[A] = \mu$ and $Var(A) = \sigma^2$, we can obtain

$$E[A^2] = \text{Vax}(A) + E^2[A] = \sigma^2 + \mu^2$$

(a) The mean of $X(t)$ is

$$m_X(t) = E[A \sin \pi t/2] = E[A] \sin \pi t/2 = \mu \sin \pi t/2$$

The autocorrelation of $X(t_1)$ and $X(t_2)$ is

$$R_X(t_1, t_2) = E[A \sin(\pi t_1/2) A \sin(\pi t_2/2)] = E[A^2] \sin(\pi t_1/2) \sin(\pi t_2/2)$$
$$= (\sigma^2 + \mu^2) \sin(\pi t_1/2) \sin(\pi t_2/2)$$

The autocovariance is

$$C_X(t_1, t_2) = R_X(t_1, t_2) - m_X(t_1) m_X(t_2) = \sigma^2 \sin(\pi t_1/2) \sin(\pi t_2/2)$$

(b) $X(1) = A \sin \pi(1)/2 = A$

$$F_X(x_1, t_1) = P[X(1) \le x_1] = P[A \le x_1] = F_A(a)$$

where $a = x_1$

$$f_X(x_1) = \frac{\partial F(x_1; t_1)}{\partial x_1} = \frac{dF_A(a)}{da} \frac{da}{dx_1} = f_A(a)$$

Since $A = N(\mu,\sigma)$,

$$f_A(a) = \frac{1}{\sigma\sqrt{2\pi}} e^{-(a-\mu)^2/(2\sigma^2)}$$

$$f_X(x_1) = \frac{1}{\sigma\sqrt{2\pi}} e^{-(x_1-\mu)^2/(2\sigma^2)}$$

Similarly, $X(3) = A \sin \pi 3/2 = -A$

$$F_X(x_3, t_1) = P[X(3) \le x_3] = P[-A \le x_3] = P[A \ge -x_3] = 1 - P[A \le -x_3]$$
$$= 1 - F_A(a)$$

where $a = -x_3$.

$$f_X(x_3) = \frac{\partial F(x_3; t_1)}{\partial x_3} = \frac{dF_A(a)}{da}\frac{da}{dx_3} = f_A(a)$$

Hence

$$f_X(x_3) = \frac{1}{\sigma\sqrt{2\pi}}e^{-(x_3+\mu)^2/(2\sigma^2)}$$

(c) Since the mean of X(t) is a function of time, the process is not stationary in any sense.

3.3 Time Averages of Random Processes and Ergodicity

For a random process X(t), we can define two types of averages: ensemble and time averages. The ensemble averages (or statistical averages) of a random process X(t) may be regarded as "averages across the process" because they involve all sample functions of the process observed at a particular instant of time. The time averages of a random process X(t) may be regarded as "averages along the process" because they involve long-term sample averaging of the process.

To define the time averages, consider the sample function x(t) of random process X(t), which is observed within the time interval $-T \leq t \leq T$. The *time average* (or *time mean*) of the sample function is

$$\bar{x} = <x(t)> = \lim_{T \to \infty} \frac{1}{2T}\int_{-T}^{T}x(t)dt \tag{3.23}$$

where $<\bullet>$ denotes time-averaging operation. Similarly, the *time autocorrelation* of the sample function x(t) is given by

$$\bar{R}_X(\tau) = <x(t)x(t+\tau)> = \lim_{T \to \infty} \frac{1}{2T}\int_{-T}^{T}x(t)x(t+\tau)dt \tag{3.24}$$

Note that both $\bar{x}$ and $\bar{R}_X(\tau)$ are random variables since their values depend on the observation interval and on the sample function x(t) used.

If all time averages are equal to their corresponding ensemble averages, then the stationary process is *ergodic*, i.e.

$$\bar{x} = <x(t)> = E[X(t)] = m_X \tag{3.25}$$

$$\bar{R}_X(\tau) = <x(t)x(t+\tau)> = E[X(t)X(t+\tau)] = R_X(\tau) \tag{3.26}$$

An **ergodic process** is one for which time and ensemble averages are interchangeable.

The concept of ergodicity is a very powerful tool and it is always assumed in many engineering applications. This is due to the fact that it is impractical to have a large number of sample functions to work with. Ergodicity suggests that if a random process is ergodic, only one sample function is necessary to determine the ensemble averages. This seems reasonable because over infinite time each sample function of a random process would take on, at one time or another, all the possible values of the process. We will assume throughout this text that the random processes we will encounter are ergodic and WSS.

Basic quantities such as dc value, rms value, and average power can be defined in terms of time averages of an ergodic random process as follows:

1. $\bar{x} = m_X$ is the dc value of x(t).
2. $[\bar{x}]^2 = m_X^2$ is the normalized dc power.
3. $\bar{R}_X(0) = \overline{x^2}$ is the total average normalized power
4. $\bar{\sigma}_X^2 = \overline{x^2} - [\bar{x}]^2$ is the average normalized power in the ac or time-varying component of the signal.
5. $X_{rms} = \sqrt{\overline{x^2}} = \sqrt{\bar{\sigma}_X^2 + [\bar{x}]^2}$ is the rms value of x(t).

Example 3.4 Consider the random process in Example 3.2. Show that the process is stationary and ergodic.

Solution

We already showed that the process is stationary because the statistical or ensemble averages do not depend on time. To show that the process is ergodic, we compute the first and second moments. Since $\omega = 2\pi/T$,

$$\bar{x} = \lim_{T \to \infty} \frac{1}{2T} \int_{-T}^{T} A \cos(\omega t + \theta) dt = 0$$

$$\overline{x^2} = \lim_{T \to \infty} \frac{1}{2T} \int_{-T}^{T} A^2 \cos^2(\omega t + \theta) dt = \lim_{T \to \infty} \frac{A^2}{2T} \int_{-T}^{T} \frac{1}{2}[1 + \cos 2(\omega t + \theta)] dt = \frac{A^2}{2}$$

indicating that the time averages are equal to the ensemble averages we obtained in Example 3.2. Hence the process is ergodic.

3.4 Multiple Random Processes

The joint behavior of two or more random processes is dictated by their joint distributions. For example, two random processes X(t) and Y(t) are said to be *independent* if for all t_1 and t_2, the random variables $X(t_1)$ and $Y(t_2)$ are independent. That means that their nth order joint PDF factors, i.e.

$$F_{XY}(x_1, y_1, x_2, y_2, \ldots, x_n, y_n; t_1, t_2, \ldots, t_n)$$
$$= F_X(x_1, x_2, \ldots, x_n; t_1, t_2, \ldots, t_n) F_Y(y_1, y_2, \ldots, y_n; t_1, t_2, \ldots, t_n) \qquad (3.27)$$

The *crosscorreleration* between two random processes X(t) and Y(t) is defined as

$$\boxed{R_{XY}(t_1, t_2) = E[X(t_1)Y(t_2)]}$$ (3.28)

Note that

$$R_{XY}(t_1, t_2) = R_{YX}(t_2, t_1)$$ (3.29)

The processes X(t) and Y(t) are said to be *orthogonal* if

$$R_{XY}(t_1, t_2) = 0 \quad \text{for all } t_1 \text{ and } t_2$$ (3.30)

If X(t) and Y(t) are jointly stationary, then their crosscorrelation function becomes

$$R_{XY}(t_1, t_2) = R_{XY}(\tau)$$

where $\tau = t_2 - t_1$. Other properties of the crosscorrelation of jointly stationary processes are:

1. $R_{XY}(-\tau) = R_{XY}(\tau)$, i.e. it is symmetric.
2. $|R_{XY}(\tau)| \leq \sqrt{R_X(0)R_Y(0)}$, i.e. it is bounded.
3. $|R_{XY}(\tau)| \leq \frac{1}{2}[R_X(0) + R_Y(0)]$, i.e. it is bounded.

The *crosscovariance* of X(t) and Y(t) is given by

$$\boxed{C_{XY}(t_1, t_2) = E[\{X(t_1) - m_X(t_1)\}\{Y(t_2) - m_Y(t_2)\}] = R_{XY}(t_1, t_2) - m_X(t_1)m_Y(t_2)}$$

(3.31)

Just like with random variables, two random processes X(t) and Y(t) are *uncorrelated* if

$$C_{XY}(t_1, t_2) = 0 \quad \text{for all } t_1 \text{ and } t_2$$ (3.32)

which implies that

$$R_{XY}(t_1, t_2) = m_X(t_1)m_Y(t_2) \quad \text{for all } t_1 \text{ and } t_2$$ (3.33)

Finally, for jointly ergodic random processes X(t) and Y(t),

$$\overline{R}_{XY}(\tau) = \lim_{T \to \infty} \frac{1}{2T} \int_{-T}^{T} x(t)x(t + \tau)dt = R_{XY}(\tau)$$ (3.34)

Thus, two random processes X(t) and Y(t) are:

(a) **Independent** if their joint PDF factors.
(b) **Orthogonal** if $R_{XY}(t_1, t_2) = 0$ for all t_1 and t_2
(c) **Uncorrelated** if $R_{XY}(t_1, t_2) = m_X(t_1)m_Y(t_2)$ for all t_1 and t_2.

Example 3.5 Two random processes are given by

$$X(t) = \sin(\omega t + \Theta), \qquad Y(t) = \sin(\omega t + \Theta + \pi/4)$$

where Θ is random variable that is uniformly distributed over $(0,2\pi)$. Find the cross correlation function $R_{XY}(t,t+\tau)$

Solution

$$R_{XY}(t,t+\tau) = R_{XY}(\tau) = E[X(t)Y(t+\tau)] = \int_0^{2\pi} x(t)y(t+\tau)f_\Theta(\theta)d\theta$$

$$= \int_0^{2\pi} \sin(\omega t + \theta) \sin[\omega(t+\tau) + \theta + \pi/4]\frac{1}{2\pi}d\theta$$

$$= \int_0^{2\pi} \frac{1}{2}\left[\cos(\omega\tau + \pi/4) - \cos(2\omega t + \omega\tau + 2\theta + \pi/4)\right]\frac{1}{2\pi}d\theta$$

$$= \frac{1}{2}\cos(\omega\tau + \pi/4)$$

where we have applied the trigonometric identity $\sin A \sin B = \frac{1}{2}[\cos(A-B) - \cos(A+B)]$.

Example 3.6 A received signal X(t) consists of two components: desired signal S(t) and noise N(t), i.e.

$$X(t) = S(t) + N(t)$$

If the autocorrelation of the random signal is

$$R_S(\tau) = e^{-2|\tau|}$$

while that of the random noise is

$$R_N(\tau) = 3e^{-|\tau|}$$

Assume that they are independent and they both have zero mean.

(a) Find the autocorrelation of X(t). (b) Determine the cross correlation between X(t) and S(t).

Solution

(a) $R_X(t_1, t_2) = E[X(t_1)X(t_2)] = E[\{S(t_1) + N(t_1)\}\{S(t_2) + N(t_2)\}]$
$= E[S(t_1)S(t_2)] + E[N(t_1)S(t_2)] + E[S(t_1)N(t_2)] + E[N(t_1)N(t_2)]$

Since S(t) and N(t) are independent and have zero mean,

$$E[N(t_1)S(t_2)] = E[N(t_1)]E[S(t_2)] = 0$$

$$E[S(t_1)N(t_2)] = E[S(t_1)]E[N(t_2)] = 0$$

Hence,

$$R_X(\tau) = R_S(\tau) + R_N(\tau) = e^{-2|\tau|} + 3e^{-|\tau|}$$

where $\tau = t_1 - t_2$.

(b) Similarly,

$$
\begin{aligned}
R_{XS}(t_1, t_2) &= E[X(t_1)S(t_2)] = E[\{S(t_1) + N(t_1)\}\{S(t_2)\}] \\
&= E[S(t_1)S(t_2)] + E[N(t_1)S(t_2)] \\
&= R_S(t_1, t_2) + 0
\end{aligned}
$$

Thus,

$$R_{XS}(\tau) = R_S(\tau) = e^{-2|\tau|}$$

3.5 Sample Random Processes

We have been discussing random processes in general. Specific random processes include Poisson counting process, Wiener process or Brownian motion, random walking process, Bernoulli process, birth-and-death process, and Markov process [4, 5]. In this section, we consider some of these specific random processes.

3.5.1 Random Walks

A random walk (or drunkard's walk) is a stochastic process in which the states are integers X_n representing the position of a particle at time n. Each state change according to

$$X_n = X_{n-1} + Z_n \tag{3.35}$$

where Z_n is a random variable which takes values of 1 or -1. If $X_0 = 0$, then

$$X_n = \sum_{i=1}^{n} Z_i \tag{3.36}$$

A *random walk* on X corresponds to a sequence of states, one for each step of the walk. At each step, the walk switches from its current state to a new state or remains at the current state. Thus,

Fig. 3.4 A typical
random walk

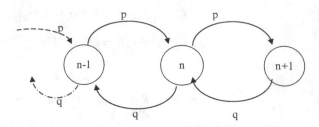

Random walks constitute a random process consisting of a sequence of discrete steps of fixed length.

Random walks are usually *Markovian*, which means that the transition at each step is independent of the previous steps and depends only on the current state. Although random walks are not limited to one-dimensional problems, the one-dimensional random walk is one of the simplest stochastic processes and can be used to model many gambling games. Random walks also find applications in potential theory. A typical one-dimensional random walk is illustrated in Fig. 3.4.

Example 3.7 Consider the following standard Markovian random walk on the integers over the range $\{0, \ldots, N\}$ that models a simple gambling game, where a player bets the same amount on each hand (i.e., step). We assume that if the player ever reaches 0, he has lost all his money and stops, but if he reaches N, he has won a certain amount of money and stops. Otherwise, at each step, one moves from state i (where $i \neq 0, N$) to $i + 1$ with probability p (the probability of winning the game), to $i - 1$ with probability q (the probability of losing the game), and stays at the same state with probability $1 - p - q$ (the probability of a draw).

3.5.2 Markov Processes

If the future state of a process depends only on the present (and independent of the past), the process is called a *Markov process*. A Markov process is made possible only if the state time has a memoryless (exponential) distribution. This requirement often limits the applicability of Markov processes.

Formally, a stochastic process X(t) is a Markov process if

$$\text{Prob}\big[X(t) = x \big| X(t_n) = x_n, X(t_{n-1}) = x_{n-1} \cdots, X(t_o) = x_o\big]$$
$$= \text{Prob}\big[X(t) = x \big| X(t_n) = x_n\big] \quad \text{for } t_o < t_1 < \cdots < t_n < t \qquad (3.37)$$

A discrete-state Markov process is called a *Markov chain* [4]. We use the state transition diagram to represent the evolution of a Markov chain. An example of three-state Markov chain is shown in Fig. 3.5.

Fig. 3.5 State transition diagram for a three-state Markov chain

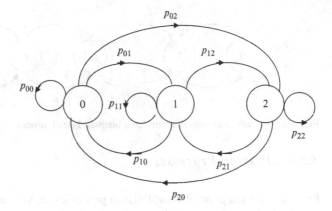

The conditional probability

$$\text{Prob}\left[X_{n+1} = i \mid X_n = j\right] = p_n(i,j)$$

is called the *transition probability* from state i to state j. Since a Markov chain must go somewhere with a probability of 1, the sum of $p_n(i,j)$'s over all j's is equal to 1. If $p_n(i,j)$ is independent of n, the Markov chain is said to be time-homogeneous and in this case, the transition probability becomes $p(i,j)$. When we arrange $p(i,j)$ into an square array, the resulting matrix is called the *transition matrix*.

For a simple example, consider four possible states as 0, 1, 2, and 3. The transition matrix is

$$P = \begin{bmatrix} p(0,0) & p(0,1) & p(0,2) & p(0,3) \\ p(1,0) & p(1,1) & p(1,2) & p(1,3) \\ p(2,0) & p(2,1) & p(2,2) & p(2,3) \\ p(3,0) & p(3,1) & p(3,2) & p(3,3) \end{bmatrix} \tag{3.38}$$

3.5.3   Birth-and-Death Processes

Birth-death processes describe the stochastic evolution in time of a random variable whose value increases or decreases by one in a single event. These are discrete-space Markov processes in which the transitions are restricted to neighboring states only. A typical example is shown in Fig. 3.6.

For example, the number of jobs in a queue with a single server and the individual arrivals can be represented as a birth-death process. An arrival to the queue (a birth) causes the state to change by +1, while a departure (a death) causes the state to change by -1. Although the birth-death processes are used in modeling population, they are useful in the analysis of communication networks. They are also used in physics, biology, sociology, and economics.

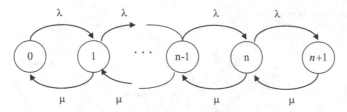

Fig. 3.6 The state transition diagram for a birth-and-death process

3.5.4   Poisson Processes

From application point of view, Poisson processes are very useful. They can be used to model a large class of stochastic phenomena. Poisson process is one in which the number of events which occur in any time interval t is distributed according to a Poisson random variable, with mean λt. In this process, the interarrival time is distributed exponentially.

> A process is called a **Poisson process** when the time intervals between successive events are exponentially distributed.

Given a sequence of discrete events occurring at times $t_0, t_1, t_2, t_3, \ldots$, the intervals between successive events are $\Delta t_1 = (t_1 - t_0), \Delta t_2 = (t_2 - t_1), \Delta t_3 = (t_3 - t_2), \ldots$, and so on. For a Poisson process, these intervals are treated as independent random variables drawn from an exponentially distributed population, i.e., a population with the density function $f(x) = \lambda e^{-\lambda x}$ for some fixed constant λ. The interoccurrence times between successive events of a Poisson process with parameter λ are independent identical distributed (IID) exponential random variable with mean $1/\lambda$.

The Poisson process is a counting process for the number of randomly occurring point-events observed in a given time interval. For example, suppose the arrival process has a Poisson type distribution. If N(t) denotes the number of arrivals in time interval (0,t], the probability mass function for N(t) is

$$p_n(t) = P[N(t) = n] = \frac{(\lambda t)^n}{n!} e^{-\lambda t} \tag{3.39}$$

Thus, the number of events N(t) in the interval (0,t] has a Poisson distribution with parameter λt and the parameter λ is called the arrival rate of the Poisson process.

Two properties of the Poisson process are the superposition property and decomposition property [6, 7].

The superposition (additive) property states that the superposition of Poisson processes is also a Poisson process, as illustrated in Fig. 3.7.

Thus, the sum of n independent Poisson processes with parameters $\lambda_k, k = 1, 2, \cdots, n$ is a Poisson process with parameter $\lambda = \lambda_1 + \lambda_2 + \cdots + \lambda_n$.

The decomposition (splitting) property is just the reverse of the superposition property. If a Poisson stream is split into k substreams, each substream is also Poisson, as illustrated in Fig. 3.8.

Fig. 3.7 Superposition of
Poisson streams

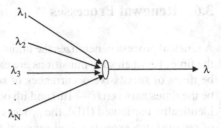

Fig. 3.8 Decomposition of
a Poisson stream

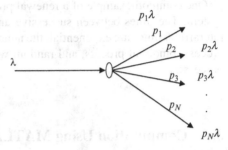

Fig. 3.9 Relationship
between various types of
stochastic processes

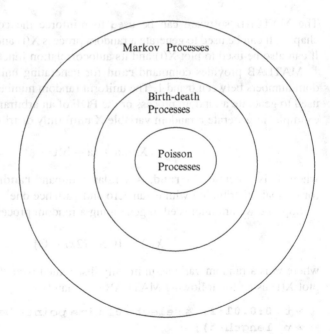

The Poisson process is related to the exponential distribution. If the interarrival
times are exponentially distributed, the number of arrival-points in a time interval is
given by the Poisson distribution and the process is a Poisson arrival process. The
converse is also true—if the number of arrival-points in any interval is a Poisson
process, the interarrival times are exponentially distributed.

The relationship among various types of stochastic processes is shown in Fig. 3.9.

3.6 Renewal Processes

A renewal process generalizes the notion of a Markov process. In a Markov process, the times between state transitions are exponentially distributed. Let $X_1, X_2, X_3, \cdots$ be times of successive occurrences of some phenomenon and let $Z_i = X_i - X_{i-1}$ be the times between $(i - 1\text{th})$ and ith occurrences, then if $\{Z_i\}$ are independent and identically distributed (IID), the process $\{X_i\}$ is called a *renewal process*. The study of renewal processes is called *renewal theory*.

One common example of a renewal process is the arrival process to a queueing system. The times between successive arrivals are IID. In a special case that the interarrival times are exponential, the nenewal process is a Poisson process. Poisson process, binomial process, and random walk process are special cases of renewal processes.

3.7 Computation Using MATLAB

The MATLAB software can be used to reinforce the concepts learned in this chapter. It can be used to generate a random process X(t) and calculate its statistics. It can also be used to plot X(t) and its autocorrelation function.

MATLAB provides command **rand** for generating uniformly distributed random numbers between 0 and 1. The uniform random number generator can then be used to generate a random process or the PDF of an arbitrary random variable. For example, to generate a random variable X uniformly distributed over (a,b), we use

$$X = a + (a - b)U \tag{3.40}$$

where U is generated by **rand**. A similar command **randn** generates a Gaussian (or normal) distribution with mean zero and variance one.

Suppose we are interested in generating a random process

$$X(t) = 10 \cos (2\pi t + \Theta) \tag{3.41}$$

where Θ is a random variable uniformly distributed over $(0, 2\pi)$. We generate and plot X(t) using the following MATLAB commands.

```
» t=0:0.01:2; % select 201 time points between 0 and 2.
» n=length(t);
» theta=2*pi*rand(1,n);   % generates n=201 uniformly
  distributed theta
» x=10*cos(2*pi*t +theta);
» plot(t,x)
```

The plot of the random process is shown in Fig. 3.10.

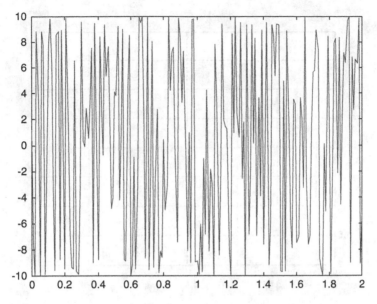

Fig. 3.10 MATLAB generation of the random process $X(t) = 10 \cos(2\pi t + \Theta)$

We may find the mean and standard deviation using MATLAB commands **mean** and **std** respectively. For example, the standard deviation is found using

```
» std(x)
ans =
    7.1174
```

where the result is a bit off from the exact value of 7.0711 obtained from Example 3.2. The reason for this discrepancy is that we selected only 201 points. If more points, say 10,000, are selected the two results should be very close.

We will now use MATLAB to generate a Bernoulli random process, which is used in data communication. The process consists of random variables which assume only two states or values: +1 and −1 (or +1 and 0). In this particular case, the process may also be regarded as *random binary process*. The probability of X(t) being +1 is p and −1 is q = 1 − p. Therefore, to generate a Bernoulli random variable X, we first use MATLAB **rand** to generate a random variable U that uniformly distributed over (0,1). Then, we obtain

$$X = \begin{cases} 1, & \text{if } U \leq p \\ -1, & \text{if } U > p \end{cases} \tag{3.42}$$

i.e. we have partitioned the interval (0,1) into two segments of length p and 1 − p. The following MATLAB program is used to generate a sample function for the random process. The sample function is shown in Fig. 3.11.

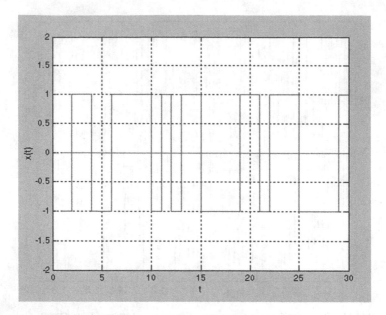

Fig. 3.11 A typical sample function of a Bernoulli random process

```
% Generation of a Bernoulli process
% Ref: D. G. Childers, "Probability of Random Processes,"
Irwin, 1997, p.164
  p=0.6;    % probability of having +1
  q=1-p;      % probability of having -1
  n=30;        % length of the discrete sequence
  t=rand(1,n); %  generate  random  numbers  uniformly
distributed over (0,1)
  x=zeros(length(t)); % set initial value of x equal to zero
  for k=1:n
   if( t(k) <= p )
     x(k)=1;
    else
      x(k)= -1;
    end
  end
  stairs(x);
  xlabel('t')
  ylabel('x(t)')
  a=axis;
  axis([a(1) a(2) -2 2]);
  grid on
```

3.8 Summary

1. A random process (also known as stochastic process) is a mapping from the sample space into an ensemble of time functions known as sample functions. At any instant of time, the value of a random process is a random variable.
2. A continuous-time random process X(t) is a family of sample functions of continuous random variables that are a function of time t, where t is a continuum of values. A random process is deterministic if future values of any sample function can be predicted from past values.
3. A random process is stationary if all its statistical properties does not change with time, i.e $m_X(t)$ is constant and $R_X(t_1,t_2)$ depends only on $\tau = |t_2 - t_1|$.
4. For an ergodic process, the statistical and time averages are the same and only one sample function is needed to compute ensemble averages.
5. For two stationary random processes X(t) and Y(t), the cross-correlation function is defined as

$$R_{XY}(\tau) = E[X(t)Y(t+\tau)]$$

Widely used random processes in communication include random walk, birth-and-death process, Poisson process, Markov process, and renewal process.
6. Some of the concepts covered in the chapter are demonstrated using MATLAB.

For more information on the material covered in this chapter, one should see [8–10].

Problems

3.1 If X(t) = A sin4t, where A is random variable uniformly distributed between 0 and 2, find $E[X(t)]$ and $E[X^2(t)]$.

3.2 Given a random process X(t) = At + 2, where A is a random variable uniformly distributed over the range (0,1),

(a) sketch three sample functions of X(t),
(b) find $\overline{X(t)}$ and $\overline{X^2(t)}$,
(c) determine $R_X(t_1,t_2)$,
(d) Is X(t) WSS?

3.3 If a random process is given by

$$X(t) = A \cos \omega t - B \sin \omega t,$$

where ω is a constant and A and B are independent Gaussian random variables with zero mean and variance σ^2, determine: (a) $E[X]$, $E[X^2]$ and $Var(X)$, (b) the autocorrelation function $R_X(t_1,t_2)$.

3.4 Let $Y(t) = X(t - 1) + \cos 3t$, where $X(t)$ is a stationary random process. Determine the autocorrelation function of $Y(t)$ in terms of $R_X(\tau)$.

3.5 If $Y(t) = X(t) - X(t - \alpha)$, where α is a constant and $X(t)$ is a random process. Show that

$$R_Y(t_1, t_2) = R_x(t_1, t_2) - R_x(t_1, t_2 - \alpha) - R_x(t_1 - \alpha, t_2) + R_x(t_1 - \alpha, t_2 - \alpha)$$

3.6 A random stationary process $X(t)$ has mean 4 and autocorrelation functon

$$R_X(\tau) = 5e^{-2|\tau|}$$

(a) If $Y(t) = X(t - 1)$, find the mean and autocorrelation function of $Y(t)$.
(b) Repeat part (a) if $Y(t) = tX(t)$.

3.7 Let $Z(t) = X(t) + Y(t)$, where $X(t)$ and $Y(t)$ are two independent stationary random processes. Find $R_Z(\tau)$ in terms of $R_X(\tau)$ and $R_Y(\tau)$.

3.8 Repeat the previous problem if $Z(t) = 3X(t) + 4Y(t)$.

3.9 If $X(t) = A\cos\omega t$, where ω is a constant and A random variables with mean μ and variance σ^2, (a) find $< x(t) >$ and $m_X(t)$. (b) Is $X(t)$ ergodic?

3.10 A random process is defined by

$$X(t) = A\cos\omega t - B\sin\omega t,$$

where ω is a constant and A and B are independent random variable with zero mean. Show that $X(t)$ is stationary and also ergodic.

3.11 $N(t)$ is a stationary noise process with zero mean and autocorrelation function

$$R_N(\tau) = \frac{N_o}{2}\delta(\tau)$$

where N_o is a constant. Is $N(t)$ ergodic?

3.12 $X(t)$ is a stationary Gaussian process with zero mean and autocorrelation function

$$R_X(\tau) = \sigma^2 e^{-\alpha|\tau|}\cos\omega\tau$$

where σ, ω, and α are constants. Show that $X(t)$ is ergodic.

3.13 If $X(t)$ and $Y(t)$ are two random processes that are jointly stationary so that $R_{XY}(t_1, t_2) = R_{XY}(\tau)$, prove that

$$R_{XY}(\tau) = R_{YX}(-\tau)$$

where $\tau = |t_2 - t_1|$.

3.14 For two stationary processes $X(t)$ and $Y(t)$, show that

(a)
$$|R_{XY}(\tau)| \le \frac{1}{2}[R_X(0) + R_Y(0)]$$

(b)
$$|R_{XY}(\tau)| \le \sqrt{R_X(0)R_Y(0)}$$

3.15 Let X(t) and Y(t) be two random processes given by

$$X(t) = \cos(\omega t + \Theta)$$
$$Y(t) = \sin(\omega t + \Theta)$$

where ω is a constant and Θ is a random variable uniformly distributed over $(0, 2\pi)$. Find

$$R_{XY}(t, t + \tau) \quad \text{and} \quad R_{YX}(t, t + \tau).$$

3.16 X(t) and Y(t) are two random processes described as

$$X(t) = A\cos\omega t + B\sin\omega t$$
$$Y(t) = B\cos\omega t - A\sin\omega t$$

where ω is a constant and $A = N(0, \sigma^2)$ and $B = N(0, \sigma^2)$. Find $R_{XY}(\tau)$.

3.17 Let X(t) be a stationary random process and Y(t) = X(t) − X(t − a), where a is a constant. Find $R_{XY}(\tau)$.

3.18 Let $\{N(t), t \ge 0\}$ be a Poisson process with rate λ. Find $E[N(t).N(t + s)]$.

3.19 For a Poisson process, show that if s < t,

$$\text{Prob}[N(s) = k | N(t) = n] = \binom{n}{k}\left(\frac{s}{t}\right)^k\left(1 - \frac{s}{t}\right)^{n-k}, k = 0, 1, \cdots, n$$

3.20 Let N(t) be a renewal process where renewal epochs are Erlang with parameters (m, λ). Show that

$$\text{Prob}[N(t) = n] = \sum_{k=nm}^{nm+m-1} \frac{(\lambda t)^k}{k!} e^{-\lambda t}$$

3.21 Use MATLAB to generate a random process $X(t) = A\cos(2\pi t)$, where A is a Gaussian random variable with mean zero and variance one. Take $0 < t < 4$ s.

3.22 Repeat the previous problem if A is random variable uniformly distributed over $(-2, 2)$.

3.23 Given that the autocorrelation function $R_X(\tau) = 2 + 3e^{-\tau^2}$, use MATLAB to plot the function for $-2 < \tau < 2$.

3.24 Use MATLAB to generate a random process

$$X(t) = 2\cos\left(2\pi t + B[n]\frac{\pi}{4}\right)$$

where B[n] is a Bernoulli random sequence taking the values of +1 and −1. Take $0 < t < 3$ s.

References

1. X. R. Li, *Probability, Random Signals, and Statistics*. Boca Raton, FL: CRC Press, 1999, pp. 259-313.
2. G. R. Grimmett and D. R. Stirzaker, *Probability and Random Processes*. New York: Oxford University Press, 3rd ed., 2001, pp. 360-374.
3. R. Nelson, *Probability, Stochastic Processes, and Queueing Theory*. New York: Springer-Verlag, 1995, pp. 235-282.
4. D. Claiborne, *Mathematical Preliminaries for Computer Networking*. New York: John Wiley & Sons, 1990, pp. 35-42.
5. S. M. Ross, *Stochastic Processes*. New York: John Wiley & Sons, 1983.
6. R. Jain, *The Art of Computer Systems Performance Analysis*. New York: John Wiley, 1991, pp. 516-517.
7. J. Medhi, *Stochastic Models in Queueing Theory*. Boston, MA: Academic Press, 1991, p. 31.
8. R. Goodman, *Introduction to Stochastic Models*. Mineola, NY: Dover Publications, 2nd ed., 2006.
9. O. C. Ibe, *Fundamentals of Applied Probability and Random Processes*. Burlington, MA: Elsevier Academic Press, 2005.
10. J. C. Falmagne, *Lectures in Elementary Probability Theory and Stochastic Processes*. New York: McGraw-Hill, 2003.

Chapter 4
Queueing Theory

The priest persuades humble people to endure their hard lot,
a politician urges them to rebel against it, and a scientist
thinks of a method that does away with the hard lot
altogether.

—Max Percy

Queueing is simply waiting in lines such as stopping at the toll booth, waiting in line for a bank cashier, stopping at a traffic light, waiting to buy stamps at the post office, and so on.

A **queue** consists of a line of people or things waiting to be served and a service center with one or more servers.

For example, there would be no need of queueing in a bank if there are infinite number of people serving the customers. But that would be very expensive and impractical.

Queueing theory is applied in several disciplines such as computer systems, traffic management, operations, production, and manufacturing. It plays a significant role in modeling computer communication networks. Since the mid-1960s performance evaluation of computer communication systems are usually made using queueing models.

Reduced to its most basic form, a computer network consists of communication channels and processors (or nodes). As messages flow from node to node, queues begin to form different nodes. For high traffic intensity, the waiting or queueing time can be dominant so that the performance of the network is dictated by the behavior of the queues at the nodes. Analytical derivation of the waiting time requires a knowledge of queueing theory. Providing the basic fundamentals of queueing theory needed for the rest of the book will be our objective in this chapter.

M.N.O. Sadiku and S.M. Musa, *Performance Analysis of Computer Networks*,
DOI 10.1007/978-3-319-01646-7_4, © Springer International Publishing Switzerland 2013

4.1   Kendall's Notation

In view of the complexity of a data network, we first examine the properties of a single queue. The results from a single queue model can be extended to model a network of queues. A single queue is comprised of one or more servers and customers waiting for service. As shown in Fig. 4.1, the queue is characterized by three quantities:

- the input process,
- the service mechanism, and
- the queue discipline.

The *input process* is expressed in terms of the probability distribution of the interarrival times of arriving customers. The *service mechanism* describes the statistical properties of the service process. The *queue discipline* is the rule used to determine how the customers waiting get served. To avoid ambiguity in specifying these characteristics, a queue is usually described in terms of a well-known shorthand notation devised by D. G. Kendall [1]. In Kendall's notation, a queue is characterized by six parameters as follows:

$$A/B/C/K/m/z \tag{4.1}$$

where the letters denote:

A: Arrival process, i.e. the interarrival time distribution
B: Service process, i.e. the service time distribution
C: Number of servers
K: Maximum capacity of the queue (default $= \infty$)
m: Population of customers (default $= \infty$)
z: Service discipline (default $=$ FIFO)

The letters A and B represent the arrival and service processes and assume the following specific letters depending on which probability distribution law is adopted:

D: Constant (deterministic) law, i.e. interarrival/service times are fixed
M: Markov or exponential law, i.e. interarrival/service times are exponentially distributed
G: General law, i.e. nothing is known about the interarrival/service time distribution

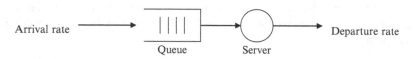

Fig. 4.1 A typical queueing system

GI: General independent law, i.e. all interarrival/service times are independent
E_k: Erlang's law of order k
H_k: Hyperexponential law of order k

The most commonly used service disciplines are:

FIFO: first-in first-out
FCFS: first-come first-serve
LIFO: last-in first-out
FIRO: first-in random-out.

It is common in practice to represent a queue by specifying only the first three symbols of Kendall's notation. In this case, it is assumed that $K = \infty, m = \infty$, and $z = $ FIFO. Thus, for example, the notation M/M/1 represents a queue in which arrival times are exponentially distributed, service times are exponentially distributed, there is one server, the queue length is infinite, the customer population is infinite, and the service discipline is FIFO. In the same way, an M/G/n queue is one with Poisson arrivals, general service distribution, and n servers.

Example 4.1 A single-queue system is denoted by M/G/4/10/200/FCFS. Explain what the operation of the system is.

Solution

The system can be described as follows:

1. The interval arrival times is exponentially distributed.
2. The services times follow a general probability distribution.
3. There are four servers.
4. The buffer size of the queue is 10.
5. The population of customers to be served is 200, i.e. only 200 customers can occupy this queue.
6. The service discipline is first come, first served.

4.2 Little's Theorem

To obtain the waiting or queueing time, we apply a useful result, known as *Little's theorem* after the author of the first formal proof in 1961. The theorem relates the mean number of customers in a queue to the mean arrival rate and the mean waiting time. It states that a queueing system, with average arrival rate λ and mean waiting time per customer $E(W)$, has a mean number of customers in the queue (or average queue length) $E(N_q)$ given by

$$E(N_q) = \lambda E(W) \tag{4.2}$$

The theorem is very general and applies to all kinds of queueing systems. It assumes that the system is in statistical equilibrium or steady state, meaning that the

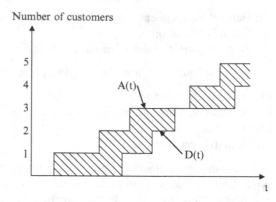

Fig. 4.2 Plot of arrival time and departure time

probabilities of the system being in a particular state have settled down and are not changing with time.

It should be noted that Eq. (4.2) is valid irrespective of the operating policies of the queueing system. For example, it holds for an arbitrary network of queues and serves. It also applies to a single queue, excluding the server.

The theorem can be proved in many ways [2–4]. Three proofs of the theorem are given by Robertazzi [2]. One of them, the graphical proof, will be given here. Suppose we keep track of arrival and departure times of individual customers for a long time t_o. If t_o is large, the number of arrivals would approximately equal to the number of departures. If this number is N_a, then

$$\text{Arrival Rate} = \lambda = \frac{N_a}{t_o} \tag{4.3}$$

Let $A(t)$ and $D(t)$ be respectively the number of arrivals and departures in the interval $(0, t_o)$. Figure 4.2 shows $A(t)$ and $D(t)$. If we subtract the departure curve from the arrival curve at each time instant, we get the number of customers in the system at that moment. The hatched area in Fig. 4.2 represents the total time spent inside the system by all customers. If this is represented by J,

$$\text{Mean time spent in system} = T = \frac{J}{N_a} \tag{4.4}$$

From Eqs. (4.3) and (4.4),

$$\text{Mean number of customers in the system} = N = \frac{J}{t_o} = \frac{N_a}{t_o} \times \frac{J}{N_a} \tag{4.5}$$

or

$$\boxed{N = \lambda T} \tag{4.6}$$

which is Little's theorem.

4.3 M/M/1 Queue

Consider the M/M/1 queue shown in Fig. 4.3.

This is a single-server system with infinite queue size, Poisson arrival process with arrival rate λ, and exponentially distributed service times with service rate μ. The queue discipline is FCFS.

The probability of k arrivals in a time interval t is given by the Poisson distribution:

$$p(k) = \frac{(\lambda t)^k}{k!} e^{-\lambda t}, \quad k = 0, 1, 2, \cdots \tag{4.7}$$

(Note that the Poisson arrival process has exponential arrival times.) It is readily shown that the mean or expected value and variance are given by

$$E(k) = \sum_{k=0}^{\infty} kp(k) = \lambda t \tag{4.8a}$$

$$\text{Var}(k) = E\left[(k - E(k))^2\right] = \lambda t \tag{4.8b}$$

One way of analyzing such a queue is to consider its state diagram [5–8] in Fig. 4.4.

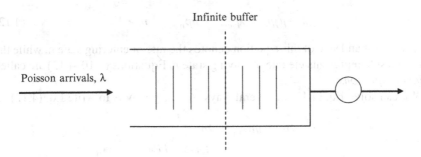

Fig. 4.3 M/M/1 queue

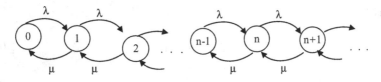

Fig. 4.4 State diagram for M/M/1 queue

We say that the system is in state n where there are n customers in the system (in the queue and the server). Notice from Fig. 4.4 that λ is the rate of moving from state n to n+1 due to an arrival in the system, whereas μ is the rate of moving from state n to n − 1 due to departure when service is completed. If N(t) is the number of customers in the system (in the queue and the server) at time t, the probability of the queue being in state n at steady state is given by

$$p_n = \lim_{t \to \infty} \text{Prob}[N(t) = n], \quad n = 0, 1, 2, \cdots \tag{4.9}$$

Our goal is to find p_n and use it to find some performance measures of interest.

Consider when the system is in state 0. Due to an arrival, the rate at which the process leaves state 0 for state 1 is λp_o. Due to a departure, the rate at which the process leaves state 1 for state 0 is μp_1. In order for stationary probability to exist, the rate of leaving state 0 must equal the rate of entering it. Thus

$$\lambda p_o = \mu p_1 \tag{4.10}$$

When the system is in state 1. Since p_1 is the proportion of time the system is in state 1, the total rate at which arrival or departure occurs is $\lambda p_1 + \mu p_1$, which is the rate at which the process leaves state 1. Similarly, the total rate at which the process enters state 1 is $\lambda p_0 + \mu p_2$. Applying the rate-equality principle gives

$$\lambda p_1 + \mu p_1 = \lambda p_0 + \mu p_2 \tag{4.11}$$

We proceed in this manner for the general case of the system being in state n and obtain

$$(\lambda + \mu)p_n = \lambda p_{n-1} + \mu p_{n+1}, \quad n \geq 1 \tag{4.12}$$

The right-hand side of this equation denotes the rate of entering state n, while the left-hand side represents the rate of leaving state n. Equations (4.10–4.12) are called *balance equations*.

We can solve Eq. (4.12) in several ways. An easy way is to write Eq. (4.12) as

$$\begin{aligned}
\lambda p_n - \mu p_{n+1} &= \lambda p_{n-1} - \mu p_n \\
&= \lambda p_{n-2} - \mu p_{n-1} \\
&= \lambda p_{n-3} - \mu p_{n-2} \\
&\vdots \quad \vdots \\
&= \lambda p_0 - \mu p_1 = 0
\end{aligned} \tag{4.13}$$

Thus

$$\lambda p_n = \mu p_{n+1} \tag{4.14}$$

or

$$p_{n+1} = \rho p_n, \quad \rho = \lambda/\mu \tag{4.15}$$

If we apply this repeatedly, we get

$$p_{n+1} = \rho p_n = \rho^2 p_{n-1} = \rho^3 p_{n-2} = \cdots = \rho^{n+1} p_0, \quad n = 0, 1, 2, \cdots \quad (4.16)$$

We now apply the probability normalization condition,

$$\sum_{n=0}^{\infty} p_n = 1 \qquad (4.17)$$

and obtain

$$p_0 \left[1 + \sum_{n=1}^{\infty} \rho^n \right] = 1 \qquad (4.18)$$

If $\rho < 1$, we get

$$p_0 \frac{1}{1 - \rho} = 1 \qquad (4.19)$$

or

$$p_0 = 1 - \rho \qquad (4.20)$$

From Eqs. (4.15) and (4.20),

$$\boxed{p_n = (1 - \rho)\rho^n, \quad n = 1, 2, \cdots} \qquad (4.21)$$

which is a geometric distribution.

Having found p_n, we are now prepared to obtain some performance measures or measures of effectiveness. These include utilization, throughput, the average queue length, and the average service time [5, 6].

The *utilization* U of the system is the fraction of time that the server is busy. In other words, U is the probability of the server being busy. Thus

$$U = \sum_{n=1}^{\infty} p_n = 1 - p_0 = \rho$$

or

$$\boxed{U = \rho} \qquad (4.22)$$

The *throughput R* of the system is the rate at which customers leave the queue after service, i.e. the departure rate of the server. Thus

$$R = \mu(1 - p_0) = \mu\rho = \lambda \tag{4.23}$$

This should be expected because the arrival and departure rates are equal at steady state for the system to be stable.

The average number of customers in the system is

$$E(N) = \sum_{n=0}^{\infty} np_n = \sum_{n=0}^{\infty} n(1 - \rho)\rho^n = (1 - \rho)\sum_{n=0}^{\infty} n\rho^n$$
$$= (1 - \rho)\frac{\rho}{(1 - \rho)^2}$$

or

$$E(N) = \frac{\rho}{1 - \rho} \tag{4.24}$$

Applying Little's formula, we obtain the *average response time* or *average delay* as

$$E(T) = \frac{E(N)}{\lambda} = \frac{1}{\lambda}\frac{\rho}{1 - \rho} \tag{4.25}$$

or

$$E(T) = \frac{1}{\mu(1 - \rho)} \tag{4.26}$$

This is the mean value of the total time spent in the system (i.e. queue and the server).

As shown in Fig. 4.5, the average delay $E(T)$ is the sum of the average waiting time $E(W)$ and the average service time $E(S)$, i.e.

$$E(T) = E(W) + E(S) \tag{4.27}$$

Equivalently, the average number of customers $E(N)$ in the system equals the sum of the average of customers waiting $E(N_q)$ in the queue and the average number of customers $E(N_s)$ being served, i.e.

$$E(N) = E(N_q) + E(N_s) \tag{4.28}$$

Fig. 4.5 Little's formula applied to M/M/1 queue thrice

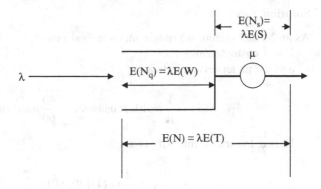

But the mean service $E(S) = \frac{1}{\mu}$. Thus

$$E(W) = E(T) - \frac{1}{\mu} \tag{4.29}$$

or

$$\boxed{E(W) = \frac{\rho}{\mu(1 - \rho)}} \tag{4.30}$$

We now apply Little's theorem to find the *average queue length* or the average number of customers waiting in the queue, i.e.

$$\boxed{E(N_q) = \lambda E(W) = \frac{\rho^2}{1 - \rho}} \tag{4.31}$$

Finally, since $E(N) = \lambda E(T)$, it is evident from Eqs. (4.27) and (4.28) that

$$E(N_s) = \lambda E(S) = \lambda \frac{1}{\mu} = \rho \tag{4.32}$$

Notice from Eqs. (4.25), (4.31), (4.32) that the Little's theorem is applied three times. This is also shown in Fig. 4.5.

Example 4.2 Service at a bank may be modeled as an M/M/1 queue at which customers arrive according to Poisson process. Assume that the mean arrival rate is 1 customer/min and that the service times are exponentially distributed with mean 40 s/customer. (a) Find the average queue length. (b) How long does a customer have to wait in line? (c) Determine the average queue size and the waiting time in the queue if the service time is increased to 50 s/customer.

Solution

As an M/M/1 queue, we obtain mean arrival rate as
$\lambda = 1$ customer/min
and the mean service rate as

$$E(S) = \frac{1}{\mu} = 40\,\text{s/customer} = \frac{40}{60}\,\text{min/customer}$$

Hence, the traffic intensity is

$$\rho = \frac{\lambda}{\mu} = (1)(40/60) = \frac{2}{3}$$

(a) The mean queue size is

$$E[N_q] = \frac{\rho^2}{1-\rho} = \frac{(2/3)^2}{1-2/3} = 1.333\,\text{customers}$$

(b) The mean waiting time is

$$E[W] = \frac{\rho}{\mu(1-\rho)} = \frac{2/3(4/6)}{(1-2/3)} = 1.333\,\text{min}$$

(c) If the mean service time E(S) = 50 s/customer = 50/60 min/customer, then

$$\rho = \frac{\lambda}{\mu} = (1)(50/60) = \frac{5}{6}$$

$$E[N_q] = \frac{\rho^2}{1-\rho} = \frac{(5/6)^2}{1-5/6} = 4.1667\,\text{customers}$$

$$E[W] = \frac{\rho}{\mu(1-\rho)} = \frac{5/6(5/6)}{(1-5/6)} = 4.1667\,\text{min}$$

We expect the queue size and waiting time to increase if it takes longer time for customers to be served.

4.4   M/M/1 Queue with Bulk Arrivals/Service

In the previous section, it was assumed that customers arrive individually (or one at a time) and are provided service individually. In this section, we consider the possibility of customers arriving in bulk (or in groups or batch) or being served in bulk. Bulk arrivals/service occur in practice because it is often more economical to collect a number of items (jobs, orders, etc.) before servicing them.

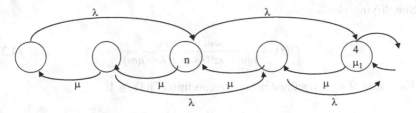

Fig. 4.6 Transition diagram of $M^X/M/1$ queue with m = 2

4.4.1 $M^x/M/1$ (Bulk Arrivals) System

Here we consider the situation where arrivals occur in batches of more than one customer, i.e. in bulk. Although the process is not birth-and-death process, the arrival instants still occur as a Poisson process with constant rate λ. Each of the arriving customers is served in standard fashion (first-come, first served, one at a time) by a server with exponentially distributed service times with parameter μ. Suppose the size of the batch is fixed at $m \geq 1$ customers. Then only two transitions can occur as

$$n \to n + m \quad \text{(arrival)}$$

or

$$n + 1 \to n \quad \text{(departure)}$$

The state transition diagram is shown in Fig. 4.6 for m = 2. The balance equation for n = 0 is

$$\lambda p_0 = m\mu p_1 \tag{4.33}$$

and for $n \geq 1$ is

$$(\lambda + \mu m)p_n = \mu m p_{n+1} + \lambda p_{n-m} \tag{4.34}$$

We now apply the method of z-transforms to solve for p_n. We define the generating function

$$G(z) = \sum_{i=0}^{\infty} p_n z^n \tag{4.35}$$

Multiplying the balance equation for state n by z^n and summing, we obtain

$$\sum_{n=1}^{\infty} (\lambda + \mu m)p_n z^n = \sum_{n=1}^{\infty} \mu m p_{n+1} z^n + \sum_{n=1}^{\infty} \lambda p_{n-m} z^n \tag{4.36}$$

Simplifying yields

$$G(z) = \frac{\mu m(1-z)p_0}{\mu m + \lambda z^{m+1} - z(\lambda + \mu m)} \tag{4.37}$$

The value of p_0 is obtained using the condition $G(1) = 1$.

$$p_0 = 1 - \frac{\lambda m}{\mu} = 1 - \rho, \quad \rho = \frac{\lambda m}{\mu} \tag{4.38}$$

4.4.2   M/M^Y/1 (Bulk Service) System

This kind of model is used to analyze systems that wait until a certain message size is reached before releasing the data for transmission. We will assume that customers are served in bulk of size m, i.e. customers are served m at a time. At equilibrium, the balance equations are [8, 9]:

$$(\lambda + \mu)p_n = \lambda p_{n-1} + \mu p_{n+m}, \quad n \geq 1 \tag{4.39a}$$

$$\lambda p_0 = \mu p_m + \mu p_{m-1} + \cdots + \mu p_1 \tag{4.39b}$$

Equation (4.39a) can be written in terms of an operator D so

$$\left[\mu D^{m+1} - (\lambda + \mu)D + \lambda\right]p_n = 0, \quad n \geq 0 \tag{4.40}$$

If the roots of the characteristic equation are $r_1, r_2, \cdots, r_{m+1}$, then

$$p_n = \sum_{I=1}^{m+1} C_i r_i^n, \quad n \geq 0 \tag{4.41}$$

Using the fact that $\sum_{n=0}^{\infty} p_n = 1$, we obtain

$$p_n = (1 - r_0)r_0^n, \quad n \geq 0, 0 < r_0 < 1 \tag{4.42}$$

where r_0 is the one and only one root of Eq. (4.40) that is less than one. Comparing this with Eq. (4.21) shows the similarity between this solution and that of M/M/1. Hence,

$$E[N] = \frac{r_0}{1 - r_0} \tag{4.43}$$

$$E[T] = \frac{r_0}{\lambda(1 - r_0)} \tag{4.44}$$

4.5 M/M/1/k Queueing System

In this case, we have situations similar to M/M/1 but the number of customers that can be queued is limited to k. In other words, this is a system with limited waiting space. If an arriving customer finds the queue full, it is lost or blocked, as shown in Fig. 4.7.

Hence,

$$\lambda_n = \begin{cases} \lambda, & \text{if } 0 \le n < k \\ 0, & n \ge k \end{cases} \tag{4.45}$$

$$\mu_n = \mu, \quad 0 \le n \le k \tag{4.46}$$

The state transition diagram is given in Fig. 4.8.

The balance equations are

$$\lambda p_0 = \mu p_1$$

$$\lambda p_n + \mu p_n = \lambda p_{n-1} + \mu p_{n+1}, \quad 1 \le n \le k-1 \tag{4.47}$$

$$\lambda p_{k-1} = \mu p_k$$

We solve these equations recursively and apply the normalization condition. If we define $\rho = \lambda/\mu$, the state probabilities at steady state are given by

$$p_n = \begin{cases} \dfrac{(1-\rho)\rho^n}{1-\rho^{k+1}}, & 0 \le n \le k \\ 0, & n > k \end{cases} \tag{4.48}$$

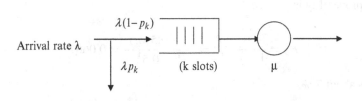

Fig. 4.7 M/M/1/k queueing system

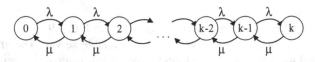

Fig. 4.8 State transition diagram for the M/M/1/k queue

The utilization of the server is given by

$$U = 1 - p_0 = \frac{\rho(1 - \rho^k)}{1 - \rho^{k+1}} \tag{4.49}$$

The average queue length is

$$E(N_q) = \sum_{n=0}^{k} np_n = \frac{\rho}{1 - \rho^{k+1}} \left[\frac{1 - \rho^k}{1 - \rho} - k\rho^k \right] \tag{4.50}$$

Since there can be blocking in this system, the blocking probability is

$$\boxed{P_B = p_k = \frac{(1 - \rho)\rho^k}{1 - \rho^{k+1}}} \tag{4.51}$$

This is the probability that arriving customer is blocked, i.e. it is lost because it finds the queue full.

Example 4.3 A system consists of a packet buffer and a communication server and can hold not more than three packets. Arrivals are Poisson with rate 15 packets/ms and the server follows exponential distribution with mean 30 packets/ms. Determine the blocking probability of the system.

Solution

This is an M/M/1/k system with k = 3.

$$\rho = \lambda \frac{1}{\mu} = \frac{15}{30} = 0.5$$

The probability is

$$P_B = \frac{(1 - \rho)\rho^k}{1 - \rho^{k+1}} = \frac{(1 - 0.5)0.5^3}{1 - 0.5^4} = 0.0667$$

which is about 7 %.

4.6   M/M/k Queueing System

This is the case where we have k servers, as shown in Fig. 4.9.

Upon arrival, a customer is served by any available server. The arriving customer is queued when all servers are found busy, i.e. no customer is queued until the number of arrivals exceeds k. The state transition diagram is shown in Fig. 4.10.

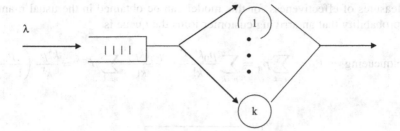

Fig. 4.9 The M/M/k queue

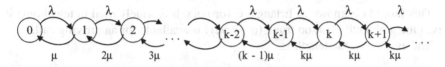

Fig. 4.10 State transition diagram for M/M/k system

The system can be modeled as a birth-and-death process with

$$\lambda_n = \lambda \tag{4.52}$$

$$\mu_m = \begin{cases} n\mu, & 0 \le n \le k \\ k\mu, & n \ge k \end{cases}$$

At steady state,

$$\lambda p_{n-1} = n\mu p_n, \quad n \le k \tag{4.53a}$$

$$\lambda p_{n-1} = k\mu p_n, \quad n > k \tag{4.53b}$$

From these, we obtain the state probabilities as

$$p_n = \begin{cases} p_0 \dfrac{(k\rho)^n}{n!}, & n \le k \\ p_0 \dfrac{\rho^n k^k}{k!}, & n \ge k \end{cases} \tag{4.54}$$

where $\rho = \frac{\lambda}{k\mu} < 1$. Solving for p_0, we get

$$p_0 = \left[\sum_{n=0}^{k-1} \frac{(k\rho)^n}{n!} + \left(\frac{k^k \rho^k}{k!} \right) \frac{1}{1-\rho} \right]^{-1} \tag{4.55}$$

Measures of effectiveness for this model can be obtained in the usual manner. The probability that an arriving customer joins the queue is

$$\text{Prob[queueing]} = P_Q = \sum_{n=k}^{\infty} p_n = \sum_{n=k}^{\infty} \frac{p_0 k^k \rho^n}{k!} = \frac{p_0 (k\rho)^k}{k!} \sum_{n=k}^{\infty} \rho^{n-k} = \frac{k^k \rho^k}{k!} \left(\frac{p_0}{1-\rho} \right)$$

or

$$\boxed{P_Q = \frac{k^k \rho^k}{k!} \left(\frac{p_0}{1-\rho} \right)} \tag{4.56}$$

This formula is known as Erlang's C formula. It is widely used in telephony; it gives the probability that no trunk (or server) is available for an arriving call.

The average queue length is

$$E[N] = \sum_{n=0}^{\infty} n p_n = k\rho + \frac{\rho}{(1-\rho)} P_Q \tag{4.57}$$

Using Little's theorem, the average time spent E[T] in the system can be obtained as

$$E[T] = \frac{E[N]}{\lambda} = \frac{1}{\mu} + \frac{1}{\mu k} \frac{P_Q}{(1-\rho)} \tag{4.58}$$

4.7 M/M/∞ Queueing System

This is the case in which we have infinite number of servers so that an arriving customer can always find a server and need not queue This model can be used to study the effect of delay in large systems. The state transition diagram for the M/M/ ∞ system is shown in Fig. 4.11.

Like we did before, we assume a Poisson arrivals at rate λ and exponentially distributed service times with mean 1/μ. We adopt a birth-and-death process with parameters

$$\lambda_n = \lambda, \quad n = 0, 1, 2, \cdots \tag{4.59}$$

Fig. 4.11 State transition diagram for M/M/∞ queueing system

$$\mu_n = n\mu, \quad n = 1, 2, \cdots \tag{4.60}$$

The balance equation is

$$\lambda p_n = (n+1)\mu p_{n+1} \tag{4.61}$$

which can be solved to give

$$p_n = \frac{\rho^n}{n!} p_0 \tag{4.62}$$

where $\rho = \lambda/\mu$. Applying the normalization condition $\sum_{n=0}^{\infty} p_n = 1$ gives

$$p_0 = e^{-\rho} \tag{4.63}$$

The utilization of the server is

$$U = 1 - p_0 = 1 - e^{-\rho} \tag{4.64}$$

The average number of customers in the system is

$$E[N] = \sum_{n=0}^{\infty} n p_n = \rho \tag{4.65}$$

We apply Little's theorem in finding the average time spent in the system.

$$E[T] = \frac{E[N]}{\lambda} = \frac{1}{\mu} \tag{4.66}$$

Also,

$$E[N_q] = 0 = E[W_q] \tag{4.67}$$

i.e. the average waiting time and the average number of customers waiting in the queue are both zero.

4.8 M/G/1 Queueing System

The M/G/1 queueing system is the simplest non-Markovian system. We analyze it assuming that it is in the steady state. An M/G/1 system assumes a FIFO service discipline, an infinite queue size, a Poisson input process (with arrival rate λ), a general service times (with arbitrary but known distribution function H, mean

$\tau = 1/\mu$, and variance σ^2), and one server. To derive the average waiting time of the M/G/1 model requires some effort beyond the scope of this book. The derivation involves applying the *method of z-transform* or generating functions and is provided in the Appendix A for the curious student. The result is [10–12]:

$$E(W) = \frac{\rho\tau}{2(1-\rho)}\left(1+\frac{\sigma^2}{\tau^2}\right)$$

(4.68)

where $\rho = \lambda/\mu = \lambda\tau$. This is known as *Pollaczek-Khintchine formula* after two Russian mathematicians Pollaczek and Khintchine who derived the formula independently in 1930 and 1932 respectively. The average number of customers $E(N_q)$ in the queue is

$$E(N_q) = \lambda E(W) = \frac{\rho^2}{2(1-\rho)}\left(1+\frac{\sigma^2}{\tau^2}\right)$$

(4.69)

The average response time is

$$E(T) = E(W) + \tau = \frac{\rho\tau}{2(1-\rho)}\left(1+\frac{\sigma^2}{\tau^2}\right) + \tau$$

(4.70)

and the mean number of customers in the system is

$$E(N) = \lambda E(T) = E(N_q) + \rho$$

(4.71)

or

$$E(N) = \frac{\rho^2}{2(1-\rho)}\left(1+\frac{\sigma^2}{\tau^2}\right) + \rho$$

(4.72)

We may now obtain the mean waiting time for the M/M/1 and M/D/1 queue models as special cases of the M/G/1 model.

For the M/M/1 queue model, a special case of the M/G/1 model, the service times follow an exponential distribution with mean $\tau = 1/\mu$ and variance σ^2. That means,

$$H(t) = \text{Prob}[X \le t] = 1 - e^{-\mu t}$$

(4.73)

Hence,

$$\sigma^2 = \tau^2$$

(4.74)

Substituting this in Pollaczek-Khintchine formula in Eq. (4.68) gives the mean waiting time as

$$E(W) = \frac{\rho\tau}{(1-\rho)}$$

(4.75)

The M/D/1 queue is another special case of the M/G/1 model. For this model, the service times are constant with the mean value $\tau = 1/\mu$ and variance $\sigma = 0$. Thus Pollaczek-Khintchine formula in Eq. (4.68) gives the mean waiting time as

$$E(W) = \frac{\rho\tau}{2(1-\rho)} \tag{4.76}$$

It should be noted from Eqs. (4.75) and (4.76) that the waiting time for the M/D/1 model is one-half that for the M/M/1 model, i.e.

$$E(W)_{M/D/1} = \frac{\rho\tau}{2(1-\rho)} = \frac{1}{2}E(W)_{M/M/1} \tag{4.77}$$

Example 4.4 In the M/G/1 system, prove that:

(a) Prob (the system is empty) $= 1 - \rho$
(b) Average length of time between busy periods $= 1/\lambda$
(c) Average no. of customers served in a busy period $= \frac{1}{1-\rho}$

where $\rho = \lambda\overline{X}$ and $\overline{X}$ is the mean service time.

Solution

(a) Let p_b = Prob. that the system is busy. Then p_b is the fraction of time that the server is busy. At steady state, arrival rate = departure rate

$$\lambda = p_b\mu$$

or

$$p_b = \frac{\lambda}{\mu} = \rho$$

The Prob. that the system is empty is

$$p_e = 1 - p_b = 1 - \rho$$

(b) The server is busy only when there are arrivals. Hence the average length of time between busy periods = average interarrival rate = $1/\lambda$.
   Alternatively, we recall that if t is the interarrival time,

$$f(t) = \lambda e^{-\lambda t}$$

   Hence E(t) = $1/\lambda$.

(c) Let E(B) = average busy period, E(I) = average idle period. From part (a),

$$p_b = \rho = \frac{E(B)}{E(B) + E(I)}$$

From part (b),

E(I) = average length of time between busy periods = $1/\lambda$

Hence

$$\rho = \frac{E(B)}{E(B) + \frac{1}{\lambda}}$$

Solving for E(B) yields

$$E(B) = \frac{\rho}{\lambda(1-\rho)} = \frac{\overline{X}}{1-\rho}$$

as required.

The average no. of customers served in a busy period is

$$N_b = \frac{\text{Average length of busy period}}{\text{Average service time}}$$

Hence

$$N_b = E(B)/\overline{X} = \frac{1}{1-\rho}$$

4.9 M/E$_k$/1 Queueing System

In this case, the service time distribution is Erlang distribution with parameters μ and k, i.e.

$$f_X(x) = \frac{\mu(\mu x)^{k-1}}{(k-1)!} e^{-\mu x}, \quad x \geq 0 \tag{4.78}$$

with mean and variance

$$E[X] = \frac{k}{\mu}, \quad \mathrm{Var}[X] = \frac{k}{\mu^2} \tag{4.79}$$

This should be regarded as another special case of M/G/1 system so that Pollaczek-Khintchine formula in Eq. (4.68) applies. Thus,

$$E[W_q] = \frac{1+k}{2k} \frac{\lambda}{\mu(\mu-\lambda)} = \frac{1+k}{2k} \frac{\rho}{\mu(1-\rho)} \tag{4.80}$$

$$E[N_q] = \lambda E(W_q) = \frac{1+k}{2k} \frac{\lambda^2}{\mu(\mu-\lambda)} = \frac{1+k}{2k} \frac{\rho^2}{1-\rho} \tag{4.81}$$

$$E[T] = E[W_q] + \frac{1}{\mu} \qquad (4.82)$$

$$E[N] = \lambda E[T] \qquad (4.83)$$

where $\rho = \lambda/\mu$.

4.10 Networks of Queues

The queues we have considered so far are isolated. In real life, we have a network of queues interconnected such as shown in Fig. 4.12. Such networks of queues are usually complicated and are best analyzed using simulation. However, we consider two simple ones here [13–15].

4.10.1 Tandem Queues

Consider two M/M/1 queues in tandem, as shown in Fig. 4.13. This is an example of open queueing network.

The state diagram is shown in Fig. 4.14. From the sate diagram, we can obtain the balance equations.

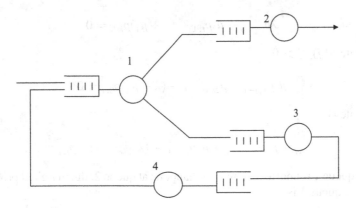

Fig. 4.12 A typical network of queues

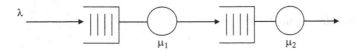

Fig. 4.13 Two M/M/1 queues in tandem

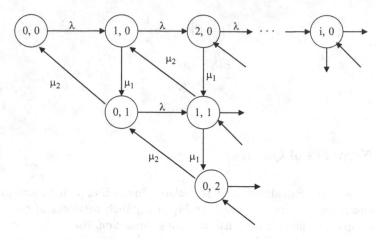

Fig. 4.14 The state diagram for two M/M/1 queues in tandem

Let

$$p_{i,j} = \text{Prob}[\,i \text{ jobs at server 1 and } j \text{ jobs at server 2}]$$

For state (0,0),

$$\lambda p_{0,0} = \mu_2 p_{0,1} \tag{4.84}$$

For state $(i,0)$, $i > 0$,

$$\lambda p_{i-1,0} + \mu_2 p_{i,1} - (\lambda + \mu_1)p_{i,0} = 0 \tag{4.85}$$

For state $(0,j)$, $j > 0$,

$$\mu_1 p_{1,j-1} + \mu_2 p_{0,j+1} - (\lambda + \mu_2)p_{0,j} = 0 \tag{4.86}$$

For state (i,j),

$$\lambda p_{i-1,j} + \mu_1 p_{i+1,j-1} + \mu_2 p_{i,j+1} - (\lambda + \mu_1 + \mu_2)p_{i,j} = 0 \tag{4.87}$$

Since queue 1 is unaffected by what happens at queue 2, the marginal probability of i jobs at queue 1 is

$$p_i = (1 - \rho_1)\rho_1^i, \quad \rho_1 = \frac{\lambda}{\mu_1} \tag{4.88}$$

Similarly, for queue 2

$$p_j = (1 - \rho_2)\rho_2^j, \quad \rho_2 = \frac{\lambda}{\mu_2} \tag{4.89}$$

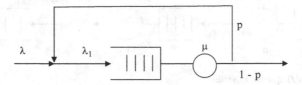

Fig. 4.15 A queueing system with a (Bernoulli) feedback

A simple product form solution for this two-node network is

$$p_{i,j} = (1 - \rho_1)(1 - \rho_2)\rho_1^i \rho_2^j, \quad \rho_1 = \frac{\lambda}{\mu_1} \tag{4.90}$$

The analysis of even this simplest case is extremely complicated.

4.10.2 Queueing System with Feedback

Queuing systems with feedback are applicable to a fairly limited set of circumstances. A typical example is shown in Fig. 4.15. The problem here is that the combination of the external Poisson process and the feedback process is not Poisson because the processes being superposed are not independent due to the feedback. However, consideration of the steady state diagram shows us that, as far as queue length is concerned, the system behaves like an M/M/1 queue with arrival rate λ and service rate $p\mu$. Also, the traffic equation for this network is

$$\lambda_1 = \lambda + \lambda_1 p \rightarrow \lambda_1 = \frac{\lambda}{1 - p} \tag{4.91}$$

4.11 Jackson Networks

A Jackson network has a steady state solution in product form. Such product-form queueing networks can be open or closed. The nature of such networks allows us to decouple the queues, analyze them separately as individual systems, and then combine the results. For example, consider a series of k single-server queues with exponential service time and Poisson arrivals, as shown in Fig. 4.16.

Customers entering the system join queue at each stage. It can be shown that each queue can be analyzed independently of other queues. Each queue has an arrival and a departure rate of λ. If the ith server has a service rate of μ_i, the utilization of the ith server is

$$\rho_i = \frac{\lambda}{\mu_i} \tag{4.92}$$

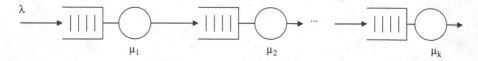

Fig. 4.16 k M/M/1 queues in series

and

$$\text{Prob}[n_i \text{ customers in the ith queue}] = P(n_i) = (1 - \rho_i)\rho_i^{n_i} \qquad (4.93)$$

The joint probability of queue lengths of k queues is the product of individual probabilities.

$$P(n_1, n_2, \cdots, n_k) = (1 - \rho_1)\rho_1^{n_1}(1 - \rho_2)\rho_2^{n_2}\cdots(1 - \rho_k)\rho_k^{n_k}$$
$$= P_1(n_1)P_2(n_2)\cdots P_k(n_k) \qquad (4.94)$$

This is known as *Jackson theorem*, after J.R. Jackson who first proved the property. The queueing network is therefore a product-form network. A network to which Jackson's theorem is applicable is known as *Jackson network*. In general, for a product-form network

$$P(n_1, n_2, \cdots, n_k) = \frac{1}{G}\prod_{i=1}^{k}\rho_i^{n_i} \qquad (4.95)$$

where G is a normalization constant and is a function of the total number of jobs in the system. The product-form networks are easier to solve than nonproduct-form networks.

4.12   Summary

1. A simple introduction to queueing theory was presented.
2. Beginning with the M/M/1 queue, we derived the closed form expressions for some performance measures.
3. We also considered the case of an M/M/1 queue with bulk arrivals or service. We considered M/M/1/k, M/M/k, and M/M/∞ queueing systems.
4. Using the more general queueing model M/G/1, we derived the Pollaczek-Khintchine formula for the mean waiting time. The corresponding mean waiting times for the M/M/1, M/D/1, M/E$_k$/1 queue models were derived as special cases of the M/G/1 model.

A more in depth introduction to queueing theory can be found in [11, 12, 16–22]. We will apply the ideas in this chapter to model computer networks in the following chapters.

Problems

4.1 For the M/M/1 system, find: (a) $E(N^2)$, (b) $E(N(N - 1))$, (c) $Var(N)$.

4.2 In an M/M/1 queue, show that the probability that the number of messages waiting in the queue is greater than a certain number m is

$$P(n > m) = \rho^{m+1}$$

4.3 For an M/M/1 model, what effect will doubling λ and μ have on $E[N]$, $E[N_q]$, and $E[W]$?

4.4 Customers arrive at a post office according to a Poisson process with 20 customers/h. There is only one clerk on duty. Customers have exponential distribution of service times with mean of 2 min. (a) What is the average number of customers in the post office? (b) What is the probability that an arriving customer finds the clerk idle?

4.5 From the balance equation for the M/M/1 queue, obtain the probability generating function.

4.6 An air-line check-in counter at Philadelphia airport can be modeled as an M/M/1 queue. Passengers arrive at the rate of 7.5 customers per hour and the service takes 6 min on the average. (a) Find the probability that there are fewer than four passengers in the system. (b) On the average, how long does each passenger stay in the system? (c) On the average, how many passengers need to wait?

4.7 An observation is made of a group of telephone subscribers. During the 2-h observation, 40 calls are made with a total conversation time of 90 min. Calculate the traffic intensity and call arrival rate assuming M/M/1 system.

4.8 Customers arrive at a bank at the rate of 1/3 customer per minute. If X denotes the number of customers to arrive in the next 9 min, calculate the probability that: (a) there will be no customers within that period, (b) exactly three customers will arrive in this period, and (c) at least four customers will arrive. Assume this is a Poisson process.

4.9 At a telephone booth, the mean duration of phone conversation is 4 min. If no more than 2-min mean waiting time for the phone can be tolerated, what is the mean rate of the incoming traffic that the phone can support?

4.10 For an M/M/1 queue operating at fixed $\rho = 0.75$, answer the following questions: (a) Calculate the probability that an arriving customer finds the queue empty. (b) What is the average number of messages stored? (c) What is the average number of messages in service? (d) Is there a single time at which this average number is in service?

4.11 At a certain hotel, a lady serves at a counter and she is the only one on duty. Arrivals to the counter seem to follow the Poisson distribution with mean of 10 customers/h. Each customer is served one at a time and the service time follows an exponential distribution with a mean of 4 min.

(a) What is the probability of having a queue?

(b) What is the average queue length?

(c) What is the average time a customer spends in the system?

(d) What is the probability of a customer spending more than 5 min in the queue before being attended to?

Note that the waiting time distribution for an M/M/1 queue is

$$\text{Prob}(W > t) = W(t) = 1 - \rho e^{-\mu(1-\rho)t}, \quad t \geq 0$$

4.12 (a) The probability p_n that an infinite M/M/2 queue is in state n is given by

$$
p_n = \begin{cases}
\dfrac{(1-\rho)}{(1+\rho)}, & n = 0 \\[2mm]
\dfrac{2(1-\rho)}{(1+\rho)}\rho^2, & n \geq 0
\end{cases}
$$

where $\rho = \frac{\lambda}{2\mu}$. Find the average occupancy E(N) and the average time delay in the queue E(T).

4.13 Consider M/M/k model. Show that the probability of any server is busy is $\lambda / k\mu$.

4.14 For the M/M/1/k system, let q_n be the probability that an arriving customer finds n customers in the system. Prove that

$$q_n = \frac{p_n}{1 - p_k}$$

4.15 Derive Eq.(4.62) from Eq. (4.61).

4.16 Find the mean and variance of the number of customers in the system for the M/M/∞ queue.

4.17 At a toll booth, there is only one "bucket" where each driver drops 25 cents. Assuming that cars arrive according to a Poisson probability distribution at rate 2 cars per minute and that each car takes a *fixed* time 15 s to service, find: (a) the long-run fraction of time that the system is busy, (b) the average waiting time for each car, (c) the average number of waiting cars, (d) how much money is collected in 2 h.

4.18 An M/E$_k$/1 queue has an arrival rate of 8 customers/s and a service rate of 12 customers/s. Assuming that k = 2, find the mean waiting time.

4.19 Consider two identical M/M/1 queueing systems in operation side by side in a facility with the same rates λ and μ ($\rho = \lambda/\mu$). Show that the distribution of the total number N of customers in the two systems combined is

$$\text{Prob}(N = n) = (n + 1)(1 - \rho)^2 \rho^n, \quad n > 0$$

References

1. D. G. Kendall, "Some problems in the theory of queues," *J. Roy. Statis. Soc.* Series B, vol. 13, 1951, pp. 151–185.
2. T. G. Robertazzi, *Computer Networks and Systems: Queueing Theory and Performance Evaluation.* New York: Springer-Verlag, 1990, pp. 43-47.
3. S. Eilon, "A Simpler Proof of L = λW," *Operation Research*, vol. 17, 1969, pp. 915–916.
4. R. Jain, *The Art of Computer Systems Performance Analysis.* New York: John Wiley, 1991, pp. 513-514.
5. J. Medhi, *Stochastic Models in Queueing Theory.* San Diego, CA: Academic Press, 1991, pp. 71–75.
6. G. C. Cassandras, *Discrete Event Systems.* Boston, MA: Irwin, 1993, pp.349-354, 404-413.
7. M. Schartz, *Telecommunication Networks.* Reading, MA: Addison-Wesley, 1987, pp. 21-69.
8. D. Gross and C. M. Harris, *Fundamentals of Queueing Theory.* New York: John Wiley, 1998, 3rd ed., pp. 116-164.
9. E. Gelenbe and G. Pujolle, *Introduction to Queueing Networks.* Chichester, UK: John Wiley & Sons, 1987, pp. 94-95.
10. R. Nelson, *Probability, Stochastic Processes, and Queueing Theory.* New York: Springer-Verlag, 1995, pp. 295–309.
11. R. B. Cooper, *Introduction to Queueing Theory.* New York: North-Holland, 2nd ed., 1981, pp. 208-222.
12. R. B. Cooper, "Queueing Theory," in D. P. Heyman (ed.), *Handbooks in Operations Research and Management Science.* New York: North-Holland, 1990, chap. 10, pp. 469-518.
13. P. J.B. King, *Computer and Communication System Performancd Modelling.* New York: Prentice Hall,1989.pp.124-130
14. P. G. Harrison and N. M. Patel, *Performance Modelling of Communication Networks and Computer Architecture.* Wokingham, UK: Addison-Wesley, 1993, pp. 258-297.
15. M. K. Molloy, *Fundamentals of Performance Modeling.* New York: MacMillan, 1989, pp. 193-248.
16. L. Kleinrock, *Queueing Systems.* New York: John Wiley, 1975, vol. I.
17. J. D. Claiborne, *Mathematical Preliminaries for Computer Networking.* New York: John Wiley, 1990.
18. O. C. Ibe, *Markov Processes for Stochastic Modeling.* Burlington, MA: Elsevier Academic Press, 2009, pp. 105-152.
19. —, *Fundamentals of Stochastic Networks.* New York: John Wiley & Sons, 2011.
20. J. F. Hayes and T. V. J. G. Babu, *Modeling and Analysis of Telecommunications Networks.* New York: Wiley-Interscience, 2004, pp. 67-112.
21. A. M. Haghighi and D. P. Mishev, *Queueing Models in Industry and Business.* New York: Nova Science Publishers, 2008.
22. G. R. Dattatreya, *Performance Analysis of Queuing and Computer Networks.* Boca Raton, FL: CRC Press, 2008.

Chapter 5
Simulation

*Science without religion is lame, religion without
science is blind.*

—Albert Einstein

The previous chapter dealt with one of the tools for performance analysis—queueing theory. This chapter concentrates on another tool—simulation. In this chapter, we provide an overview of simulation: its historical background, importance, characteristics, and stages of development.

There is a lot of confusion among students as to what simulation is really about. Some confuse simulation with emulation or numerical modeling. While emulation is building a prototype (either hardware or software or combination of both) to mimic the real system, simulation is "the process of designing a mathematical or logical model of a real system and then conducting computer-based experiments with the model to describe, explain, and predict the behavior of the real system" [1]. In other words, simulation is modeling the real system, while emulation is an imitation of the system.

Simulation is designing a model that resembles a real system in certain important aspects.

It can be viewed as the act of performing experiments on a model of a given system. It is a cost-effective method of solving engineering problems. With computers, simulations have been used with great success in solving diverse scientific and engineering problems.

Simulation emerged as a numerical problem-solving approach during World War II when the so-called *Monte Carlo methods* were successfully used by John Von Neumann and Stanislaw Ulam of Los Alamos laboratory. The Monte Carlo methods were applied to problems related to atomic bomb. Simulation was introduced into university curricula in the 1960s during which books and periodicals on simulation began to appear. The system that is being modeled is deterministic in Monte Carlo simulation, and stochastic in case of simulation [2].

M.N.O. Sadiku and S.M. Musa, *Performance Analysis of Computer Networks*,
DOI 10.1007/978-3-319-01646-7_5, © Springer International Publishing Switzerland 2013

Computer systems can be modeled at several levels of detail [3]: circuit-level, gate-level, and system-level. At the circuit-level, we employ simulation to analyze the switching behavior of various components of the circuit such as resistors, capacitors, and transistors. In the gate-level simulation, the circuit components are aggregated into a single element so that the element is analyzed from a functional standpoint. At the system-level, the system is represented as a whole rather than as in segments as in gate-level simulation. System-level simulation involves analyzing the entire system from a performance standpoint. It is this kind of simulation that we shall be concerned with in this chapter.

5.1   Why Simulation?

A large number of factors influence the decision to use any particular scientific technique to solve a given problem. The appropriateness of the technique is one consideration, and economy is another. In this section, we consider the various advantages of using simulation as a modeling technique.

A system can be simplified to an extent that it can be solved analytically. Such an analytical solution is desirable because it leads to a closed form solution (such as in Chap. 4) where the relationship between the variables is explicit. However, such a simplified form of the system is obtained by many several assumptions so as to make the solution mathematically tractable. Most real-life systems are so complex that some simplifying assumptions are not justifiable, and we must resort to simulation. Simulation imitates the behavior of the system over time and provides data as if the real system were being observed.

Simulation as a modeling technique is attractive for the following reasons [4, 5]:

(1) It is the next best thing to observing a real system in operation.
(2) It enables the analysis of very complicated systems. A system can be so complex that its description by a mathematical model is beyond the capabilities of the analyst. "When all else fails" is a common slogan for many such simulations.
(3) It is straightforward and easy to understand and apply. It does not rely heavily on mathematical abstractions which require an expert to understand and apply. It can be employed by many more individuals.
(4) It is useful in experimenting with new or proposed design prior to implementation. Once constructed, it may be used to analyze the system under different conditions. Simulation can also be used in assessing and improving an existing system.
(5) It is useful in verifying or reinforcing analytic solutions.

A major disadvantage of simulation is that it may be costly because it requires large expenditure of time in construction, running, and validation.

5.2 Characteristics of Simulation Models

As mentioned earlier, a model is a representation of a system. It can be a replica, a prototype, or a smaller-scale system [6]. For most analysis, it is not necessary to account for all different aspects of the system. A model simplifies the system to sufficiently detailed level to permit valid conclusions to be drawn about the system. A given system can be represented by several models depending on the objectives being pursued by the analyst. A wide variety of simulation models have been developed over the years for system analysis. To clarify the nature of these models, it is necessary to understand a number of characteristics.

5.2.1 Continuous/Discrete Models

This characteristic has to do with the model variables. A *continuous* model is one in which the state variables change continuously with time. The model is characterized by smooth changes in the system state. A *discrete* model is one in which state variables assume a discrete set of values. The model is characterized by discontinuous changes in the system state. The arrival process of messages in the queue of a LAN is discrete since the state variable (i.e. the number of waiting messages) changes only at the arrival or departure of a message.

5.2.2 Deterministic/Stochastic Models

This characteristic deals with the system response. A system is *deterministic* if its response is completely determined by its initial state and input. It is *stochastic* (or non-deterministic) if the system response may assume a range of values for given initial state and input. Thus only the statistical averages of the output measures of a stochastic model are true characteristics of the real system. The simulation of a LAN usually involves random interarrival times and random service times.

5.2.3 Time/Event Based Models

Since simulation is the dynamic portray of the states of a system over time, a simulation model must be driven by an automatic internal clock. In *time-based* simulation, the simulation clock advances one "tick" of Δt. Figure 5.1 shows the flowchart of a typical time-based simulation model.

Fig. 5.1 Typical time-based simulation model

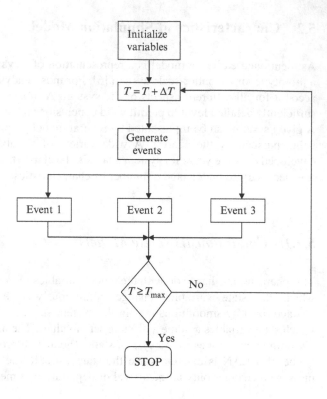

Although time-based simulation is simple, it is inefficient because some action must take place at each clock "tick." An event signifies a change in state of a system. In *event-based* simulation model, updating only takes place at the occurrence of events and the simulation clock is advanced by the amount of time since the last event. Thus no two events can be processed at any pass. The need of determining which event is next in event-based simulation makes its programming complex. One disadvantage of this type of simulation is that the speed at which the simulation proceeds is not directly related to real time; correspondence to real time operation is lost. Figure 5.2 is the flow chart of a typical event-based simulation.

The concepts of *event, process*, and *activity* are important in building a system model. As mentioned earlier, an event is an instantaneous occurrence that may change the state of the system. It may occur at an isolated point in time at which decisions are made to start or end an activity.

A process is a time-ordered sequence of events. An activity represents a duration of time. The relationship of the three concepts is depicted in Fig. 5.3 for a process that comprises of five events and two activities. The concepts lead to three types of discrete simulation modeling [7]: *event scheduling, activity scanning*, and *process interaction* approaches.

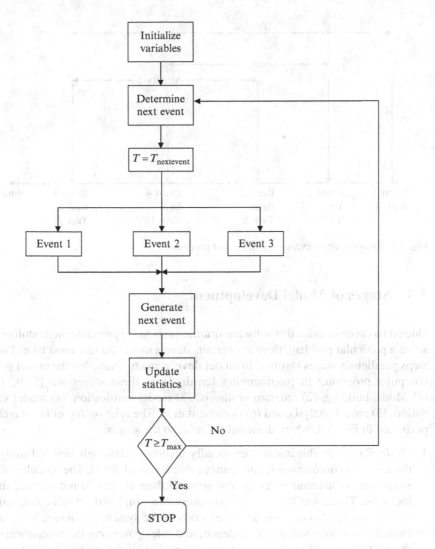

Fig. 5.2 Typical event-based simulation model

5.2.4 Hardware/Software Models

Digital modeling may involve either hardware or software simulation. Hardware simulation involves using a special purpose equipment, and detailed programming is reduced to a minimum. This equipment is sometimes called a *simulator*. In software simulation, the operation of the system is modeled using a computer program. The program describes certain aspects of the system that are of interest.

In this chapter, we are mainly concerned with software models that are discrete, stochastic, and event-based.

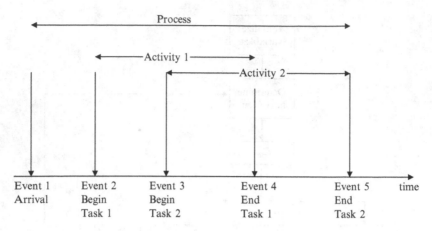

Fig. 5.3 Relationship of events, activities, and processes

5.3 Stages of Model Development

Once it has been decided that software simulation is the appropriate methodology to solve a particular problem, there are certain steps a model builder must take. These steps parallel six stages involved in model development. (Note that the model is the computer program.) In programming terminology, these stages are [5, 9, 10]: (1) Model building, (2) program synthesis, (3) model verification, (4) model validation, (5) model analysis, and (6) documentation. The relationship of the stages is portrayed in Fig. 5.4, where the numbers refer to the stages.

1. *Model Building:* This initial stage usually involves a thorough, detailed study of the system to decompose it into manageable levels of detail. The modeler often simplifies components or even omit some if their effects do not warrant their inclusion. The task of the modeler is to produce a simplified yet valid abstraction of the system. This involves a careful study of the system of interest. The study should reveal interactions, dependence, and rules governing the components of the system. It should also reveal the estimation of the system variables and parameters. The modeler may use flowcharts to define or identify subsystems and their interactions. Since flowcharting is a helpful tool in describing a problem and planning a program, commonly used symbols are shown in Fig. 5.5. These symbols are part of the flowcharting symbols formalized by the American National Standards Institute (ANSI). The modeler should feel free to adapt the symbols to his own style.

2. *Program Synthesis*: After a clear understanding of the simplified system and the interaction between components is gained, all the pieces are synthesized into a coherent description, which results in a computer program. The modeler must decide whether to implement the model in a general-purpose language such as FORTRAN or C++ or use a special-purpose simulation language such GASP,

Fig. 5.4 Stages in model development

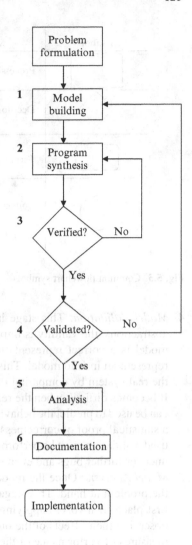

GPSS, SLAM, SIMULA, SIMSCRIPT, NS2 or OPNET. A special-purpose simulation language usually require lesser amount of development time, but executes slower than a general-purpose language. However, general-purpose languages so speed up programming and verification stages that they are becoming more and more popular in model development [5]. The selection of the type of computer and language to be used depends on resources available to the programmer.

3. *Model Verification*: This involves a logical proof of the correction of the program as a model. It entails debugging the simulation program and ensuring that the input parameters and logical structure of the model are correctly represented in the code. Although the programmer may know precisely what the program is intended to accomplish, the program may be doing something else.

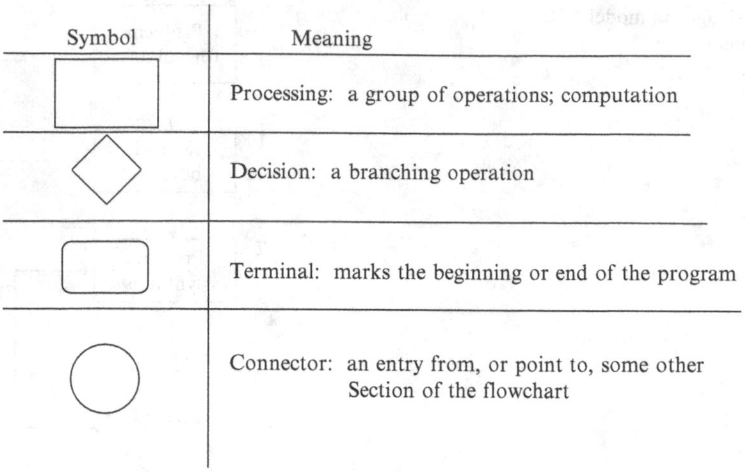

Symbol	Meaning
☐	Processing: a group of operations; computation
◇	Decision: a branching operation
☐	Terminal: marks the beginning or end of the program
◯	Connector: an entry from, or point to, some other Section of the flowchart

Fig. 5.5 Common flowchart symbols

4. *Model Validation*: This stage is the most crucial. Since models are simplified abstractions, the validity is important. A model is validated by proving that the model is a correct representation of the real system. A verified program can represent an invalid model. This stage ensures that the computer model matches the real system by comparing the two. This is easy when the real system exists. It becomes difficult when the real system does not exist. In this case, a simulator can be used to predict the behavior of the real system. Validation may entail using a statistical proof of correctness of the model. Whichever validation approach is used, validation must be performed before the model can be used. Validation may uncover further bugs and even necessitate reformulation of the model.

5. *Model Analysis:* Once the model has been validated, it can be applied to solve the problem at hand. This stage is the reason for constructing the model in the first place. It involves applying alternate input parameters to the program and observing their effects of the output parameters. The analysis provides estimate measures of performance of the system.

6. *Documentation*: The results of the analysis must be clearly and concisely documented for future references by the modeler or others. An inadequately documented program is usually useless to everyone including the modeler himself. Thus the importance of this step cannot be overemphasized.

5.4   Generation of Random Numbers

Fundamental to simulations is the need of having available sequences of numbers which appear to be drawn at random from a particular probability law. The method by which random numbers are generated is often called the random *number generator* [8, 10–12]. A simple way of generating random numbers is by casting a dice with six faces numbered 1 to 6. Another simple way is to use the roulette wheel (similar to the "wheel of fortune"). These simple ways, however, will not generate enough numbers to make them truly random.

The almost universally used method of generating random numbers is to select a function G(Z) that maps integers into random numbers. Select some guessed value Z_0, and generate the next random number as $Z_{n+1} = G(Z_n)$. The commonest function G(Z) takes the form

$$G(Z) = (aZ + c) \bmod m \tag{5.1}$$

where

$$Z_0 = \text{a starting value or a seed } (Z_0 \geq 0) \tag{5.2}$$

$$a = \text{multiplier}(a \geq 0),$$
$$c = \text{increment } (c \geq 0),$$
$$m = \text{the modulus}$$

The modulus m is usually 2^t for t-digit binary integers. For a 31-bit computer machine, for example, m may be $2^{31} - 1$. Here Z_0, a, and c are integers in the same range as $m > a$, $m > c$, $m > Z_0$.

The desired sequence of random numbers Z_n is obtained from

$$Z_{n+1} = (aZ_n + c) \bmod m \tag{5.3}$$

This is called a *linear congruential sequence*. For example, if $Z_0 = a = c = 7$ and m = 10, the sequence is

$$7, 6, 9, 0, 7, 6, 9, 0, \ldots \tag{5.4}$$

In practice, we are usually interested in generating random numbers U from the uniform distribution in the interval (0,1).

$$U = \frac{Z_{n+1}}{m} \tag{5.5}$$

U can only assume values from the set $\{0, 1/m, 2/m, \ldots, (m - 1)/m\}$. A set of uniformly distributed random numbers can be generated using the following procedure:

(a) Select an odd number as a seed value Z_0.
(b) Select the multiplier a = 8r ± 3, where r is any positive integer and a is close to $2^{t/2}$. If t = 31, a = $2^{15} + 3$ is a good choice.
(c) Compute Z_{n+1} using either the multiplicative generator

$$Z_{n+1} = aZ_n \bmod m \tag{5.6}$$

or the mixed generator

$$Z_{n+1} = (aZ_n + c) \bmod m \qquad (5.7)$$

(d) Compute $U = Z_{n+1}/m$.

U is uniformly distributed in the interval (0,1). For generating random numbers X uniformly distributed over the interval (A,B), we use

$$X = A + (B - A)U \qquad (5.8)$$

Random numbers based on the above mathematical relations and computer-produced are not truly random. In fact, given the seed of the sequence, all numbers U of the sequence are completely predictable or deterministic. Some authors emphasize this point by calling such computer-generated sequences *pseudorandom numbers*.

Example 5.1 (a) Using linear congruential scheme, generate ten pseudorandom numbers with a = 573, c = 19, m = 10^3, and seed value Z_0 = 89. Use these numbers to generate uniformly distributed random numbers $0 < U < 1$. (b) Repeat the generation with c = 0.

Solution

(a) This is a multiplicative generator. Substituting a = 573, c = 19, m = 1,000, and Z_0 = 89 in Eq. (5.3) leads to

$Z_1 = 573 \times 89 + 19 \;(\bmod\; 1{,}000) = 16$
$Z_2 = 573 \times 16 + 19 \;(\bmod\; 1{,}000) = 187$
$Z_3 = 573 \times 187 + 19 \;(\bmod\; 1{,}000) = 170$
$Z_4 = 573 \times 170 + 19 \;(\bmod\; 1{,}000) = 429$
$Z_5 = 573 \times 429 + 19 \;(\bmod\; 1{,}000) = 836$
$Z_6 = 573 \times 836 + 19 \;(\bmod\; 1{,}000) = 47$
$Z_7 = 573 \times 47 + 19 \;(\bmod\; 1{,}000) = 950$
$Z_8 = 573 \times 950 + 19 \;(\bmod\; 1{,}000) = 369$
$Z_9 = 573 \times 369 + 19 \;(\bmod\; 1{,}000) = 456$
$Z_{10} = 573 \times 456 + 19 \;(\bmod\; 1{,}000) = 307$

Dividing each number by m = 1,000 gives U as

0.016, 0.187, 0.170, ...,0.307

(b) For c = 0, we have the mixed generator. Thus, we obtain

$Z_1 = 573 \times 89 \;(\bmod\; 1{,}000) = 997$
$Z_2 = 573 \times 997 \;(\bmod\; 1{,}000) = 281$
$Z_3 = 573 \times 281 \;(\bmod\; 1{,}000) = 13$
$Z_4 = 573 \times 13 \;(\bmod\; 1{,}000) = 449$
$Z_5 = 573 \times 449 \;(\bmod\; 1{,}000) = 277$
$Z_6 = 573 \times 277 \;(\bmod\; 1{,}000) = 721$
$Z_7 = 573 \times 721 \;(\bmod\; 1{,}000) = 133$
$Z_8 = 573 \times 133 \;(\bmod\; 1{,}000) = 209$

$Z_9 = 573 \times 209 \pmod{1,000} = 757$
$Z_{10} = 573 \times 757 \pmod{1,000} = 761$

with the corresponding U as

$0.997, 0.281, 0.013, \ldots, 0.761$

5.5   Generation of Random Variables

It is often required in a simulation to generate random variable X from a given probability distribution F(x). The most commonly used techniques are the inverse transformation method and the rejection method [10, 13].

The inverse transformation method basically entails inverting the cumulative probability function $F(x) = P[X \leq x]$ associated with the random variable X. To generate a random variable X with cumulative probability distribution F(x), we set $U = F(x)$ and obtain

$$X = F^{-1}(U) \tag{5.9}$$

where X has the distribution function F(x).

If, for example, X is a random variable that is exponentially distributed with mean μ, then

$$F(x) = 1 - e^{-x/\mu}, \quad 0 < x < \infty \tag{5.10}$$

Solving for X in $U = F(X)$ gives

$$X = -\mu \ln(1 - U) \tag{5.11}$$

Since $(1 - U)$ is itself a random number in the interval (0,1), we can write

$$X = -\mu \ln U \tag{5.12}$$

A number of distributions which can be generated using the inverse method are listed in Table 5.1.

The rejection method can be applied to the probability distribution of any bounded variable. To apply the method, we let the probability density function of the random variable $f(x) = 0$ for $a > x > b$, and let f(x) be bounded by M (i.e. $f(x) \leq M$) as shown in Fig. 5.6.

We generate random variate by taking the following steps:

(1) Generate two random numbers (U_1, U_2) in the interval (0,1).
(2) Compute two random numbers with uniform distributions in (a,b) and (0,M) respectively, i.e.

$X = a + (b - a) U_1$ (scale the variable on the x-axis)
$Y = U_2 M$ (scale the variable on the y-axis).

Table 5.1 Applications
of the inverse-transform
method [14]

Distribution	F(x)	Inverse
Exponential	$1 - e^{-x/\mu}$	$-\mu \ln U$
Geometric	$1 - (1 - p)^x$	$\frac{\ln U}{\ln(1-p)}$
Logistic	$1 - \frac{1}{1+e^{(x-\mu)/b}}$	$\mu - b\ln\left(\frac{1}{U} - 1\right)$
Pareto	$1 - x^{-\mu}$	$\frac{1}{U^{1/\mu}}$
Weibull	$1 - e^{(x/a)^b}$	$a(\ln U)^{1/b}$

Fig. 5.6 The rejection
method of generating a
random variate from f(x)

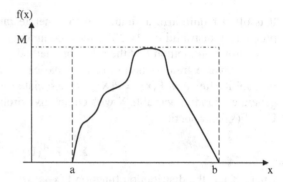

(3) If $Y \leq f(X)$, accept X as the next random variate, otherwise reject X and return
   to Step 1.

Thus in the rejection technique all points falling above f(x) are rejected while those
points falling on or below f(x) are utilized to generate X through $X = a + (b - a)U_1$.

The C codes for generating uniform and exponential variates using Eqs. (5.8)
and (5.12) are shown in Fig. 5.7. RAND_MAX is defined in stdlb.h and defines the
maximum random number generated by the rand() function. Also, EX represents
the mean value of the exponential variates.

Other random variables are generated as follows [14]:

- Bernoulli variates: Generate U. If $U \leq p$, return 0. Otherwise, return 1.
- Erlang variates: Generate U in m places and then

$$\text{Erlang}(a, m) \sim -a\ln\left(\prod_{k=1}^{m} U_k\right)$$

- Geometric variates: Generate U and compute

$$G(p) = \left\lceil \frac{\ln U}{\ln(1 - p)} \right\rceil$$

where [.] denotes rounding up to the next larger integer.
- Gaussian (or normal) variates: Generate twelve U, obtain $Z = \sum_{k=1}^{12} U_k - 6$ and

  set $X = \sigma Z + \mu$

Fig. 5.7 Subroutines
for generating random:
(a) uniform, (b) exponential
variates

X=rand()/RAND_MAX;

X=A+(B-A)*X;

X=rand()/RAND_MAX;

X=-EX*log(X);

5.6   Simulation of Queueing Systems

For illustration purposes, we now apply the ideas in the previous sections specifically to M/M/1 and M/M/n queueing systems. Since this section is the heart of this
chapter, we provide a lot of details to make the section as interesting, self-
explanatory, and self-contained as possible.

5.6.1   Simulation of M/M/1 Queue

As shown in Fig. 5.8, the M/M/1 queue consists of a server which provides service
for the customers who arrive at the system, receive service, and depart. It is a single-
server queueing system with exponential interarrival times and exponential service
times and first-in-first-out queue discipline. If a customer arrives when the server is
busy, it joins the queue (the waiting line).

There are two types of events: customer arrivals (A) and departure events (D).
The following quantities are needed in representing the model [15, 16]:

AT = arrival time
DT = departure time
BS = Busy server (a Boolean variable)
QL = queue length
RHO = traffic intensity
ART = mean arrival time
SERT = mean service time
CLK = simulation global clock
CITs = customer interarrival times (random)
CSTs = customer service times (random)
TWT = total waiting time
NMS = total no. of messages (or customers) served

The global clock CLK always has the simulated current time. It is advanced by
AT, which is updated randomly. The total waiting time TWT is the accumulation of
the times spent by all customers in the queue.

The simulator works as shown in the flowchart in Fig. 5.9a and explained as
follows. As the first step, we initialize all variables.

Fig. 5.8 M/M/1 queue

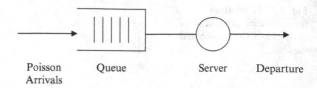

Poisson   Queue   Server   Departure
Arrivals

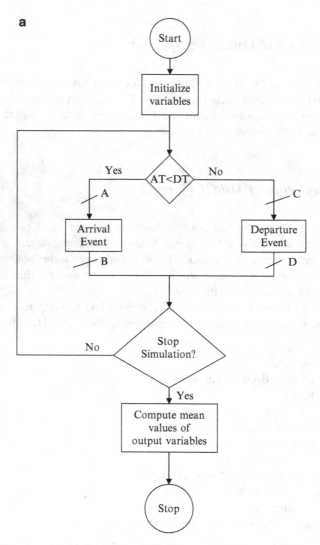

Fig. 5.9 (**a**) Flowchart for the simulation of M/M/1 queue, (**b**) flowchart of the arrival event, (**c**) flowchart for the departure event

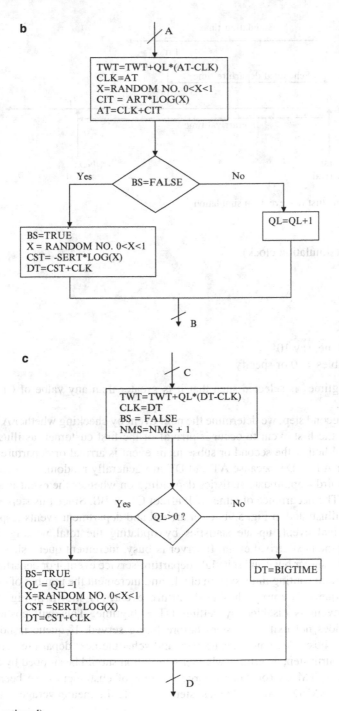

Fig. 5.9 (continued)

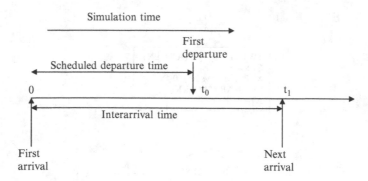

Fig. 5.10 The first few events in simulation

CLK = 0 (simulation clock)
QL = 0
TWT = 0
NMS = 0
AT = 0
BS = false
DT = bigtime, say 10^{25}
other variables = 0 or specify

The "bigtime" is selected such that it is greater than any value of CLK in the simulation.

As the second step, we determine the next event by checking whether AT > DT. By default the first event to occur is arrival of the first customer, as illustrated in Fig. 5.10. Whether the second or subsequent event is arrival or departure depends on whether AT < DT because AT and DT are generally random.

As the third step, update statistics depending on whether the event is arrival or departure. The occurrence of either will affect QL or BS. Since this step is crucial, the step is illustrated in Fig. 5.9b, c for arrival and department events respectively. For an arrival event, update statistics by updating the total waiting time and scheduling the next arrival event. If server is busy, increment queue size. If server is idle, make server busy and schedule departure/service event. For departure event, update the total waiting time, system clock, and increment the number of customers served. If queue is empty, disable departure event. As shown in Fig. 5.9c, the departure event is disabled by setting DT = bigtime. This will ensure that a customer does not exit the system before being served. If queue is not empty, make server busy, decrement queue size, and schedule next departure event.

As the fourth step, determine whether simulation should be stopped by checking when CLK ≤ TMAX (or when a large number of customers have been served, i.e. NMS ≤ NMAX). And as the last step, compute the mean/average values, i.e.

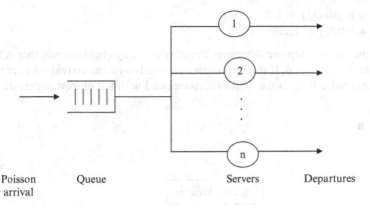

Fig. 5.11 M/M/n queue

$$\text{Average queue length} = \frac{\text{TWT}}{\text{CLK}} \qquad (5.13)$$

$$\text{Average waiting time} = \frac{\text{TWT}}{\text{NMS}} \qquad (5.14)$$

5.6.2 Simulation of M/M/n Queue

Figure 5.11 shows a M/M/n queue, in which n servers are attached to a single queue. Customers arrive following a Poisson counting process (i.e., exponential interarrival times). Each server serves the customers with exponentially distributed service times. Here, we assume that the mean service time is the same for all of the servers. If all the servers are busy, a new customer joins the queue. Otherwise, it will be served by one of the free servers. After serving a customer, the server can serve the customer waiting ahead of queue, if any.

With a careful observation of the way that the customers are served, we can extend the C program for M/M/1 queue to take care of the more general, M/M/n queue. The following quantities should be defined as arrays instead of scalar quantities:

DT[j]—departure time from the jth server, j = 1,2,..., n
BS[j]—busy server jth, j = 1,2,..., n

We also define a variable named SERVER which is associated with the current event. The other quantities remain unchanged from the M/M/1 model. Figure 5.12a illustrates the flowchart of simulator for M/M/n queue.

As the first step, we initialize all variables at the start of the program just like for the M/M/1 queue (Fig. 5.9). The only difference here is with the two arrays for BS and DT.

DT[j] = bigtime, j = 1,2, ..., n
BS[j] = false, j = 1,2,..., n

As the second step, we determine the next event by checking whether AT < DT
[j] for all j = 1,2,...,n. If so, the program proceeds with the arrival event in the third
step. Otherwise it finds the SERVER associated with the closest departure event.

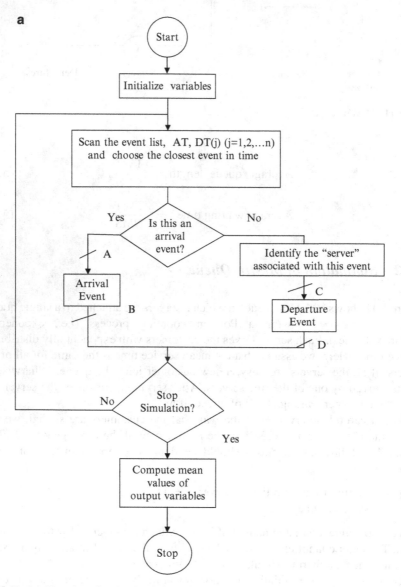

Fig. 5.12 (a) Flowchart for the simulation of M/M/n queue, (b) flowchart of the arrival event,
(c) flowchart for the departure event

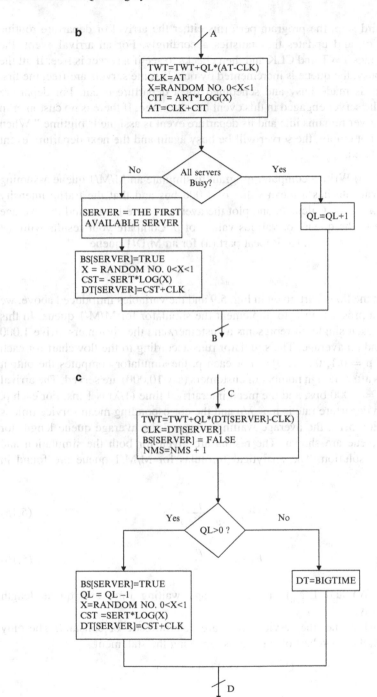

b

TWT=TWT+QL*(AT-CLK)
CLK=AT
X=RANDOM NO. 0<X<1
CIT = ART*LOG(X)
AT=CLK+CIT

All servers
Busy?

No   Yes

SERVER = THE FIRST
AVAILABLE SERVER

QL=QL+1

BS[SERVER]=TRUE
X = RANDOM NO. 0<X<1
CST= -SERT*LOG(X)
DT[SERVER]=CST+CLK

B

c

C

TWT=TWT+QL*(DT[SERVER]-CLK)
CLK=DT[SERVER]
BS[SERVER] = FALSE
NMS=NMS + 1

QL>0 ?

Yes   No

BS[SERVER]=TRUE
QL = QL –1
X=RANDOM NO. 0<X<1
CST =SERT*LOG(X)
DT[SERVER]=CST+CLK

DT=BIGTIME

D

Fig. 5.12 (continued)

As the third step, the program performs either the arrival or departure routine (Fig. 5.12b, c), and updates the statistics accordingly. For an arrival event, the program updates TWT and CLK and then checks to see if a server is free. If all the servers are busy, the queue is incremented by one. If some servers are free, the first available one is made busy and scheduled for a departure event. For departure event, only the server engaged in this event becomes free. If there is no customer in queue, this server remains idle and its departure event is assigned "bigtime." When the queue is not empty, the server will be busy again and the next departure event will be scheduled.

Example 5.2 (a) Write a computer program to simulate an M/M/1 queue assuming that the arrival rate has a mean value of 1,000 bps and that the traffic intensity $\rho = 0.1, 0.2, \ldots, 0.9$. Calculate and plot the average queue length and the average waiting time in the queue for various values of ρ. Compare your results with the exact analytical formulas. (b) Repeat part (a) for an M/D/1 queue.

Solution

(a) Based on the flowchart given in Fig. 5.9 and the variables introduced above, we develop a program in C to implement the simulator for M/M/1 queue. In this example each single bit represents a customer, and the customers arrive 1,000 per second on average. The simulator runs according to the flowchart for each value of $\rho = 0.1, 0.2, \ldots, 0.9$. For each ρ, the simulator computes the output variables after enough number of customers (say 10,000) are served. The arrival rate is $\lambda = 1,000$ bps, and the mean interarrival time $(1/\lambda)$ is 1 ms. For each ρ, the mean departure rate is $\mu = \lambda/\rho$ and the corresponding mean service time is $1/\mu$. In Fig. 5.13, the average waiting time and the average queue length for M/M/1 queue are shown. The results are given for both the simulation and analytical solution. The analytical formulas for M/M/1 queue are found in Chap. 4:

$$E(W) = \frac{\rho}{\mu(1 - \rho)} \tag{5.15}$$

$$E(N_q) = \frac{\rho^2}{1 - \rho} \tag{5.16}$$

where $E(W)$ and $E(N_q)$ are the average waiting time and queue length respectively.

(b) For M/D/1 queue, the service times are deterministic or constant. The only change in the flowchart of Fig. 5.9 is replacing the statement

$$CST = -SERT*LOG(X)$$

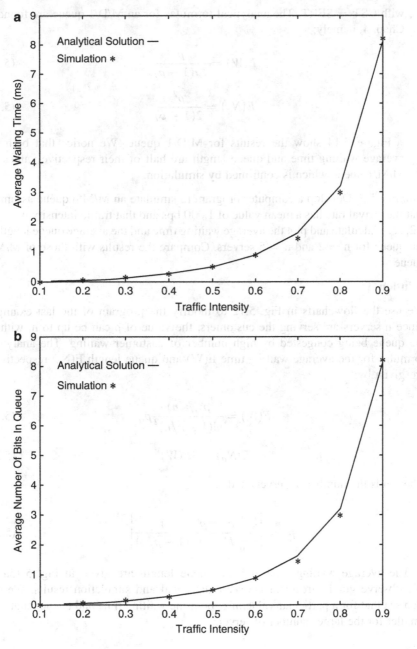

Fig. 5.13 (a) Average waiting time for M/M/1 queue; (b) Average queue length for M/M/1 queue

with CST = SERT. The analytical formulas for an M/D/1 queue are found in Chap. 4, namely:

$$E(W) = \frac{\rho}{2\mu(1-\rho)} \tag{5.17}$$

$$E(N_q) = \frac{\rho^2}{2(1-\rho)} \tag{5.18}$$

Figure 5.14 show the results for M/D/1 queue. We notice that both the average waiting time and queue length are half of their respective values for M/M/1 queue which is confirmed by simulation.

Example 5.3 Develop a computer program to simulate an M/M/n queue assuming that the arrival rate has a mean value of 1,000 bps and that traffic intensity $\rho = 0.1$, 0.2, ... Calculate and plot the average waiting time and the average queue length in the queue for n = 2 and n = 5 servers. Compare the results with those of M/M/1 queue.

Solution

We use the flowcharts in Fig. 5.12 to modify the program of the last example. Since n servers are serving the customers, the value of ρ can be up to n, without the queue being congested by high number of customer waiting. The analytical formulas for the average waiting time E(W) and queue length $E(N_q)$ respectively are given by:

$$E(W) = \frac{\rho^n(\rho/n)}{n!(1-\rho/n)^2}p_0 \tag{5.19}$$

$$E(N_q) = \lambda E(W) \tag{5.20}$$

where n is the number of servers and

$$p_0 = \left[\sum_{k=0}^{n-1}\frac{\rho^k}{k!} + \frac{\rho^n}{n!}\frac{1}{(1-\rho/n)}\right]^{-1} \tag{5.21}$$

The average waiting time and the queue length are given in Fig. 5.15a, b. We observe good agreement between analytical and simulation results. We can also see that for a particular value of ρ, both the waiting time and queue length are smaller for the larger number of servers.

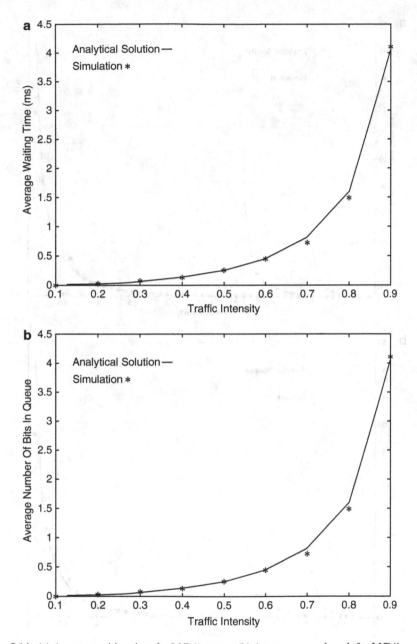

Fig. 5.14 (a) Average waiting time for M/D/1 queue; (b) Average queue length for M/D/1 queue

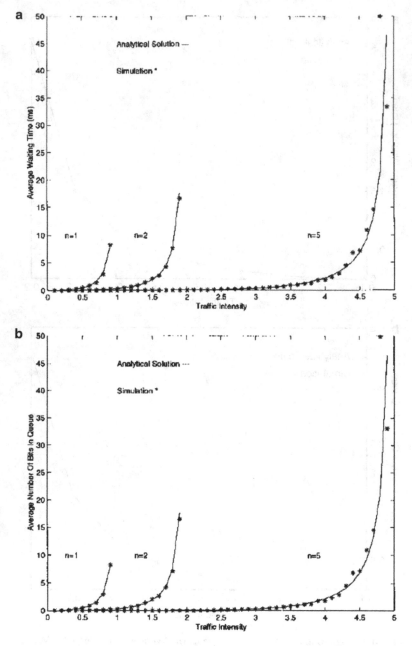

Fig. 5.15 (a) Average waiting time for M/M/n queue, n = 1, 2, 5. (b) Average queue length for M/M/n queue, n = 1, 2, 5

5.7 Estimation of Errors

Simulation procedures give solutions which are averages over a number of tests. For this reason, it is important to realize that the sample statistics obtained from simulation experiments will vary from one experiment to another. In fact, the sample statistics themselves are random variables and, as such, have associated probability distributions, means, variances, and standard deviation. Thus the simulation results contain fluctuations about a mean value and it is impossible to ascribe a 100 % confidence in the results. To evaluate the statistical uncertainty or error in a simulation experiment, we must resort to various statistical techniques associated with random variables and utilize the central limit theorem.

Suppose that X is a random variable. You recall that we define the expected or mean value of X as

$$\mu = \int_{-\infty}^{\infty} xf(x)dx \tag{5.22}$$

where f(x) is the probability density distribution of X. If we draw random and independent samples, $x_1, x_2, \cdots, x_N$ from f(x), our estimate of x would take the form of the mean of N samples, namely,

$$\widetilde{\mu} = \frac{1}{N} \sum_{n=1}^{N} x_n \tag{5.23}$$

Whereas μ is the true mean value of X, $\widetilde{\mu}$ is the unbiased estimator of μ—an unbiased estimator being one with the correct expectation value. Although expected value $\widetilde{\mu}$ is close to μ but $\widetilde{\mu} \neq \mu$. The standard deviation, defined as

$$\sigma(x) = \left[E(X^2) - \mu^2\right]^{1/2} \tag{5.24}$$

provides a measure of the spread in the values of $\widetilde{\mu}$ about μ; it yields the order of magnitude of the error. The confidence we place in the estimate of the mean is given by the variance of $\widetilde{\mu}$. The relationship between the variance of $\widetilde{\mu}$ and the variance of x is

$$\sigma(\widetilde{\mu}) = \frac{\sigma(x)}{\sqrt{N}} \tag{5.25}$$

This shows that if we use $\widetilde{\mu}$ constructed from N values of x_n according to Eq. (5.23) to estimate μ, then the spread in our results of $\widetilde{\mu}$ about μ is proportional to $\sigma(x)$ and falls off as the number of N of samples increases.

In order to estimate the spread in $\widetilde{\mu}$ we define the *sample variance*

$$S^2 = \frac{1}{N-1} \sum_{n=1}^{N} (x_n - \tilde{x})^2 \tag{5.26}$$

Again, it can be shown that the expected value of S^2 is equal to $\sigma^2(x)$. Therefore the sample variance is an unbiased estimator of $\sigma^2(x)$. Multiplying out the square term in Eq. (5.26), it is readily shown that the *sample standard deviation* is

$$S = \left(\frac{N}{N-1}\right)^{1/2} \left[\frac{1}{N} \sum_{n=1}^{N} x_n^2 - \tilde{x}^2\right]^{1/2} \tag{5.27}$$

For large N, the factor N/(N − 1) is set equal to one.

According to the central limit theorem, the sum of a large number of random variables tends to be normally distributed, i.e.

$$f(\tilde{\mu}) = \sqrt{\frac{N}{2\pi}} \frac{1}{\sigma(x)} \exp\left[-\frac{N(\tilde{\mu} - \mu)^2}{2\sigma^2(x)}\right] \tag{5.28}$$

The normal (or Gaussian) distribution is very useful in various problems in engineering, physics, and statistics. The remarkable versatility of the Gaussian model stems from the central limit theorem. For this reason, the Gaussian model often applies to situations in which the quantity of interest results from the summation of many irregular and fluctuating components.

Since the number of samples N is finite, absolute certainty in simulation is unattainable. We try to estimate some limit or interval around μ such that we can predict with some confidence that $\tilde{\mu}$ falls within that limit. Suppose we want the probability that $\tilde{\mu}$ lies between $\mu - \varepsilon$ and $\mu + \varepsilon$. By definition,

$$\text{Prob}[\mu - \varepsilon < \tilde{\mu} < \mu + \varepsilon] = \int_{\mu-\varepsilon}^{\mu+\varepsilon} f(\tilde{\mu})d\tilde{\mu} \tag{5.29}$$

By letting $\lambda = \frac{(\tilde{\mu}-\mu)}{\sqrt{2/N}\sigma(x)}$, we get

$$\text{Prob}[\mu - \varepsilon < \tilde{\mu} < \mu + \varepsilon] = \frac{2}{\sqrt{\pi}} \int_{0}^{(\sqrt{N/2})(\varepsilon/\sigma)} e^{-\lambda^2} d\lambda = \text{erf}\left(\sqrt{N/2}\frac{\varepsilon}{\sigma(x)}\right) \tag{5.30}$$

or

$$\text{Prob}\left[\mu - z_{\alpha/2}\frac{\sigma}{\sqrt{N}} < \tilde{\mu} < \mu + z_{\alpha/2}\frac{\sigma}{\sqrt{N}}\right] = 1 - \alpha \tag{5.31}$$

where erf(x) is the error function and $z_{\alpha/2}$ is the upper $\alpha/2 \times 100$ percentile of the standard normal deviation. The random interval $\tilde{x} \pm \varepsilon$ is called a *confidence interval* and $\text{erf}\left(\sqrt{N/2}\ \varepsilon/\sigma(x)\right)$ is the *confidence level*. Most simulation experiments use error $\varepsilon = \sigma(x)/\sqrt{N}$ which implies that $\widetilde{\mu}$ is within one standard deviation of μ, the true mean. From Eq. (5.31), the probability that the sample mean $\widetilde{\mu}$ lies within the interval $\widetilde{\mu} \pm \sigma(x)/\sqrt{N}$ is 0.6826 or 68.3 %. If higher confidence levels are desired, two or three standard deviations may be used. For example,

$$\text{Prob}\left[\mu - M\frac{\sigma}{\sqrt{N}} < \widetilde{\mu} < \mu + M\frac{\sigma}{\sqrt{N}}\right] = \begin{cases} 0.6826, & M = 1 \\ 0.954, & M = 2 \\ 0.997 & M = 3 \end{cases} \qquad (5.32)$$

where M is the number of standard deviations. In Eqs. (5.31) and (5.32), it is assumed that the population standard deviation σ is known. Since this is rarely the case, σ must be estimated by the sample standard S calculated from Eq. (5.27) so that the normal distribution is replaced by Student's t-distribution. It is well known that the t-distribution approaches the normal distribution as N becomes large, say $N > 30$. Thus Eq. (5.31) is equivalent to

$$\text{Prob}\left[\mu - \frac{St_{\alpha/2;N-1}}{\sqrt{N}} < \widetilde{\mu} < \mu + z_{\alpha/2}\frac{St_{\alpha/2;N-1}}{\sqrt{N}}\right] = 1 - \alpha \qquad (5.33)$$

where $t_{\alpha/2;N-1}$ is the upper $100 \times \alpha/2$ percentage point of Student's t-distribution with $(N - 1)$ degrees of freedom. Its values are listed in any standard statistics text.

The confidence interval $\widetilde{x} - \varepsilon < x < \widetilde{x} + \varepsilon$ contains the "true" value of the parameter x being estimated with a prespecified probability $1 - \alpha$. Therefore, when we make an estimate, we must decide in advance that we would like to be, say, 90 or 95 % confident of the estimate. The confidence of interval helps us to know the degree of confidence we have in the estimate. The upper and lower limits of the confidence interval (known as *confidence limits*) are given by

$$\text{upper limit} = \mu + \varepsilon \qquad (5.34a)$$
$$\text{lower limit} = \mu - \varepsilon \qquad (5.34b)$$

where

$$\varepsilon = \frac{St_{\alpha/2;N-1}}{\sqrt{N}} \qquad (5.35)$$

Thus, if a simulation is performed N times by using different seed values, then in $(1 - \alpha)$ cases, the estimate $\widetilde{\mu}$ lies within the confidence interval and in α cases the estimate lies outside the interval, as illustrated in Fig. 5.16. Equation (5.35) provides the error estimate for a given number N of simulation experiments or observations.

If, on the other hand, an accuracy criterion ε is prescribed and we want to estimate μ by $\widetilde{\mu}$ within tolerance of ε with at least probability $1 - \alpha$, we must ensure that the sample size N satisfies

Fig. 5.16 Confidence
of interval

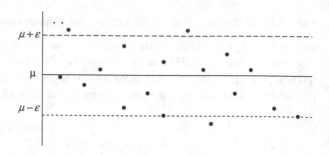

$$\text{Prob}\left[\left|\widetilde{\mu} - \mu\right| < \varepsilon\right] \geq 1 - \alpha \qquad (5.36)$$

To satisfy this requirement, N must be selected as the small integer satisfying

$$N \geq \left(\frac{St_{\alpha/2;N-1}}{\sqrt{\varepsilon}}\right)^2 \qquad (5.37)$$

For further discussion on error estimates in simulation, one should consult [17, 18].

Example 5.4 In a simulation experiment, an analyst obtained the mean values of a certain parameter as 7.60, 6.60, 7.50, and 7.43 for five simulations runs using different seed values. Calculate the error estimate using a 95 % confidence interval.

Solution

We first get the sample mean

$$\mu = \frac{7.60 + 6.60 + 6.97 + 7.50 + 7.43}{5} = 7.22$$

From Eq. (5.26), the sample variance is obtained as

$$S^2 = \frac{(7.60 - 7.22)^2 + \cdots + (7.43 - 7.22)^2}{4} = 0.23793$$

or S = 0.48778. Using a 95 % confidence interval, $1 - \alpha = 95\%$ (i.e., $\alpha = 0.05$). For five runs (N = 5), the t-distribution table gives $t_{\alpha/2;N-1} = 2.776$. Using Eq. (5.35), the error is estimated as

$$\varepsilon = \frac{0.48778x2.776}{\sqrt{5}} = 0.6056$$

Thus, the 95 % confidence interval for the parameter is

$$\mu - \varepsilon < \widetilde{\mu} < \mu + \varepsilon = 6.6144 < \widetilde{\mu} < 7.78265$$

5.8   Simulation Languages

The purpose of this section is to present the characteristics of common simulation languages and provide the analyst with the criteria for choosing a suitable language. Once the analyst has acquired a throughout understanding of the system to be simulated and is able to describe precisely how the model would operate, the next step is to decide on the language to use in the simulation. This step should not be taken lightly since the choice of a language would have several implications, some of which will be discussed later. After deciding on the language to apply, the analyst needs to consult the language reference manual for all the details.

There are basically two types of languages used in simulation: multipurpose languages and special-purpose languages. The former are *compiler languages* while the latter are *interpretive languages* [19]. A compiler language comprises of macrostatements and requires compilation and assembly before execution can occur. An interpretive language consists of symbols which denote commands to carry out operations directly without the need for compilation and assembly. Thus the major difference between the two types of languages is the distinction between a *source* program and an *object* program. An analyst usually submits a source program to a computer. If the source program is in a compiler language, an object program is needed for execution. If the source program is in interpretive language, execution is done directly without any object program.

Some analysts tend to select multipurpose or general-purpose languages such as FORTRAN, BASIC, PASCAL, and C for the simulation of computer networks. Although these languages are far from ideal for discrete simulation, they are widely been used. Why? There are at least three reasons. First, there is conservatism on the part of the analysts and organizations that support them. Many organizations are committed to multipurpose languages and do not want to be vulnerable to a situation where a code written in a language only familiar to an analyst may have to be rewritten when the analyst leaves the organization. Second, the widespread availability of multipurpose languages and the libraries of routines that have been developed over the years makes them more desirable. It is easy to gain technical support since experts of multipurpose languages are everywhere. Third, high speed in the simulation is possible if a general-purpose language is used. Analysts who prefer fast-running simulations use a general-purpose language. In view of the problem of learning another set of syntactic rules, a decision in favor of a general-purpose language is often considered wise by analysts.

The development of special-purpose simulation languages began in the late 1950s. The need came from the fact that many simulation projects required similar functions across various applications. The purpose of simulation languages is to provide the analyst with a relatively simple means of modeling systems. Unlike using the general-purpose language such as C++ where the analyst is responsible for all the details in the model, special-purpose languages are meant to eliminate the major portion of the programming effort by providing a simulation-oriented framework about which a model is constructed in a simple fashion. Although many such languages have been developed, only few have gained wide acceptance.

Before deciding which type of language to use in a simulation, the analyst must carefully weigh the advantages of the multipurpose languages against the almost guaranteed longer program development and debugging time required in special-purpose languages. Irrespective of the language used in the simulation of a computer network, the language must be capable of performing functions including:

- generating random numbers,
- executing events,
- managing queues,
- collecting and analyzing data, and

Commonly used special-purpose, discrete simulation languages include GPSS, SIMSCRIPT, GASP, SLAM, RESQ, NS2, and OPNET. No attempt will be made to include the many instructions available in these languages. Interested readers must consult the manuals and references for more details on the languages [20–28]. Only OPNET and NS2 will be covered.

The development of new simulation languages has slowed considerably in the last few years, and the well established languages have not changed dramatically for the past few years. This notwithstanding, it is expected that new languages will be developed and old ones will be improved. At present, there is a growing interest in combined discrete-continuous simulations. Also, the use of ADA and C as simulation languages is receiving active attention [32].

5.9 OPNET

Optimized Network Engineering Tools (OPNET) is a window-based comprehensive engineering system that allows you to simulate large communication networks with detailed protocol modeling. It allows you to design and study communication networks, devices, protocols, and applications with great flexibility. OPNET key features include graphical specification of models, a dynamic, event-scheduled simulation kernel, integrated data analysis tools, and hierarchical, object-based modeling. Modeler's object-oriented modeling approach and graphical editors mirror the structure of actual networks and network components. Modeler supports all network types and technologies [29].

Here, we focus on the modeling using OPNET IT Guru which is user-friendly interface with drag-and-drop features that enable users to effectively model, manage, and troubleshoot real-world network infrastructures. For example, we illustrate here how OPNET is used to examine the Medium Access Control (MAC) sublayer of the IEEE 802.11 standard for wireless local area network (WLAN). The performance of different options is analyzed under different scenarios [30].

The model's concept is overviewed as following: The IEEE 802.11 standard provides wireless connectivity to computerized stations that require rapid deployment such as portable computers. The Medium Access Control (MAC) sublayer in the standard includes two fundamental access methods: distributed coordination function

(DCF) and the point coordination function (PCF). DCF utilizes the carrier sense multiple access with collision avoidance (CSMA/CA) approach; it is implemented in all stations in the wireless local area network (WLAN). PCF is based on polling to determine the station that can transmit next. Stations in an infrastructure network optionally implement the PCF access method. In addition to the physical CSMA/CD, DCF and PCF utilize virtual carrier-sense mechanism to determine the state of the medium. This virtual mechanism is implemented by means of the network allocation vector (NAV). The NAV provides each station with a prediction of future traffic on the medium. Each station uses NAV as an indicator of time periods during which transmission will not be installed even if the station senses that the wireless medium is not busy. NAV gets the information about future traffic from management frames and the header of regular frames being exchanged in the network.

With DCF, every station senses the medium before transmitting. The transmitting station defers as long as the medium is busy. After deferral and while the medium is idle, the transmitting station has to wait for a random backoff interval. After the backoff interval and if the medium is still idle, the station initiates data transmission or optionally exchanges RTS (request to send) and CTS (clear to send) frames with the receiving station. With PCF, the access point (AP) in the network acts as a point coordinator (PC). The PC uses polling to determine which station can initiate data transmission. It is optional for the stations in the network to participate in PCF and hence respond to poll received from the PC. Such stations are called CF-pollable stations. The PCF requires control to be gained of the medium by the PC. To gain such control, the PC utilizes the Beacon management frames to set the network allocation vector (NAV) in the network stations. As the mechanism used to set NAV is based on the DCF, all stations comply with the PC request to set their NAV whether or not they are CF-pollable. This way the PC can control frame transmissions in the network by generating contention free periods (CFP). The PC and the CF_pollable stations do not use RTSCTS in the CFP.

The standard allows for fragmentation of the MAC data units into smaller frames. Fragmentation is favorable in case the wireless channel is not reliable enough to transmit longer frames. Only frames with a length greater than a fragmentation and will be separately acknowledged. During a contention period, all fragments of a single frame will be sent as burst with a single invocation of the DCF medium access procedure. In case of PCF and during a contention free period, fragments are sent individually following the rules of the point coordinator (PC), which will based on the following steps:

5.9.1 Create a New Project

To create a new project for the Ethernet network:

1. Start *OPNET IT Guru Academic Edition* → Choose *New* from the *File* menu.
2. Select   *Project* → Click   ok → Name   the   project < *your   initials* >
   _*WirelessLAN* and the scenario *DCF* → Click ok

Fig. 5.17 Workspace to create and configure the network

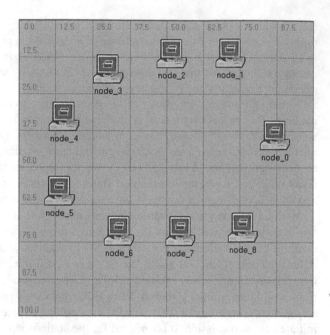

3. In the Startup Wizard Initial Topology dialog box, make sure that *Create Empty Scenario* is selected → click next → choose *Office* from the Network *Scale* list and check *Use Metric Units* → Click next twice → click ok.

5.9.2 Create and Configure the Network

To create the wireless network:

1. The *Object Palette* dialog box should be now on the top of your project workspace.
2. Add to project workspace the following objects from the palette: *9 wlan_station_adv (fix)*.

   To add an object from a palette, click its icon in the object palette → move the mouse to the workspace → left-click to place the object. Right-click when finished.
3. Close the Object Palette dialog box → Arrange the stations in the workspace as shown in Fig. 5.17 → Save your project.

Table 5.2 Assignment of destination address to the node name

Node name	Destination address
Node_1	5
Node_2	8
Node_3	6
Node_4	7
Node_5	1
Node_6	3
Node_7	4
Node_8	2

Fig. 5.18 Values assigned to the Destination Address and Wireless LAN MAC Address attributes for node1

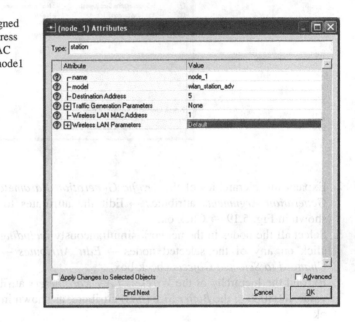

5.9.2.1 Configure the Wireless Nodes

Repeat the following for each of the nine nodes in Fig. 5.17:

1. Right-click on the node → *Edit Attributes* → Assign to the *Wireless LAN MAC Address* attribute a value equal to the node number. Assign to the *Destination Address* attribute the corresponding value shown in Table 5.2 → Click ok.

Figure 5.18 shows the values assigned to the *Destination Address* and *Wireless LAN MAC Address* attributes for node_1.

5.9.2.2 Traffic Generation Parameters

1. Select all the nodes in the network simultaneously *except node_0* → Right-click on any of the selected nodes (i.e. node_1 to node_8) → *Edit Attributes* → Check the Apply Changes to *Selected Objects* check box.

Fig. 5.19 Traffic
generation parameters
for node 1

2. Expand the hierarchies of the *Traffic Generation Parameters* and the *Packet Generation Arguments* attributes → Edit the attributes to match the values shown in Fig. 5.19 → Click ok.
3. Select all the nodes in the network simultaneously *including node_0* → Right-click on any of the selected nodes → *Edit Attributes* → Check the *Apply Changed to Selected Objects* check box.
4. Expand the hierarchy of the *Wireless LAN Parameters* attribute → Assign the value 4608000 to the *Buffer Size (bits)* attribute, as shown in Fig. 5.20 → Click ok.
5. Right-click on *node_0* → *Edit Attributes* → Expand the *Wireless LAN Parameters* hierarchy and set the *Access Point Functionality to Enabled,* as shown in Fig. 5.21 → Click ok.

5.9.3   Select the Statistics

To test the performance of the network in our DCF scenario, we collect some of the available statistics as follows:

1. Right-click anywhere in the project workspace and select *Choose Individual Statistics* from the pop-up menu.
2. In the Choose Results dialog box, expand the *Global Statistics* and *Node Statistics* hierarchies → choose the five statistics, as shown in Fig. 5.22.
3. Click ok and then save your project.

Fig. 5.20 Editing
buffer size

Fig. 5.21 Enabled the
access point functionality
for node 0

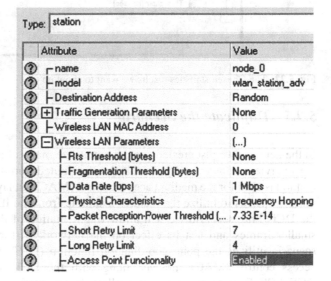

5.9.4 Configure the Simulation

Here we will configure the simulation parameters:

1. Click on the Configure Simulation button.
2. Set the duration to be 10.0 min.
3. Click ok and then save your project.

Fig. 5.22 The Chosen statistics results we want to show up

5.9.5 Duplicate the Scenario

In the network we just created, we did not utilize many of the features explained in the overview. However, by default the distributed coordination function (DCF) method is used for the medium access control (MAC) sublayer. We will create three more scenarios to utilize the features available from the IEEE 802.11 standard. In the DCF_Frag scenario we will allow fragmentation of the MAC data units into smaller frames and test its effect on the network performance. The DCF_PCF scenario utilizes the point coordination function (PCF) method for the medium access control (MAC) sublayer along with the DCF method. Finally, in the DCF_PCF_Frag scenario we will allow fragmentation of the MAC data and check its effect along with PCF.

5.9.5.1 The DCF_Frag Scenario

1. Select *Duplicate Scenario* from the *Scenarios* menu and give it the name *DCF_Frag* → click ok.

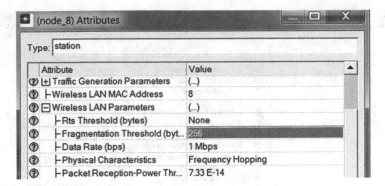

Fig. 5.23 DCF_Frag Scenario for node 8

⑦ ⌐name	node_0	
⑦ ⊢model	wlan_station_adv	
⑦ ⊢Destination Address	Random	
⑦ ⊞ Traffic Generation Parameters	None	
⑦ ⊢Wireless LAN MAC Address	0	
⑦ ⊟Wireless LAN Parameters	(...)	
⑦ ⊢Rts Threshold (bytes)	None	
⑦ ⊢Fragmentation Threshold (bytes)	256	
⑦ ⊢Data Rate (bps)	1 Mbps	
⑦ ⊢Physical Characteristics	Frequency Hopping	
⑦ ⊢Packet Reception-Power Threshold (...	7.33 E-14	
⑦ ⊢Short Retry Limit	7	
⑦ ⊢Long Retry Limit	4	
⑦ ⊢Access Point Functionality	Enabled	

Fig. 5.24 Enabled the access point functionality for node 0

2. Select all the nodes in the *DCF_Frag scenario* simultaneously → Right-click on anyone of them → *Edit Attributes* → Check the *Apply Changes to Selected Objects* check box.
3. Expand the hierarchy of the *Wireless LAN Parameters* attribute → Assign the value 256 to the *Fragmentation Threshold (bytes)* attribute, as shown in Fig. 5.23 → Click ok.
4. Right-click on *node_0* → *Edit Attributes* → Expand the *Wireless LAN Parameters* hierarchy and set the *Access Point Functionality* to *Enabled* as shown in Fig. 5.24 → Click ok.

Fig. 5.25 Enabling PCF
Parameters for node 0

5.9.5.2 The DCF_PCF Scenario

1. Switch to the *DCF scenario*, select *Duplicate Scenario* from the *Scenarios* menu and give it the name *DCF_PCF* → Click ok → Save your project.
2. Select node_0, node_1, node_3, node_5 and node_7 in the DCF_PCF scenario simultaneously → Right-click on anyone of the selected nodes → *Edit Attributes*.
3. Check *Apply Changes to Selected Objects* → Expand the hierarchy of the *Wireless LAN Parameters* attribute → Expand the hierarchy of the *PCF Parameters* attribute → *Enable* the *PCF Functionality* attribute, as shown in Fig. 5.25 → Click ok.
4. Right-click on *node_0* → *Edit Attributes* → Expand the *Wireless LAN Parameters* hierarchy and set the *Access Point Functionality* to *Enabled,* as shown in Fig. 5.26.
5. Click ok and save your project.

5.9.6 Run the Simulation

To run the simulation for the four scenarios simultaneously.

1. Go to the *Scenarios* menu → Select *Manage Scenarios*.

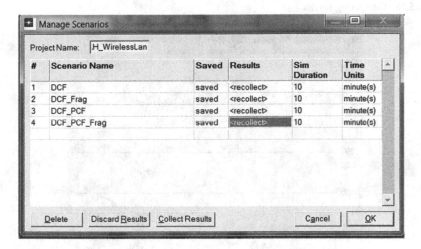

Fig. 5.26 Enabled the access point functionality for node 0

Fig. 5.27 Managing the Scenarios

2. Click on the row of each scenario and click the *Collect Results* button. This should change the values under the *Results* column to < *collect* > shown in Fig. 5.27.
3. Click ok to run the four simulations.
4. After the simulation of the four scenarios complete, click *Close* and then save your project.

5.9.7 View the Results

To view and analyze the results:

1. Select *Compare Results* from the *Results* menu.

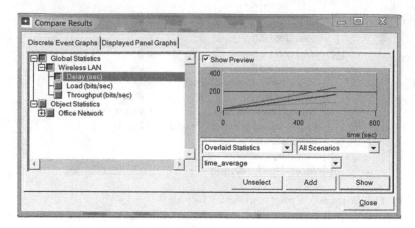

Fig. 5.28 Comparing results

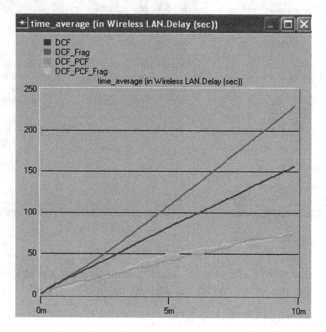

Fig. 5.29 Time average in WLAN delay (s)

2. Change the drop-down menu in the lower right part of the *Compare Results* dialog box from *As Is* to *time-average* → Select the *Delay (sec)* statistic from the *Wireless LAN* hierarchy as shown in Fig. 5.28.
3. Click *Show* to show the result in a new panel. The resulting graph should resemble that shown in Fig. 5.29.

Fig. 5.30 Time average
in WLAN load (bits/s)

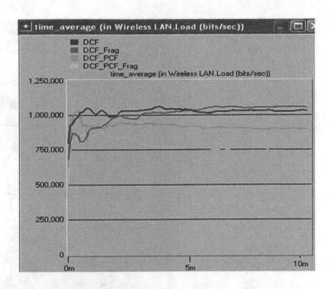

Fig. 5.31 Time average in
WLAN throughput (bits/s)

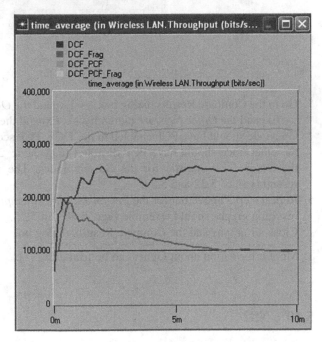

4. Go to the *Compare Results* dialog → Follow the same procedure to show the
   graphs of the following statistics from the *Wireless LAN* hierarchy: *Load (bits/s)*
   and *Throughput (bits/s)*. The resulting graphs should resemble Figs. 5.30
   and 5.31.

Fig. 5.32 Time average in
WLAN delay (s) for node 3

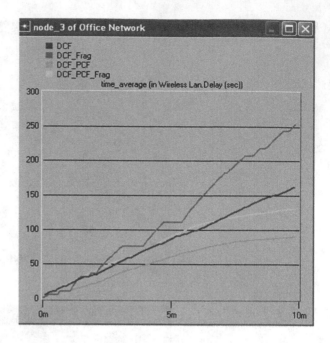

5. Go to the Compare Results dialog box → Expand the *Object Statistics* hierarchy
   → Expand the *Office Network* hierarchy → Expand the hierarchy of two nodes.
   One node should have PCF enabled in the DCF_PCF scenario (e.g., node_3) and
   the other node should have PCF disabled (e.g., node_2) → Show the result of
   the *Delay (sec)* statistic for the chosen nodes. The resulting graphs should
   resemble Figs. 5.32 and 5.33.
6. Repeat step 5 above but for the *Retransmission Attempts (packets)* statistic. The
   resulting graphs should resemble Figs. 5.34 and 5.35.
7. Close all graphs and the Compare Results dialog box → Save your project.

   More information about Opnet can be found in [31].

5.10   NS2

The Network Simulator version 2 (NS2) is targeted at networking. It is
object-oriented, discrete event driven network simulator. It was developed at UC
Berkeley written in C++ language and it uses Object-oriented extension of Tool
command language (OTcl). These two different languages are used for different
purposes in NS2 as shown in Table 5.3 and more information about NS2 can be
found in [32, 33].

Fig. 5.33 Time average in WLAN delay (s) for node 2

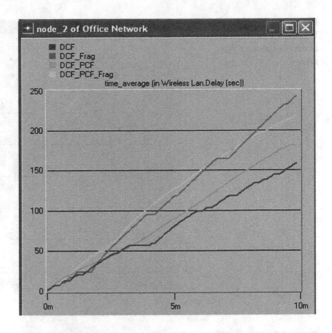

Fig. 5.34 Time average in WLAN retransmission line attempts (packets) for node 3

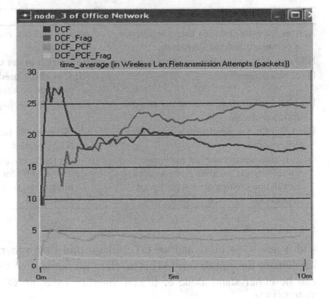

Figure 5.36 shows the process of network simulation in NS2. The simulation using NS2 can carry two levels: first level is based on configuration and construction of OTcl, and second level, is based on OTcl and C++. It is essential for NS2 to be upgraded or modified to add the required elements when the module resources needed do not exist. Therefore, the split object model of NS2 is used to

Fig. 5.35 Time average in WLAN retransmission line attempts (packets) for node 2

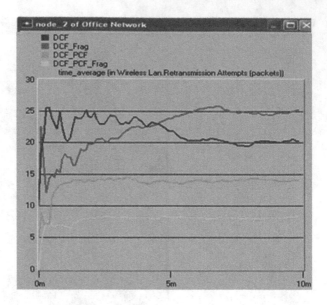

Table 5.3 Use of OTcl and C++

OTcl	C++
Acts as the front end (i.e., user interference, a command and configuration)	Acts as the back end running the actual simulation
NS2 uses it to create and configure a network	NS2 uses it to run simulation
OTcl is an interpreter	All C++ codes need to be complied and linked to create an executable file
Use OTcl for configuration, setup, and one time simulation	Use C++ for dealing with a packet
Use OTcl for run simulation with existing NS2 models	Use C++ for the need to modify existing NS2 modules
OTcl is slow to run, but fast to change, therefore, it is suitable to run a small simulation configuration over several repetitions.	C++ is fast to run and slow to change, therefore, it is suitable for the detailed protocol implementation procedures and large simulation

add a new C++ class and an OTcl class, and then program the OTcl scripts to implement the simulation [34]. The class hierarchies of C++ and OTcl languages can be either stand alone or linked together using an OTcl/C++ interface called TclCL [32].

There are three components for whole network simulation using NS2 [35]. First, modifying the source code. This step is used only when there is a need to modify the source codes which requires programming and debugging from the users. Indeed, the OTcl codes need to be modified as the source codes due to that NS2 supports the OTcl and C++. Second, writing the Tcl/OTcl scripts of network simulations. In fact,

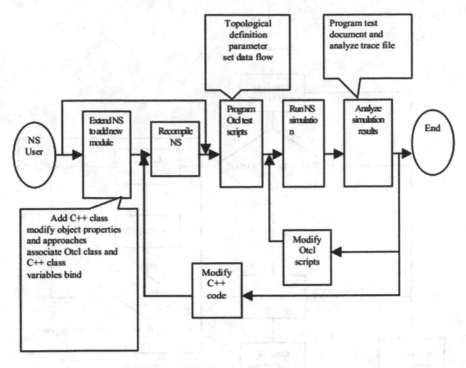

Fig. 5.36 The simulation process of NS2 [34]

in this step, it requires the user writing Tcl codes for describing the network topology types, defining nodes and network component attributes, controlling the network simulation process. Third, analyzing the network simulation results. This step requires the user to understand the structure of the NS2 Trace file and to be able to use some tools to check the outcome data and draw figures, etc. Figure 5.37 shows the flow chart for simulation in NS2. Although, the general architecture of the view of the NS2 for the general users can be presented in Fig. 5.38.

NS2 is primarily useful for simulating LAN and WAN. It has the capability of supporting the simulations of unicast node and multicast node. It is complemented by Network Animator (NAM) for packet visualization purposes such as Fig. 5.39 for simulation topology of wireless network [37]. Indeed, NS2 is widely used network simulator that has been commonly used in education and research.

NS2 has the following limitations [36]:

1. Large multi format outcome files, which require post processing.
2. Huge memory space consumption due to a very large output file.
3. Relatively slow.
4. Lack of built-in-QoS monitoring modules.
5. Lack of user friendly visual output representation.
6. Requires the users to develop tools by themselves.

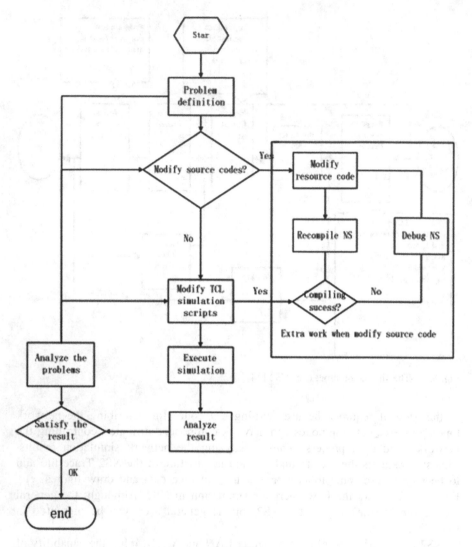

Fig. 5.37 The simulation flow chart of NS2 [35]

5.11   Criteria for Language Selection

There are two types of factors that influence the selection of the special-purpose language an analyst uses in his simulation. One set of factors is concerned with the operational characteristics of the language, while the other set is related to its problem-oriented characteristics [38, 39].

In view of the operational characteristics of a language, an analyst must consider factors such as the following:

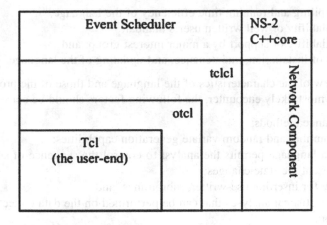

Fig. 5.38 The architectural view of NS2 [36]

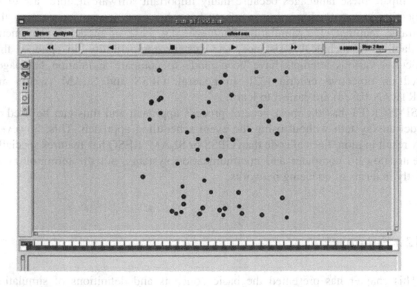

Fig. 5.39 Network animator interface (NAM) showing the simulation topology of wireless network [37]

1. the analyst's familiarity with the language;
2. the ease with which the language can be learned and used if the analyst is not familiar with it;
3. the languages supported at the installation where the simulation is to be done;
4. the complexity of the model;
5. the need for a comprehensive analysis and display of simulation results;
6. the language's provision of good error diagnostics;

7. the compiling and running time efficiency of the language;
8. the availability of well written user's manual;
9. the availability of support by a major interest group; and
10. the cost of installation, maintenance, and updating of the language.

In the view of the characteristics of the language and those of the problems the analyst will most likely encounter, the following factors should be considered:

1. time advance methods;
2. random number and random variate generation capabilities;
3. the way a language permits the analyst to control the sequence of subroutines that represent the state changes;
4. capability for inserting use-written subroutines; and
5. forms of statistical analyses that can be performed on the data collected during simulation.

No language is without some strong points as well as weak points. It is difficult to compare these languages because many important software features are quite subjective in nature. Everyone seems to have his own opinion concerning the desirable features of a simulation language, e.g. ease of model development, availability of technical assistance, and system compatibility. In spite of this difficulty, various attempts have been made to compare simulation languages based on objective criteria [22]. In general, GPSS and SLAM (which are FORTRAN-based) are easiest to learn.

SIMSCRIPT has the most general process approach and thus can be used to model any system without using the event-scheduling approach. This, however, may result in more lines of code than GPSS or SLAM. RESQ has features specially oriented toward computer and communication systems, but the terminology is strictly in terms of queueing networks.

5.12 Summary

1. This chapter has presented the basic concepts and definitions of simulation modeling of a system.
2. The emphasis of the chapter has been on discrete, stochastic, digital, software simulation modeling. It is discrete because it proceeds a step at a time. It is stochastic or nondeterministic because element of randomness is introduced by using random numbers. It is digital because the computers employed are digital. It is software because the simulation model is a computer program.
3. Because simulation is a system approach to solving a problem, we have considered the major stages involved in developing a model of a given system. These stages are model building.
4. Since simulation output is subject to random error, the simulator would like to know how close is the point estimate to the mean value μ it is supposed to estimate. The statistical accuracy of the point estimates is measured in

terms of the confidence interval. The simulator generates some number of observations, say N, and employs standard statistical method to obtain the error estimate.

5. There are basically two types of languages used in simulation: multipurpose languages and special-purpose languages. The multipurpose or general-purpose languages include FORTRAN, BASIC, ADA, PASCAL, and C++. Special-purpose languages are meant to eliminate the major portion of the programming effort by providing a simulation-oriented framework about which a model is constructed in a simple fashion.

6. A brief introduction to two commonly used special-purpose, discrete simulation packages (NS2 and OPNET) is presented.

More information about simulation can be found in the references, including [40].

Problems

5.1 Define simulation and list five attractive reasons for it?

5.2 Generate 10,000 random numbers uniformly distributed between 0 and 1. Find the percentage of numbers between 0 and 0.1, between 0.1 and 0.2, etc., and compare your results with the expected distribution of 10 % in each interval.

5.3 (a) Using the linear congruential scheme, generate ten pseudorandom numbers with $a = 1573$, $c = 19$, $m = 1000$, and seed value $X_0 = 89$.
   (b) Repeat the generation with $c = 0$.

5.4 Uniformly distributed random integers between 11 and 30, inclusive, are to be generated from the random numbers U shown below. How many of the integers are odd numbers?

0.2311	0.7919
0.2312	0.9218
0.6068	0.7382
0.4860	0.1763
0.8913	0.4057
0.7621	0.9355
0.4565	0.9169
0.0185	0.4103
0.8214	0.8936
0.4447	0.0579

5.5 Generate 500 random numbers, exponentially distributed with mean 4, using uniformly distributed random numbers U. Estimate the mean and the variance of the variate.

5.6 Using the rejection method, generate a random variable from

$$f(x) = 5x^2, \quad 0 \le x \le 1$$

5.7 (a) Using the idea presented in this chapter, generate 100 Gaussian variates
     with mean 3 and variance 2.
     (b) Repeat part (a) using MATLAB command **randn**.
     (c) By estimating the mean and variance, which procedure is more accurate?
5.8 The probability density function of Erlang distribution is

$$f(x) = \frac{\alpha^k x^{k-1}}{\Gamma(k)} e^{-\alpha x}, \quad x > 0, \alpha > 0$$

where $\Gamma(k) = (k-1)!$ and k is an integer. Take $k = 2$ and $\alpha = 1$. Use the
rejection method to describe a procedure for generating random variates from
Erlang distribution.
5.9 Write a computer program to produce variates that follow hyperexponential
distribution, i.e.

$$f(x) = p\lambda e^{-\lambda x} + (1-p)\mu e^{-\mu x}$$

Take $p = 0.6$, $\lambda = 10$, $\mu = 5$.
5.10 Write a program to simulate the $M/E_k/1$ queueing system. Take $k = 2$.
    Compare the results of the simulation with those predicted by queueing
    theory.
5.11 A random sample of 50 variables taken from a normal population has a mean
    of 20 and standard deviation of 8. Calculate the error with 95 % confidence
    limits.
5.12 In a simulation model of a queueing system, an analyst obtained the mean
    waiting time for four simulation runs as 42.80, 41.60, 42.48, and 41.80 μs.
    Calculate the 98 % confidence interval for the waiting time.
5.13 Discuss the OPNET simulation results of Fig. 5.29 results?
5.14 Discuss the OPNET simulation comparison results of Figs. 5.30 and 5.31?
5.15 Discuss the OPNET simulation comparison results Figs. 5.32 through 5.35?
5.16 What are different purposes for C++ and OTcl languages in NS2?
5.17 What are the limitations of NS2?

References

1. S. V. Hoover and R. F. Perry, *A Problem Solving Approach*. New York: Addison-Wesley,
   1989.
2. F. Neelamkavil, *Computer Simulation and Modelling*. Chichester: John Wiley & Sons, 1987,
   pp. 1-4.

3. M. H. MacDougall, *Simulating Computer Systems: Techniques and Tools*. Cambridge, MA: MIT Press, 1987, p. 1.
4. J. W. Schmidt and R. E. Taylor, *Simulation and Analysis of Industrial Systems*. Homewood, IL: R. D. Irwin, 1970, p. 5.
5. J. Banks and J. S. Carson, *Discrete-event System Simulation*. Englewood Cliffs, NJ: Prentice-Hall, 1984, pp. 3-16.
6. W. Delaney and E. Vaccari, *Dynamic Models and Discrete Event Simulation*. New York, Marcel Dekker, 1989, pp. 1,13.
7. G. S. Fishman, *Concepts and Methods in Discrete Event Digital Simulation*. New York: John Wiley & Sons, 1973, pp. 24-25.
8. W. J. Graybeal and U. W. Pooch, *Simulation: Principles and Methods*. Cambridge, MA: Winthrop Publishers, 1980, pp. 5-10.
9. T. G. Lewis and B. J. Smith, *Computer Principles of Modeling and Simulation*. Boston, MA: Houghton Mifflin, 1979, pp. 172-174.
10. M. N. O. Sadiku and M. Ilyas, *Simulation of Local Area Networks*. Boca Raton: CRC Press, 1995, pp. 44,45, 67-77.
11. A. M. Law and W. D. Kelton, *Simulation of Modeling and Analysis*. New York: McGraw-Hill, 2nd ed., 1991, pp. 420-457.
12. R. McHaney, *Computer Simulation: a Practical Perspective*. New York: Academic Press, 1991, pp. 91-95, 155-172.
13. H. Kobayashi, *Modeling and Analysis: An Introduction to System Performance Evaluation Methodology*. Reading, MA: Addison-Wesley, 1978
14. R. Jain, The Art of Computer Systems Performance Analysis. New York: John Wiley & Sons, 1991, pp. 474-501.
15. M.N.O. Sadiku and M. R. Tofighi, "A Tutorial on Simulation of Queueing Models," *International Journal of Electrical Engineering Education*, vol. 36, 1999, pp. 102-120.
16. M. D. Fraser, "Simulation," *IEEE Potential*, Feb. 1992, pp. 15-18.
17. M. H. Merel and F. J. Mullin, "Analytic Monte Carlo error analysis," *J. Spacecraft*, vol. 5, no. 11, Nov. 1968, pp. 1304 -1308.
18. A. J. Chorin, "Hermite expansions in Monte-Carlo computation," J. Comp. Phys., vol. 8, 1971, pp. 472 -482.
19. G. S. Fishman, *Concepts and Methods in Discrete Event Digital Simulation*. New York: John Wiley & Sons, 1973, pp. 92-96.
20. G. Gordon, "A General Purpose Systems Simulation Program," *Proc. EJCC*, Washington D.C. New York: Macmillan, 1961.
21. J. Banks, J. S. Carson, and J. N. Sy, *Getting Started with GPSS/H*. Annandale, VA: Wolverine Software, 1989.
22. Minuteman Software: *GPSS/PC Manual*. Stow: MA, 1988.
23. B. Schmidt, *The Simulator GPSS-FORTRAN Version 3*. New York: Springer Verlag, 1987.
24. H. M. Markowitz, B. Hausner, and H. W. Karr, *SIMSCRIPT: A Simulation Programming Language*. Englewood Cliffs, NJ: Prentice-Hall, 1963.
25. P. J. Kiviat, R. Villaneuva, and H. M. Markowitz, *The SIMSCRIPT II Programming Language*. Englewood Cliffs, NJ: Prentice-Hall, 1968.
26. A. A. B. Pritsker, *The GASP IV Simulation Language*. New York: John Wiley & Sons, 1974.
27. A. A. B. Pritsker, *Introduction to Simulation and SLAM II*. New York: John Wiley & Sons, 2nd ed., 1984.
28. J. F. Kurose et al., "A graphics-oriented modeler's workstation environment for the RESearch Queueing Package (RESQ)," *Proc. ACM/IEEE Fall Joint Computer Conf.*, 1986.
29. I. Katzela, *Modeling and Simulation Communication Networks*. Upper Saddle River, NJ: Prentice Hall, 1999.
30. E. Aboelela, *Network Simulation Experiments Manual*. London, UK: Morgan Kaufmann, 2008, pp. 173–184.
31. http://www.opnet.com/

32. T. Issarikakul and E. Hossain, "Introduction to Network Simulator NS2. Springer, 2009.

33. http://www.isi.edu/nsnam/ns/

34. L. Fan and L. Taoshen, "Implementation and performance analyses of anycast QoS routing algorithm based on genetic algorithm in NS2," *Proceedings of Second International Conference on Information and Computing Science,* 2009, pp. 368 – 371.

35. S. Xu and Y. Yang, "Protocols simulation and performance analysis in wireless network based on NS2," *Proceedings of International conference on Multimedia Technology* (ICMT), 2011, pp. 638 – 641.

36. M. J. Rahimi et al., "Development of the smart QoS monitors to enhance the performance of the NS2 network simulator," *Proceedings of 13th International Conference on computer and Information Technology,* 2010, pp. 137-141.

37. R. Huang et al., "Simulation and analysis of mflood protocol in wireless network," *Proceedings of International Symposium on Computer Science and Computational Technology,* 2008, pp. 658-662.

38. W. J. Graybeal and U. W. Pooch, *Simulation: Principles and Methods*. Cambridge, MA: Winthrop Publishers, 1980, p. 153.

39. J. R. Emshoff and R. L. Sisson, *Design and Use of Computer Simulation Models*. London: Macmillan, 1970, pp. 119-150.

40. D. Maki and M. Thompson, *Mathematical modeling and Computer Simulation*. Belmont, CA: Thomson Brooks/Cole, 2006, pp. 153-211.

Chapter 6
Local Area Networks

> *Success doesn't discriminate. It's an equal opportunity*
> *employer—available to everyone willing to pay the price.*
>
> —Anonymous

When designing a local area network (LAN), establishing performance characteristics of the network before putting it into use is of paramount importance; it gives the designer the freedom and flexibility to adjust various parameters of the network in the planning rather than the operational phase. However, it is hard to predict the performance of the LAN unless a detailed analysis of a similar network is available. Information on a similar network is generally hard to come by so that performance modeling of the LAN must be carried out.

In this chapter we focus on the analytic models of four LAN important protocols: the token-passing access methods for the ring and bus topologies, the CSMA/CD for bus, and the star. The analytic models provide an insight into the nature of the networks. It should be emphasized that for each network, we do not provide all the details; that can be found in the references. We provide enough detail to understand the performance analysis, which is our focus.

Before we present the analytic model for each network, it is expedient that we consider the OSI reference model, which applies to LANs, MANs, and WANs.

6.1 OSI Reference and IEEE Models

An effective solution to communication between diverse equipment by numerous manufacturers is to have vendors abide by a common set of rules or data-exchange protocols. In 1973, the International Standards Organization (ISO) issued a recommendation for a standard network architecture. This is known as the Open System

M.N.O. Sadiku and S.M. Musa, *Performance Analysis of Computer Networks*,
DOI 10.1007/978-3-319-01646-7_6, © Springer International Publishing Switzerland 2013

Fig. 6.1 Relationship
between the OSI model
and IEEE LAN layers

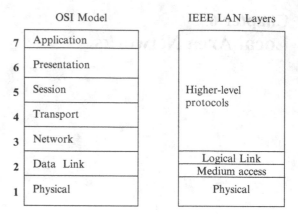

OSI Model

IEEE LAN Layers

Interconnection (OSI) reference model. "Open" refers to the ability to communicate with any other system obeying the same standards.

The OSI reference model is a structured model. It is divided into seven layers as shown in Fig. 6.1 and explained as follows.

The *application layer*, layer 7, is the one the user sees. It provides services directly comprehensible to application programs; login, password checks, network transparency for distribution of resources, file and document transfer, industry specific protocols.

The *presentation layer*, layer 6, is concerned with the interpretation of the data. It restructures data to/from standardized format used within network; text compression, code conversion, file format conversion, and encryption.

The *session layer*, layer 5, manages address translation and access security. It negotiates to establish a connection with another node on the network and then to manage the dialogue. This means controlling the start, stopping, and synchronisation of the conversion.

The *transport layer*, layer 4, performs error control, sequence checking, handling of duplicate packets, flow control, and multiplexing. Here it is determined whether the channel is to be point-to-point (virtual) with ordered messages, isolated messages with no order, or broadcast messages. It is the last of the layers which are concerned with communications between peer entities in the systems. The transport layer and above are referred to as the upper layers of the model, and they are independent of the underlying network. The lower layers are concerned with data transfer across the network.

The *network layer*, layer 3, provides a connection path between systems, including the case where intermediate nodes are involved. It deals with message packetization, message routing for data transfer between non-adjacent nodes or stations, congestion control, and accounting.

The *data-link layer*, layer 2, establishes the transmission protocol, the way in which information will be transmitted, acknowledgment of message, token possession, error detection, and sequencing. It prepares the packets passed down from the network layer for transmission on the network. It takes a raw transmission and transforms it into a line free from error. Here headers and framing information are added or removed. With these go the timing signals, check-sum, and station addresses, as well as the control system for access.

The *physical layer*, layer 1, is that part that actually touches the media or cable; the line is the point within the node or device where the data is received and transmitted. It sees to it that ones arrive as ones and zeros as zeros. It encodes and physically transfers messages (raw bits stream) between adjacent stations. It handles voltages, frequencies, direction, pin numbers, modulation techniques, signaling schemes, ground loop prevention, and collision detection in CSMA/CD access method.

A good way to remember the layers is this. Starting from the layer 1, one should remember the saying, "Please Do Not Throw Sausage Pizza Away."

The IEEE has formulated standards for the physical and logical link layers for three types of LANs, namely, token buses, token rings, and CSMA/CD protocols. Figure 6.1 illustrates the correspondence between the three layers of the OSI and the IEEE 802 reference models. The physical layer specifies means for transmitting and receiving bits across various types of media. The media access control layer performs the functions needed to control access to the physical medium. The logical link control layer is the common interface to the higher software layers.

6.2 LAN Characteristics

A local area network (LAN) is distinguished from other types of computer networks in that communication is usually confined to a moderate geographical area such as a building or a campus. It has the following characteristics:

- Short distance (up to 1 km)
- High speed (1–100 Mbps)
- Low error rate (10^{-8} to 10^{-4})
- Ease of access

A LAN is usually owned by a single organization and it is designed for the purpose of sharing resources.

The topology of a network is the way in which the nodes (or stations) are interconnected. The basic forms of LAN topologies are shown in Fig. 6.2.

The type of technology used to implement LANs are diverse as the LAN vendors. Both vendors and users are forced to make a choice. This choice is usually based on several criteria such as:

- network topology and architecture
- access control
- transmission medium
- transmission techniques (baseband/broadband signaling)
- adherence to standards
- performance in terms of channel utilization, delay, and power

The primary performance criterion is the delay-throughput characteristics of the system.

Fig. 6.2 Typical LAN
topologies

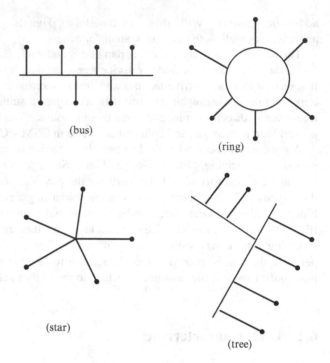

(bus)

(ring)

(star)

(tree)

The **mean transfer delay** of a message is the time interval between the instant the message
is available at the sending station and the end of its successful reception at the receiving
station.

It is convenient to regard the transfer delay as comprising of three components.
The first component, W, is called the waiting time or access time. It is the time
elapsed from the availability of a message in the source station transmit buffer until
the beginning of its transmission on the channel. The second component, T_p, called
the propagation time, is the time elapsed from the beginning of the transmission of
the message until the arrival of the first bit of the message at the destination. The
third component is the transmission or service time, S, which is the time elapsed
between the arrival of the first bit of the message at the destination and the last bit.
As soon as the last bit arrives at the destination, the transfer is complete. This
implies that the transfer delay D includes the waiting time W (or queueing delay) at
the sending station, the service (or transmission) time S of the message, and the
propagation delay T_p, i.e.

$$D = W + S + T_p \qquad (6.1a)$$

In terms of their expected values

$$E(D) = E(W) + E(S) + E(T_p) \qquad (6.1b)$$

6.3 Token-Passing Ring

The token-passing ring, developed by workers at the Zurich Research Laboratories of IBM in 1972 and standardized as an access method in the IEEE Standard 802.5, is the best-known of all the ring systems. Here we are interested in its basic operation and delay analysis [3–4].

6.3.1 Basic Operation

In a token ring, the stations are connected as in all ring networks as illustrated in Fig. 6.3.

Access to the transmission channel is controlled by means of a special eight-bit pattern called a *token*, which is passed around the ring. When the system is initialized, a designated station generates a free token, such as 11111111. If no station is ready to transmit, the free token circulates around the ring. When a station wishes to transmit, it captures the free token and changes it to a busy token, such as 11111110, thereby disallowing other stations from transmitting. The packet to be transmitted is appended to the busy token. The receiving station copies the information. When the information reaches the sending station, the station takes it off the ring and generates a new free token to be used by another station who may need the transmission channel.

This operation can be described by a single-server queueing model, as illustrated in Fig. 6.4.

The server serves as many queues as stations attached to the ring. The server attends the queues in a cyclic order as shown by the rotating switch which

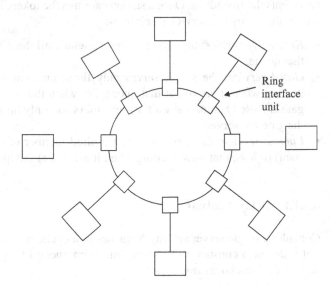

Fig. 6.3 A typical ring topology

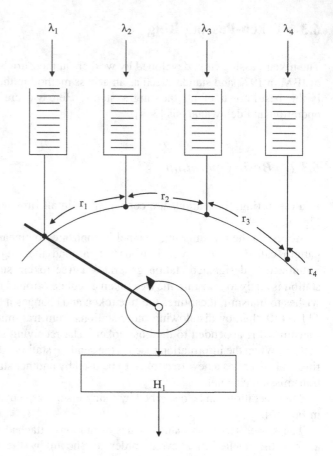

Fig. 6.4 Cyclic-service
queueing model

represents the free token. Once a station captures the token, it is served according to
one of the following service disciplines:

- *Exhaustive service*: the server serves a queue until there are no customers left in
  that queue.
- *Gated service*: the server serves only those customers in a queue that were
  waiting when it arrived at that queue, i.e. when the server arrives at a queue, a
  gate is closed behind the waiting customers and only those customers in front of
  the gate are served.
- *Limited service*: the server serves a limited number of customers, say K (constant) or less, that were waiting when it arrived at the queue.

6.3.1.1 Delay Analysis

Consider a single server serving N queues in a cyclic manner as shown in Fig. 6.4.
Let r_i denote a constant switchover time from queue i to queue i+1 and R_o be the
sum of all switchover times, i.e.

$$R_o = \sum_{i=1}^{N} r_i \qquad (6.2)$$

We examine the M/G/1 model, that is, messages arrive at queues according to independent Poisson processes with mean rates $\lambda_1, \lambda_2, \cdots, \lambda_N$ and the service times H_i of the messages from queue i are generally distributed with mean $E(S_i)$ and second moment $E(S_i^2)$. We denote the utilization of queue i by

$$\rho_i = \lambda_i E(S_i) \qquad (6.3)$$

and assume that the normalization condition:

$$\rho = \sum_{i=1}^{N} \rho_i < 1 \qquad (6.4)$$

Let V_i denote the intervisit time of queue i, also known as the server-vacation time, the time interval from the server's departure from the queue until its return to the same queue. The moment generating function for the statistical-equilibrium waiting time distribution is given by [5–7]:

Exhaustive service:

$$G_W^e(z) = E(e^{-zW_i}) = \frac{1 - \rho_i}{E(V_i)} \frac{1 - G_v(z)}{z - \lambda_i + \lambda_i G_s(z)} \qquad (6.5)$$

Gated service:

$$G_W^g(z) = \frac{G_c(z)\lambda_i[1 - G_s(z)] - G_c(z)}{E(V_i)[z - \lambda_i + \lambda_i G_s(z)]} \qquad (6.6)$$

Limited service:

$$G_W^\ell(z) = \frac{1 - \rho_i + \lambda_i E(V_i)}{E(V_i)} \frac{1 - G_v(z)}{z - \lambda_i + \lambda_i G_s(z)G_v(z)} \qquad (6.7)$$

where $G_v(z) = E(e^{-zV_i})$ is the generating function for the intervisit time; $G_s(z) = E(e^{-zS_i})$ is the generating function for the service time, $G_c(z) = E(e^{-zC_i})$ is the generating function for the cycle time.

From Eqs. (6.5)–(6.7), the mean waiting time of messages in queue i is determined by differentiating $G_W(z)$ and setting $z = 0$. The result is:

Exhaustive service:

$$E^e(W_i) = \frac{E(V_i)}{2} + \frac{Var(V_i)}{2E(V_i)} + \frac{\lambda_i E(S_i^2)}{2(1 - \rho_i)} \qquad (6.8)$$

Gated service:

$$E^g(W_i) = \frac{E(C_i)}{2} + \frac{Var(C_i)}{2E(C_i)} + \frac{\rho_i E(S_i^2)}{2(1 - \rho_i)E(S_i)} \tag{6.9}$$

Limited service:

$$E^\ell(W_i) = \frac{\lambda_i E\left[(V_i + S_i)^2\right]}{2\left[1 - \rho_i + \lambda_i E(V_i)^i\right]} \tag{6.10}$$

Hence the mean waiting time can be found provided the first two moments of the intervisit times V_i are known.

To find the first moment of V_i, let C_i be the total cycle time (i.e. the time between subsequent visits of the server to queue i) and T_i be the time spent by the server at queue i, then

$$E(V_i) = E(C_i) - E(T_i) \tag{6.11}$$

It is readily shown that [8]

$$E(C_i) = \frac{R_o}{1 - \rho} \tag{6.12}$$

Since the traffic flow must be conserved, the average number of messages serviced during one visit of queue i is equal to the average number of arriving messages at that queue in one cycle time, i.e.

$$\frac{E(T_i)}{E(S_i)} = \lambda_i E(C_i)$$

or

$$E(T_i) = \lambda_i E(C_i)E(S_i) = \rho_i E(C_i) \tag{6.13}$$

Substituting Eqs. (6.12) and (6.13) into Eq. (6.11) gives the mean intervisit time of queue i as

$$E(V_i) = \frac{1 - \rho_i}{1 - \rho}R_o \tag{6.14}$$

Introducing Eqs. (6.12) and (6.14) in Eq. (6.8) leads to

$$E^e(W_i) = \frac{Var(V_i)}{2E(V_i)} + \frac{1 - \rho_i}{2(1 - \rho)}R_o + \frac{\rho_i}{2(1 - \rho_i)}\frac{E(S_i^2)}{E(S_i)} \tag{6.15}$$

for exhaustive service. Taking similar procedure for gated service discipline results in

$$E^g(W_i) = \frac{Var(V_i)}{2E(V_i)} + \frac{1+\rho_i}{2(1-\rho)}R_o + \frac{\rho_i}{2(1-\rho_i)}\frac{E(S_i^2)}{E(S_i)} \quad (6.16)$$

For limited service, we have an explicit solution for $E(W_i)$ only in the special case of statistically symmetric conditions and $K = 1$ for all stations [5, 7]. However, an upper bound for $E(W_i)$ for any K is presented in [9].

For symmetric traffic conditions (i.e. in the case of identical stations),

$$\lambda_1 = \lambda_2 = \cdots = \lambda_N = \frac{\lambda}{N} \quad (6.17)$$

$$r_1 = r_2 = \cdots = r_N = \frac{R_o}{N} = r \quad (6.18)$$

and the mean waiting time for all the queues becomes:

Exhaustive service:

$$E^e(W_i) = \frac{\delta^2}{2r} + \frac{Nr(1-\rho/N)}{2(1-\rho)} + \frac{\rho E(S^2)}{2(1-\rho)E(S)} \quad (6.19)$$

Gated service:

$$E^g(W_i) = \frac{\delta^2}{2r} + \frac{Nr(1+\rho/N)}{2(1-\rho)} + \frac{\rho E(S^2)}{2(1-\rho)E(S)} \quad (6.20)$$

Limited service:

$$E^e(W_i) = \frac{\delta^2}{2r} + \frac{Nr(1+\rho/N) + N\lambda\delta^2}{2(1-\rho-N\lambda r)} + \frac{\rho E(S^2)}{2(1-\rho-N\lambda r)E(S)} \quad (6.21)$$

where δ^2 is the variance of the switchover time. An alternative, less rigorous means of deriving Eqs. (6.19–6.21) is the decomposition theorem [8]. Note that the only difference between Eqs. (6.19) and (6.20) is the $\pm$ signs in the terms $(1 \pm \rho)$ which implies that $E^e(W) \leq E^g(W)$. Thus, from Eqs. (6.19)–(6.21), we conclude that:

$$E^e(W) \leq E^g(W) \leq E^\ell(W) \quad (6.22)$$

The above derivations are for continuous-time systems. The corresponding derivations for discrete-time systems can be found in [5, 9–11].

The formulas in Eqs. (6.19)–(6.21) for the waiting time are valid for token ring and token bus. However, the mean value r of the switchover time and its variance δ^2 differ for each protocol. Here we evaluate these parameters for the token ring.

The token passing interval or switchover time T is given by

$$T = T_t + T_{pt} + T_b \tag{6.23}$$

where T_t is the token transmission time, T_{pt} is the token propagation delay, and T_b is the bit delay per station. Hence, the expected value $r = E(T)$ is given by

$$r = E(T_t) + E(T_{pt}) + E(T_b) \tag{6.24}$$

and, since the random variables are independent, the variance Var $(T) = \delta^2$ is given by

$$\delta^2 = \text{Var}(T_i) + \text{Var}(T_{pt}) + \text{Var}(T_b) \tag{6.25}$$

Assuming a constant token packet length L_t (including preamble bits), for a network data rate R,

$$T_t = \frac{L_t}{R}$$

Its expected value is constant. Hence

$$E(T_t) = T_t = \frac{L_t}{R}, \quad \text{Var}(T_t) = 0 \tag{6.26}$$

Assuming that the stations are equally spaced on the ring, the distance between any adjacent stations is identical to ℓ/N, where ℓ is the physical length of the ring. If P is the signal propagation delay in seconds per unit length (the reciprocal of the signal propagation delay velocity u, i.e. $P = 1/u$), the token propagation delay is

$$T_{pt} = \frac{P\ell}{N}$$

Hence

$$E(T_{pt}) = T_{pt} = \frac{P\ell}{N}, \quad \text{Var}(T_{pt}) = 0 \tag{6.27}$$

If L_b is the bit delay caused by each station,

$$T_b = \frac{L_b}{R}$$

and

$$E(T_b) = \frac{L_b}{R}, \quad \text{Var}(T_b) = 0 \tag{6.28}$$

We conclude from Eqs. (6.24)–(6.28) that

$$r = \frac{P\ell}{N} + \frac{L_b + L_t}{R}, \quad \delta^2 = 0 \tag{6.29}$$

The average propagation delay suffered from one station is the propagation delay halfway around the ring, i.e.

$$E(T_p) = \tau/2 \tag{6.30}$$

where τ is the round-trip propagation delay. Note that the sum of the switchover times (assumed to be constant) corresponds to the round-trip propagation delay and the sum of the bit-holding times at each station, i.e

$$Nr = P\ell + N(L_b + L_t)/R = \tau \tag{6.31}$$

Thus, for large N and symmetric traffic conditions, the mean transfer delay is obtained by substituting Eqs. (6.19)–(6.21), (6.29), and (6.30) in Eq. (6.1). We obtain:

Exhaustive service:

$$\boxed{E^e(D) = \frac{\tau(1 - \rho/N)}{2(1 - \rho)} + \frac{\rho E(S^2)}{2(1 - \rho)E(S)} + E(S) + \tau/2} \tag{6.32}$$

Gated service:

$$\boxed{E^g(D) = \frac{\tau(1 + \rho/N)}{2(1 - \rho)} + \frac{\rho E(S^2)}{2(1 - \rho)E(S)} + E(S) + \tau/2} \tag{6.33}$$

Limited service:

$$\boxed{E^\ell(D) = \frac{\tau(1 + \rho/N)}{2(1 - \rho - \lambda\tau)} + \frac{\rho E(S^2)}{2(1 - \rho - \lambda\tau)E(S)} + E(S) + \tau/2} \tag{6.34}$$

Finally, the mean service time E(S) is given by

$$E(S) = \frac{L_p + L_h}{R} = \rho/\lambda \tag{6.35a}$$

where L_p and L_h are the mean packet length and header length respectively. For fixed messages (requiring constant service times),

$$E(S^2) = E^2(S) \tag{6.35b}$$

and for exponential service times,

$$E(S^2) = 2E^2(S) \tag{6.35c}$$

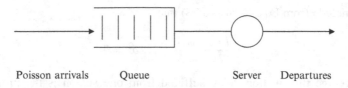

Poisson arrivals   Queue   Server   Departures

Fig. 6.5 A switching node; for Example 6.1

Example 6.1 Messages arrive at a switching node at the rate of 2 bits/min, as shown in Fig. 6.5. If the messages is exponentially distributed with an average length of 20 bytes and the node serves 10 bits/s, calculate the traffic intensity.

Solution

The arrival rate is the number of messages/second or packets/second.

$$\lambda = 2 bits/\text{minute} = \frac{2}{60} bps$$

The service time is the time taken to service 1 packet.

$$E(S) = \frac{L_p}{R} = \frac{20 \times 8}{10} = 16s$$

The traffic intensity is given by

$$\rho = \lambda E(S) = \frac{2}{60} \times 16 = 0.5333$$

Example 6.2 A token-ring LAN has a total propagation delay of 20 μs, a channel capacity of 10^6 bps and 50 stations, each of which generates Poisson traffic and has a latency of 1 bit. For a traffic intensity of 0.6, calculate:

(a) the switchover time,
(b) the mean service time,
(c) the message arrival rate per station,
(d) the average delay for exhaustive, gated, and limited service disciplines.

   Assume 10 bits for overhead and 500 bits average packet length, exponentially distributed.

Solution

(a) If the end-to-end propagation time is $\tau = 20$ μs, then the switchover time r is given by

$$r = \frac{\tau}{N} = \frac{20}{50} = 0.4 \mu s$$

(b) The mean service time is

$$E(S) = \frac{L_p + L_h}{R} = \frac{500 + 10}{10^6} = 510\mu s$$

(c) Since $\rho = \lambda E(S)$, the total arrival rate is

$$\lambda = {}^\rho/_{E(S)}$$

Hence, the arrival rate per station is

$$\lambda_i = \frac{\rho}{NE(S)} = \frac{0.6}{50 \times 510 \times 10^{-6}} = 23.53\,\text{bps}$$

(d) For exponentially distributed packet lengths,

$$E(S^2) = 2E^2(S) = 52.02 \times 10^{-8} s^2$$

Using Eqs. (6.32)–(6.34), we obtain

$$E^e(D) = \frac{20 \times 10^{-6}(1 - 0.6/50)}{2(1 - 0.6)} + \frac{0.6 \times 52.02 \times 10^{-8}}{2(1 - 0.6) \times 510 \times 10^{-6}}$$
$$+ 510 \times 10^{-6} + 10 \times 10^{-6}$$
$$= (24.7 + 765 + 520)\mu s = 1.3097\,\text{ms}$$

for exhaustive service.
For gated service,

$$E^g(D) = \frac{20 \times 10^{-6}(1 + 0.6/50)}{2(1 - 0.6)} + (765 + 520)\mu s = 1.3103\,\text{ms}$$

For limited service,

$$E^l(D) = \frac{20 \times 10^{-6}(1 + 0.6/50)}{2(1 - 0.6 - 0.02353)} + \frac{0.6 \times 52.02 \times 10^{-8}}{2(1 - 0.6 - 0.02353) \times 510 \times 10^{-6}}$$
$$+ 510 \times 10^{-6} + 10 \times 10^{-6}$$
$$= (26.881 + 812.81 + 520)\mu s = 1.3597\,\text{ms}$$

Notice that

$$E^e(D) < E^g(D) < E^l(D)$$

as stated in Eq. (6.22).

6.4   Token-Passing Bus

The token-passing bus was inspired by the token ring and standardized in the IEEE Standard 802.4. The basic operation of the token bus LAN is fully discussed in [3, 12] while its delay analysis in [13].

6.4.1   Basic Operation

The operation of the token bus is similar in many respects to that of the token ring. Although the token bus uses bus topology while the token ring uses ring, the stations on a token bus are logically ordered to form a *logical ring*, which is not necessarily the same as the physical ordering of the stations. Figure 6.6 shows a typical ordering of stations on bus with the sequence AEFHCA. Each station on the ring knows the identity of the stations preceding and following it. The right of access to the bus is controlled by the cyclic passing of a token among the stations in the logical ring. Unlike in a token ring where the token is passed implicitly, an explicit token with node addressing information is used. The token is passed in order of address. When a station receives the token, it may transmit its messages according to a service discipline (exhaustive, gated, or limited) and pass the token to the next station in the logical ring.

A token bus differs in some respects from token ring. Since token bus is a broadcast protocol, stations not in the logical ring can receive messages. Stations on a token bus are passive and thus create no station latency or delay unlike in token ring where the signal is regenerated at each station. Propagation delay on a token bus are generally longer because the token may have to travel longer distances to satisfy the logical ordering of the stations.

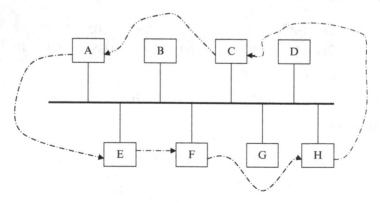

Fig. 6.6 A typical logical ordering on a physical bus

6.4.2 Delay Analysis

As mentioned earlier, the expressions for waiting time (or queueing delay) in Eqs. (6.19)–(6.21) are valid for both token ring and token bus protocols except that the mean value of r of the switchover time and its variance δ^2 are different for the two protocols. We now evaluate these parameters as they apply to the token bus.

Unlike token ring, the token bus requires that the complete token packet be transmitted, received, and identified before a data packet can be generated and transmitted. Therefore, the token passing transmission time T_t is a significant delay in token bus protocol. According to Eq. (6.26),

$$E(T_t) = T_t = \frac{L_t}{R}, \quad \mathrm{Var}(T_t) = 0 \tag{6.36}$$

Assuming bus length ℓ, uniform distribution of N stations, and an equal probability of communication between any two stations, the distance between station i and its logical successor j is given by

$$d_{ij} = jd = \frac{j\ell}{N-1}, \quad 1 \le j \le N-1 \tag{6.37}$$

The probability of station i having the token and passing it to station j is given by

$$P_{ij} = \frac{1}{\binom{N}{2}} = \frac{2}{N(N-1)} \tag{6.38}$$

If X is the token propagation distance, the expected token propagation delay is

$$E(X) = \sum d_{ij} P_{ij} = \sum_{i=1}^{N} \sum_{j=1}^{i-1} \frac{2\ell j}{N(N-1)^2} = \frac{(N+1)\ell}{3(N-1)} \tag{6.39}$$

where the identities

$$\sum_{i=1}^{n} i = \frac{n}{2}(n+1)$$

and

$$\sum_{i=1}^{n} i^2 = \frac{n}{6}(n+1)(2n+1)$$

have been applied. Corresponding to the bus length ℓ, we have an end-to-end propagation delay τ. Therefore, the expected token propagation delay is

$$E(T_{pt}) = \frac{(N+1)\tau}{3(N-1)} \tag{6.40}$$

The variance of X is given by

$$\begin{aligned}
\text{Var}(X) &= E(X^2) - [E(X)]^2 = \sum d_{ij}^2 P_{ij} - [E(X)]^2 \\
&= \frac{(N+1)\ell^2}{3(N-1)^3} - \frac{(N+1)^2 \ell^2}{9(N-1)^2}
\end{aligned} \tag{6.41}$$

where the identity

$$\sum_{i=1}^{n} i^3 = \frac{n^2}{4}(n+1)^2$$

has been incorporated. Thus the variance of the token passing propagation delay is

$$\text{Var}(T_{pt}) = \frac{(N+1)(N-2)\tau^2}{18(N-1)^2} \tag{6.42}$$

The bit delay per station adds to the token passing time a delay corresponding to token handling and address recognition. In IEEE 802.4, for example, a buffer of four or five bits may be required depending on the size of the address field. If L_b is the bit delay caused by each station,

$$T_b = \frac{L_b}{R}$$

and

$$E(T_b) = \frac{L_b}{R}, \quad \text{Var}(T_b) = 0 \tag{6.43}$$

Substitution of Eqs. (6.36), (6.40), (6.42), and (6.43) into Eqs. (6.24) and (6.25) yields

$$r = \frac{(N+1)\tau}{3(N-1)} + c, \quad \delta^2 = \frac{(N+1)(N-2)\tau^2}{18(N-1)^2} \tag{6.44}$$

with limiting values ($N \to \infty$) of

$$r = \frac{\tau}{3} + c, \quad \delta^2 = \frac{\tau^2}{18} \tag{6.45}$$

where

$$c = T_t + T_b = \frac{L_t + L_b}{R}$$

The packet propagation delay is the same as the token propagation delay so that for large N,

$$E(T_p) = \tau/3 \tag{6.46}$$

If we assume large N and symmetric traffic conditions, the mean transfer time is obtained by substituting Eqs. (6.19)–(6.21), (6.45), and (6.46) into Eq. (6.1).

Exhaustive service:

$$E^e(D) = \frac{\tau^2}{36(\tau/3 + c)} + N(\tau/3 + c)\frac{(1 - \rho/N)}{2(1 - \rho)} + \frac{\rho E(S^2)}{2(1 - \rho)E(S)} + E(S) + \tau/3$$

$$\tag{6.47}$$

Gated service:

$$E^g(D) = \frac{\tau^2}{36(\tau/3 + c)} + N(\tau/3 + c)\frac{(1 + \rho/N)}{2(1 - \rho)} + \frac{\rho E(S^2)}{2(1 - \rho)E(S)} + E(S) + \tau/3$$

$$\tag{6.48}$$

Limited service:

$$E^\ell(D) = \frac{\tau^2}{36(\tau/3 + c)} + \frac{N(\tau/3 + c)(1 + \rho/N)}{2[1 - \rho - N\lambda(\tau/3 + c)]}$$

$$+ \frac{\rho E(S^2)}{2[1 - \rho - N\lambda(\tau/3 + c)]E(S)} + E(S) + \tau/3 \tag{6.49}$$

where the mean service time E(S) is given by Eq. (6.35) and the end-to-end propagation delay by

$$\tau = P\ell \tag{6.50}$$

6.5 CSMA/CD Bus

Multiple access local area network (LAN) protocols divide broadly into two classes [14]: *random* (or *contention*) access protocols and *controlled access* protocols. In random access protocols, transmission rights are simultaneously offered to a group of stations in the hope that exactly one of the stations has a packet to send. However, if two or more stations send packets simultaneously on the channel, these messages interfere with each other and none of them are correctly received by the destination stations. In such cases, a collision has occurred and stations retransmit packets until they are successfully received by the destination stations.

Controlled-based access mechanism is one in which a token is first secured by a node in order to transmit its messages through the medium. Controlled access protocols, such as token ring and token bus considered in Sections 6.3 and 6.4 respectively, avoid collisions by coordinating access of the stations to the channel by imposing either a predetermined or dynamically determined order of access. Access coordination is done by use of the channel itself. Each station indicates with a short message on the channel whether or not it wants access. This polling mechanism consumes some channel capacity regardless of whether stations require access or not. While such protocols are efficient when traffic is heavy, under light traffic conditions they result in unnecessary packet delays as stations that want to transmit wait their turn.

In contrast, random access protocols exhibit small packet delays under light traffic conditions: stations transmit as soon as they want access to the channel, and the probability of a collision is low when traffic is light. Another attractive aspect of random access protocols is their simplicity, making them easy to implement at the stations [15].

The ALOHA family of protocols is popular due its seniority because it was the first random access mechanism to be introduced. In this type of protocols, the success of a transmission is not guaranteed in advance. When two or more packets overlap in time, even by a bit, all are lost and must be retransmitted. The carrier sense multiple access (CSMA) reduces the level of interference caused by overlapping packets by allowing users to sense the carrier due to other users' transmissions and aborting transmission when the channel is sensed busy. In CSMA, all nodes listen constantly to the bus and only transmit if there is no transmission already on the bus. This is the *carrier sense* aspect of the name. If there is no transmission on the bus, any node with available data can transmit immediately, hence the term *multiple access*. Beside the ability to sense carrier, some LANs have an additional feature of being able to detect interference among several transmissions while transmitting and abort transmission when there is collision. This additional feature produces a variation of CSMA that is known as CSMA-CD (Carrier Sense Multiple Access with Collision Detection). Because of its simplicity, CSMA-CD is perhaps the most popular contention-based protocol. It operates on a bus-type network and is sometimes referred to as the 'Ethernet' protocol.

6.5.1 Basic Operation

In a LAN employing CSMA-CD protocol, each node listens during, as well as before, transmitting its packet. Variations within the CSMA-CD protocols center about the operation mode of the station when the medium is sensed busy or idle. The most popular operation modes are [15, 16]:

- nonpersistent,
- 1-persistent, and
- p-persistent protocols

In the nonpersistent CSMA-CD scheme, a node with a packet ready for transmission senses the channel and acts as follows.

1. If the channel is sensed idle, the node initiates transmission of the packet.
2. If the channel is sensed busy, the node schedules the retransmission of its packet to some later time. It waits for a random amount of time and resenses the channel.
3. If a collision is detected during transmission, the node aborts its transmission, and schedules the retransmission of the packet later.

In the 1-persistent CSMA-CD protocol (which is a special case of the p-persistent), a node which finds the channel busy persists on transmitting as soon as the channel becomes free. If it finds the channel idle, it transmits the packet immediately with probability one. In other words, a ready node senses the channel and proceeds as in nonpersistent CSMA-CD, except that, when the channel is sensed busy, it monitors the channel until it is senses idle and then with probability one initiates transmission of its packet.

In the p-persistent protocol, a ready node senses the channel and proceeds as in non-persistent protocol except that when the channel is sensed busy, the node persists until the channel is idle, and

(i) With probability p it initiates transmission of the packet
(ii) With probability 1-p it delays transmission by τ seconds (the end-to-end propagation delay).

If at this instant, the channel is sensed idle, then the node repeats steps (i) and (ii); otherwise it schedules retransmission of its packet later.

Note that in all CSMA-CD protocols, given that a transmission is initiated on an empty channel, it takes at most one τ seconds for the packet transmission to reach all nodes. Beyond this time the channel will surely be sensed busy for as long as data transmission is in process. A collision can only occur if another transmission is initiated before the current one is sensed, and it will take at most additional τ seconds before interference reaches all devices. Moreover, Ethernet has a collision consensus reinforcement mechanism by which a device, experiencing interference, jams the channel to ensure that all other interfering nodes detect the collision.

In addition to the variations in the protocols, the transmission medium may be slotted or unslotted.

6.5.2   Delay Analysis

A widely used analytic model of CSMA-CD networks was developed by Lam [17, 18]. The analysis of the M/G/1 queue using embedded Markov chain led to a closed-form expression for the mean delay E(D). The underlying assumptions are close to the standardized CSMA-CD protocol, and the results are simple to evaluate numerically.

The underlying assumptions in Lam's model are as follows. The network consists of an infinite number of stations connected to a slotted channel in which stations can begin transmissions only at the start of a time slot. The traffic offered to the network is a Poisson process with a constant arrival rate λ. Each state is allowed to hold at most one message at a time. Message transmission times are generally distributed. The system operates under the p-persistent protocol. Following a successful transmission, all ready stations transmit within the next slot. Following a collision, stations use an adaptive retransmission algorithm such that the probability of a successful transmission within any of the slots subsequent to a collision is constant and equal to 1/e ($=0.368$).

Under these assumptions, the mean delay was found by Lam and later modified by Bux [4, 19] for non-slotted channel as:

$$
\begin{aligned}
E(D) = &\frac{\lambda\left[E(S^2) + (4e+1)\tau E(S) + 5\tau^2 + 4e(2e-1)\tau^2\right]}{2(1 - \lambda[E(S) + \tau + 2e\tau])} \\
&- \frac{(1 - e^{-2\lambda\tau})(e + \lambda\tau - 3\lambda\tau e)}{\lambda e[F(\lambda)e^{-(1+\lambda\tau)} + e^{-2\lambda\tau} - 1]} + 2\tau e + E(S) + \tau/3
\end{aligned}
\tag{6.51}
$$

where τ is the end-to-end propagation delay as in Eq. (6.50), $E(S)$ and $E(S^2)$ are respectively the first and second moments of the message transmission (or service) time as given by Eq. (6.35). The term $\tau/3$ is the mean source-destination propagation time $E(T_p)$. It is heuristically taken as $\tau/2$ in other works, but we have used $\tau/3$ to be consistent with the derivation in Eq. (6.46). The function $F(\lambda)$ is the Laplace transform of the message transmission time distribution, i.e.

$$
F(\lambda) = \int_0^\infty f(t)e^{-\lambda t}dt
\tag{6.52}
$$

For constant message lengths,

$$
F(\lambda) = e^{-\rho}, \quad E(S^2) = E^2(S)
\tag{6.53}
$$

where $\rho = \lambda E(S)$. For exponentially distributed message lengths,

$$
F(\lambda) = \frac{1}{1+\rho}, \quad E(S^2) = 2E^2(S)
\tag{6.54}
$$

It is important to note the two limiting cases of operation of CSMA/CD from Eq. (6.51). The mean delay becomes unbounded as the traffic intensity ρ approaches the maximum value of

$$
\rho_{max} = \frac{1}{1 + (2e+1)a} = \frac{1}{1 + 6.44a}
\tag{6.55}
$$

where $a = \tau/E(S)$. Also as the traffic intensity ρ approaches zero, the mean delay approaches the minimum value of

$$E(D)_{min} = E(S) + \tau/3 \qquad (6.56)$$

Example 6.3 A CSMA/CD network with a channel bit rate of 1 Mbps connects 40 stations on a 2-km cable. For fixed packet length of 1,000 bits, calculate the mean transfer delay. Assume propagation delay of 5 μs/km and an average arrival rate/station of 0.015 packets/s.

Solution

The mean service time is

$$E(S) = \frac{L_R}{R} = \frac{1,000}{10^6} = 10^{-3}s$$

The mean arrival rate for each station is

$$\lambda_i = 0.015 \times 1,000 \text{ bits/s} = 15 \text{ bps}$$

Hence, the total arrival rate is

$$\lambda = N\lambda_i = 40 \times 15 = 600 \text{ bps}$$

The traffic intensity is

$$\rho = \lambda E(S) = 10^{-3} \times 600 = 0.6$$

The end-to-end propagation delay is

$$\tau = \frac{\ell}{u} = \ell P = 2 \text{ km} \times 5\mu s/\text{km} = 10\mu s$$

For constant packet lengths,

$$F(\lambda) = e^{-\rho}, \quad E(S^2) = E^2(S) = 10^{-6}$$

Applying Eq. (6.51), we obtain the delay as

$$E(D) = \frac{600\{10^{-6} + [(4e+2) \times 10^{-5} \times 10^{-3}] + 5 \times 10^{-10} + [4e(2e-1) \times 10^{-10}]\}}{2\{1 - 600[(10^{-3} + 10^{-5} + (2e \times 10^{-5})]\}}$$

$$- \frac{\left(1 - e^{-2x6x10^{-3}}\right)[e + 6 \times 10^{-3} - (3e \times 6 \times 10^{-3}]}{600e\left[e^{-0.6}e^{-(1+6x10^{-3})} + e^{-12x10^{-3}} - 1\right]} + 2e \times 10^{-5} + 10^{-3} + \frac{10^{-5}}{3}$$

$$= (761.35 - 103.87 + 1005.77)\mu s$$

$$= 1.663 \text{ ms}$$

6.6 STAR

Due to their simplicity, the star networks evolved as the first controlled-topology networks. They are regarded as the oldest communication medium topologies because of their use in centralized telephone exchanges. As we shall see, the star topology has some disadvantages which led to its apparent unpopularity in local area networks. While the control of traffic is distributed in both the bus and the ring topologies, it is concentrated in the star.

6.6.1 Basic Operation

A star topology usually consists of a primary node (hub) and secondary nodes (the nodes on the periphery). The primary node is the central node which acts like a switch or traffic director. Communication between any two nodes is via circuit switching. When a peripheral node has data to transmit, it must first send a request to the central node which establishes a dedicated path between the node and the destination node. All links must therefore be full duplex to allow two-way communication between the primary and secondary nodes as shown in Fig. 6.7.

The use of a central node to perform all routing provides a fairly good mapping of technology, but at the expense of creating a complex routing station. The central node is a complex one from a hardware standpoint. It is also a limiting element in the star growth because it requires the hub to have a spare port to plug a new link. The delay caused by the hub affects the performance of the network. Because of the problems associated with the central switch, the star network exhibits growth

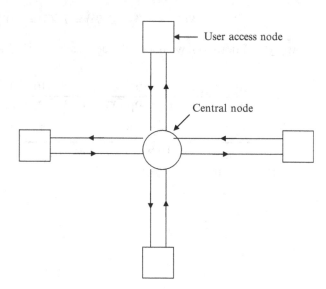

Fig. 6.7 A typical star network

limitations, low reliability, poor expandability, and a complex central node. In spite of the bottleneck caused by the central node, however, the star is one of the common topologies commonly in use. Although the star may not be as effective as the bus or ring in terms of routing, the star is effectively used for other reasons.

The star networks offer positive features that many other networks lack. For example, the interconnection in star networks is point to point which makes them suitable for optical fiber-based implementation. That is, in fiber-optic systems, star-shaped topologies are usually preferred because they allow the interconnection of more nodes, are less prone to catastrophic failure, and are relatively flexible and expandable. In fact the first optical fiber networks were built in the star configuration [20]. Also, the throughput of star networks is usually very high and can easily approach unity, which means that the bandwidth is effectively utilized. Very high data rates can be sustained on star networks. Star systems allow simple modular expansion, and their performance is in general better than the performance of other networks [21].

6.6.2 Delay Analysis

Delay analyses of star networks have been carried out by Kamal [21] and Mehmet-Ali, Hayes and Elhakeem [22]. Here we adopt the approximate analysis in [22].

The underlying assumptions of the analysis are as follows. Messages are assumed to arrive at each source node according to Poisson process with an average arrival rate of λ_i and have an arbitrary length distribution. Messages arrive to the system at one of the N nodes and are switched to one of the other $(N - 1)$ nodes. It is assumed that the source-destination line pair must be free before a message can be transmitted and that the probability that a message will have its destination as its source is zero. It is also assumed that messages are transmitted from the source queues strictly in their order of arrival. Finally, it is assumed that the traffic is symmetric. With each source modeled as an M/G/1 queue, the waiting time or queueing delay is obtained as [22]:

$$E(W) = \hat{y} + \frac{\lambda \hat{y}^2}{2(1 - \rho)} \qquad (6.57)$$

where

$$\hat{y} = [1 + (N - 2)\rho G]E(S) \qquad (6.58a)$$

$$\hat{y}^2 = 2[1 + 2(N - 2)\rho G + (N - 2)(N - 3)\rho^2 G^2]E(S^2) \qquad (6.58b)$$

$$\rho = \frac{\lambda E(S)}{1 - (N - 2)G\lambda E(S)} \qquad (6.58c)$$

$\lambda = \lambda_i$, and $G = 1/(N - 1)$ is the probability that a message from source i will have node j as its destination. From Eq. (6.57), the stability requirement $\rho \leq 1$ implies that $\lambda E(S) \leq (N - 1)(2N - 3)$. For large N, this implies $\lambda E(S) \leq 1/2$.

The source-destination propagation time $E(T_p)$ is given by

$$E\left(T_p\right) = \tau \tag{6.59}$$

where τ is the round-trip or two-way propagation delay between any node and the central hub.

By substituting Eqs. (6.57) and (6.59) into Eq. (6.1), we obtain

$$\boxed{E(D) = \hat{y} + \frac{\lambda \hat{y}^2}{2(1 - \rho)} + E(S) + \tau} \tag{6.60}$$

$E(S)$ and $E(S^2)$, the first and second moments of the message service time, are given by Eq. (6.35).

6.7   Performance Comparisons

Having examined each LAN protocol separately, it is instructive that we compare the protocols in terms of their performance under similar traffic conditions. We compare Eqs. (6.32), (6.47), (6.51), and (6.60) and present typical performance results for the four protocols. As expected, the components of the mean delay that depend on the propagation delay make a negligible contribution towards total delay. The queueing delay, on the other hand, contribute heavily to the total delay.

Figures 6.8 and 6.9 compare the delay characteristic of the four protocols. In both figures, the ordinate represents the mean delay normalized to the mean service time, $E(D)/E(S)$, while the abscissa denotes the traffic intensity or offered load, $\rho = \lambda E(S)$. In both figures, we consider:

N (no. of stations) $= 50$
ℓ (cable length) $= 2$ km
Packet length distribution: exponential
$E(L_p)$ (mean packet length) $= 1{,}000$ bits
L_h (header length) $= 24$ bits
L_b (bit delay) $= 1$ bit
L_t (token packet length) $= 0$
P (propagation delay) $= 5$ μs/km

Figure 6.8 shows the curves plotted for the four protocols when the transmission rate, R, is 1 Mb/s. It is apparent from Fig. 6.8 that the star has the worse performance; the token ring performs less well than the token bus over the entire throughput range; and the token bus and CSMA-CD protocols track one another closely over most of the throughput range.

Increasing the transmission rate to 10 Mb/s while keeping other parameters the same, we obtain the curves in Fig. 6.9. It is evident from this figure that the

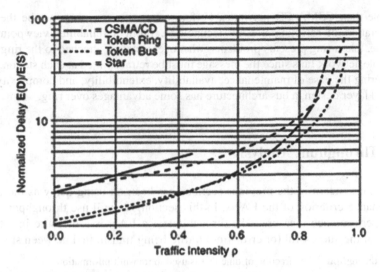

Fig. 6.8 Normalized delay versus traffic intensity at R = 1 Mbps

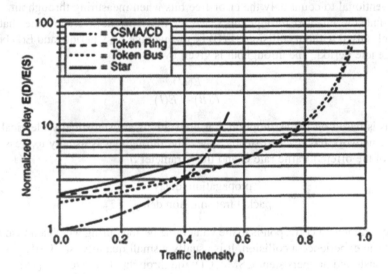

Fig. 6.9 Normalized delay versus traffic intensity at R = 10 Mbps

performance of the star is still worst, the performance of both token-passing protocols is only slightly affected by the increased network rate, thus showing little sensitivity to this parameter. However, the CSMA-CD scheme is highly sensitive to the transmission rate. This should be expected because with increase in the transmission rate, relatively more collisions take place and more transmission attempts result in collisions.

From performance grounds, CSMA-CD is better at light loading. For heavy loading, token ring seems to be more desirable than token bus, and certainly more desirable than CSMA-CD networks. Performance, however, may not be the only consideration in selecting a LAN technology. From a reliability viewpoint, for example, token ring presents problems: whenever a station attached to the ring fails, the whole network fails since the message must be retransmitted at each station. Also considering the ease of maintenance, availability, extendibility, and complexity of a physical layer design, a bus architecture has some advantages over ring.

6.8 Throughput Analysis

Our major concern in the previous sections has been on using delay as the major performance criterion of the LANs. In this section, we will use throughput as the major performance measure. The throughput of a LAN is a measure in bits per second of the successful (or error-free) traffic being transmitted between stations.

The **throughput** is the fraction of time that is used to transmit information.

Since the information can be corrupted as it travels from one station to another, it is conventional to count only the error-free bits when measuring throughput.

To find the channel throughput S, we let E(U) be the average time that the channel is used without collisions, E(B) be the average busy period, and E(I) be the average idle period. The throughput is given by

$$S = \frac{E(U)}{E(B) + E(I)} \tag{6.61}$$

This is based on the assumption that the stations are statistically identical and that the network has reached steady state. The throughput is usually expressed in terms of the offered traffic rate G and the parameter a

$$a = \frac{\text{propagation delay}}{\text{packet transmission delay}} = \frac{\tau}{T_p} \tag{6.62}$$

The parameter a corresponds to the vulnerable period during which a transmitted packet can experience a collision. It is usually a small quantity, say 0.01.

For unslotted nonpersistent CSMA/CD, the throughput is given by [15]

$$S = \frac{Ge^{-aG}}{Ge^{-aG} + bG(1 - e^{-aG}) + 2aG(1 - Ge^{-aG}) + 2(2 - e^{-aG})} \tag{6.63}$$

where b is the jamming time or the length of the jamming signal. For slotted nonpersistent CSMA/CD,

$$S = \frac{aGe^{-aG}}{aGe^{-aG} + bG(1 - e^{-aG} - aGe^{-aG}) + a(2 - e^{-aG} - aGe^{-aG})} \tag{6.64}$$

6.9 Summary

1. In this chapter, we examined the delay-throughput characteristics of four local area networks: token ring, token bus, CSMA-CD bus, and star.
2. In order to make a valid comparisons between the schemes, we presented analytical models based on similar sets of assumptions. Assuming an M/G/1 queueing model for each station in the network, we obtained closed form approximate formula(s) for the mean delay for each protocol. The protocols were then compared under the same traffic conditions.
3. Throughput analysis of CSMA/CD was also considered.

The performance analysis of LANs is presented in [23].

Problems

6.1 Describe briefly the seven layers of the OSI model.

6.2 Compare and contrast controlled access and random access protocols.

6.3 Explain how token ring works.

6.4 In a Cambridge ring with a data rate of 5 Mbps, each slot has 37 bits. If 50 stations are connected to the ring and the average internodal distance is 20 m, how many slots can the ring carry? Assume a propagation speed of 2.5×10^8 m/s and that there is a 1-bit delay at each station.

6.5 For a token-passing ring, assume the following parameters:

No. of stations	= 50
Transmission rate	= 1 Mbps
Mean packet length	= 1,000 bits (exponentially distributed)
Length of the ring	= 2 km
Token length	= 24 bits
Header length	= 0 bit
Bit delay	= 1 bit
Propagation delay	= 5 μs/km

Calculate the mean delay of a message for exhaustive service discipline for $\rho = 0.1, 0.2, \ldots, 0.9$.

6.6 For both constant exponential packet distributions, calculate the mean delay for a token bus LAN with the following parameters:

No. of stations	=	50
Transmission rate	=	5 Mbps
Mean packet length	=	1,000 bits
Bus length	=	1 km
Token length	=	96 bits
Header length	=	0 bit

(continued)

Bit latency	=	1 bit
Propagation delay	=	5 μs/km

Try cases for $\rho = 0.1, 0.2, \ldots, 0.9$ and assume exhaustive service discipline.

6.7 Explain how CSMA/CD protocol works.

6.8 Repeat problem 6.6 for the CSMA/CD protocol.

6.9 (a) Assuming an exhaustive service discipline, calculate the average transfer delay of a token bus with the following parameters.

No. of stations	=	40
Transmission rate	=	1 Mbps
Mean packet length	=	500 bits (exponentially distributed)
Cable length	=	4 km
Token length	=	96 bits
Header length	=	0 bit
Bit delay	=	1 bit
Propagation delay	=	2 μs/km
Traffic intensity	=	0.4

(b) Repeat part (a) for a CSMA/CD bus LAN.

6.10 Rework Problem 6.6 for the case of a constant packet length of 1,000 bits.

6.11 Verify Eqs. (6.55) and (6.56).

6.12 For the unslotted nonpersistent CSMA/CD, plot the throughput S versus offered local G. Take a = 0.01 and b = 5a.

6.13 Repeat 6.12 for slotted nonpersistent CSMA/CD.

References

1. J. R. Freer, *Computer Communications and Networks*. New York: Plenum Press, 1988, pp. 284, 285.
2. P. J. Fortier, *Handbook of LAN Technology*. New York: McGraw-Hill, 1989, chap. 16, pp. 305-312.
3. J. L. Hammond and P. J. P. O'Reilly, *Performance Analysis of Local Computer Networks*. Reading, MA: Addison-Wesley, 1986, pp. 225-237.
4. W. Bux, "Local-area subnetworks: a performance comparison," *IEEE Trans. Comm.*, vol. COM-29, no. 10, Oct. 1981, pp. 1465-1473.
5. H. Tagaki, *Analysis of Polling Systems*. Cambridge: MIT Press, 1986.
6. M. J. Ferguson and Y. J. Aminetzah, "Exact results for nonsymmetric token ring systems," *IEEE Trans. Comm.*, vol. COM-33, no. 3, March 1985, pp. 223-231.
7. K. S. Watson, "Performance evaluation of cyclic service strategies – a survey," in E. Gelenbe (ed.), *Performance '84*. Amsterdam: North-Holland, 1984, pp. 521-533.
8. S. W. Fuhrmann and R. B. Cooper, "Application of decomposition principle in M/G/1 vacation model to two continuum cyclic queueing models – especially token-ring LANs," *AT & T Technical Journal*, vol. 64, no. 5, May-June 1985, pp. 1091-1099.
9. I. Rubin and L. F. M. de Moraes, "Message delay analysis for polling and token multiple-access schemes for local communication networks," *IEEE Jour. Sel. Area Comm.*, vol. SAC-1, no. 5, Nov. 1983, pp. 935-947.

10. A. G. Konheim and M. Reiser, "A queueing model with finite waiting room and blocking," *J. ACM*, vol. 23, no. 2, April 1976, pp. 328-341.

11. G. B. Swartz, "Polling in a loop system," *J. ACM*, vol. 27, no. 1, Jan. 1980, pp. 42-59.

12. F. -J. Kauffels, *Practical LANs Analysed*. Chichester: Ellis Horwood, 1989.

13. S. R. Sachs et al., "Performance analysis of a token-bus protocol and comparison with other LAN protocols," *Proc. 10th Conf. on Local Computer Networks,* Oct. 1985, pp. 46-51.

14. R. Rom and M. Sidi, *Multiple Access Protocols: Performance and Analysis*. New York: Springer-Verlag, 1990.

15. G. E. Keiser, *Local Area Networks*. New York: McGraw-Hill, 1989.

16. F. A. Tobagi and V. B. Hunt, Performance analysis of carrier sense multiple access with collision detection, *Computer Networks,* vol. 4, 1980, pp. 245-259.

17. S. S. Lam, "A carrier sense multiple access protocol for local networks," *Computer Networks*, vol. 4, no. 1, Jan. 1980, pp. 21-32.

18. J. F. Hayes, *Modeling and Analysis of Computer Communications Networks*. New York: Plenum Press, 1984, pp. 226–230.

19. W. Bux, "Performance issues in local-area networks," *IBM Syst. Jour.*, vol. 23, no. 4, 1984, pp. 351-374.

20. E. S. Lee and P. I. P. Boulton, "The principles and performance of Hebnet: A 40 Mbits/s glass fiber local area network," *IEEE J. Select. Areas Comm.*, vol. SAC-1, Nov. 1983, pp. 711-720.

21. A. E. Kamal, "Star local area networks: a performance study," *IEEE Trans. Comp.,* vol. C-36, no. 4, April 1987, pp. 484-499.

22. M. K. Mehmet-Ali et al., "Traffic analysis of a local area network with a star topology," *IEEE Trans. Comm.*, vol. COM-36, no. 6, June 1988, pp. 703-712.

23. C. Androne and T. Palade, "Radio coverage and performance analysis for local area networks," *Proc. of 9th International Symposium on Electronics and Telecommunications,* 2010, pp. 213-216

Chapter 7
Metropolitan Area Networks

Experience is the worst teacher; it gives the test before presenting the lesson.

—Vernon Law

With some of the characteristics of LANs and some reflecting WANs, the metropolitan area network (MAN) technology embraces the best features of both. The motivations for MAN technology include the need for: (1) interconnection of LANs, (2) high-speed services, and (3) integrated services. The proliferation of LANs and the need for connecting them has brought MANs to the fore. The increasing customer demand for high-speed services has spawned the search for new technologies with wideband transport capabilities. For example, it is important that a travel agent gets prompt responses from the host computer when making airline reservations. The salary of the agent depends on high speed data communication.

We begin this chapter by first looking at some characteristics of MAN. We then consider various types of internetworking devices and how they are used in constructing non-standard MANs. The performance analysis of interconnected token rings is given as an example of a LAN-based MAN.

7.1 Characteristics of MANs

When a number of computer stations is distributed over a city, it is efficient to connect them in networks and then connect these networks by a high-speed network. (A high-speed system is one which operates at data rates exceeding 100 Mbps.) A metropolitan area network (MAN) is meant to accomplish the latter task. Typically, a MAN spans an entire office park, an entire campus, or an entire city and its suburbs.

M.N.O. Sadiku and S.M. Musa, *Performance Analysis of Computer Networks*,
DOI 10.1007/978-3-319-01646-7_7, © Springer International Publishing Switzerland 2013

Although the concept of a MAN is modeled after LAN principles, there are some major differences between the two types of networks. These differences can be summarized as follows [1–3]:

- *Distance*: Whereas a LAN operates within a few kilometers, a MAN spans a city and its suburbs. IEEE Project 802 set a distance optimization of 50 km diameter in order to match the dimensions of typical large metropolitan areas.
- *Backbone*: A backbone for interconnecting LANs is needed in a MAN to ease administration. The switching function is free; no large up-front expenditure for a switch is necessary in a shared-medium network.
- *Service*: It is desirable that MAN is optimized for carrying voice and video as well as computer data thus having a more demanding access requirement. Voice has stringent requirements—a guaranteed bandwidth (64 kbps per voice channel) and bounded delay (2 s at worst for round trip). These requirements for so-called isochronous channels cannot be met by conventional LANs.
- *Central Management*: MAN requires a central management for installation, operation, maintenance, and billing of users.
- *Public Operation*: MAN is shared between many user organizations rather than being privately owned. This raises privacy and security issues in addition to requiring centralized operation and a need to gain right-of-way.

In a MAN, the speed of the backbone network is anticipated to be ten to a hundred times greater than that of a LAN. This speed disparity between the high speed backbone and the lower speed LANs that are connected to it creates a bottleneck situation at the gateways.

There are two kinds of MAN:

(1) Standard MANs are fiber distributed data interface (FDDI) and distributed queue dual bus (DQDB). FDDI is ANSI standard. DQDB is IEEE 802.6 standard which has been implemented as switched multisegment data service (SMDA). It is no longer popular and will not discussed further in this chapter.
(2) Non-standard MANs involving LANs that are interconnected by bridges, routers or gateways.

7.2 Internetworking Devices

Since many organizations already have more than one LAN, the most common approach to building a MAN is the interconnection of LANs; it is more economical to interconnect them than to build a network that will serve the same purpose. This approach was taken on ad hoc basis before standard MANs were developed.

Internetworking devices are the building blocks for constructing computer networks. The primary purpose of internetworking is to enable a network user to establish communication link with a user of another network and vice versa.

To achieve the connectivity and facilitate communications between computer systems, network designers have implemented a number of interconnection

Fig. 7.1 How internetworking devices are related to the OSI model

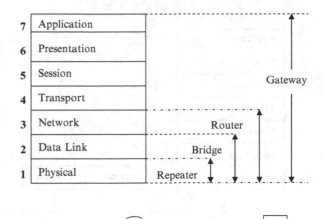

Fig. 7.2 Signal regeneration by a repeater

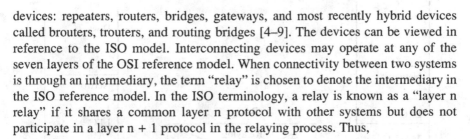

devices: repeaters, routers, bridges, gateways, and most recently hybrid devices called brouters, trouters, and routing bridges [4–9]. The devices can be viewed in reference to the ISO model. Interconnecting devices may operate at any of the seven layers of the OSI reference model. When connectivity between two systems is through an intermediary, the term "relay" is chosen to denote the intermediary in the ISO reference model. In the ISO terminology, a relay is known as a "layer n relay" if it shares a common layer n protocol with other systems but does not participate in a layer n + 1 protocol in the relaying process. Thus,

- a repeater is a physical layer relay,
- a bridge is a data link layer relay,
- a router is a network layer relay, and
- a gateway is any higher layer than network layer relay.

The relationships of these interconnecting devices and the OSI model is shown in Fig. 7.1. It should be noted that these terms are used loosely in the market-place. A vendor may call its product a "bridge" when it is capable of providing routing and protocol conversion.

7.2.1 Repeaters

The most basic and simplest interconnecting device is the repeater. The term "repeater" denotes a device that regenerate a signal received from the input and correct it to its original shape, as shown in Fig. 7.2. A repeater is a physical layer device which receives, amplifies, and retransmits all incoming signals, including collisions. It simply forwards every packet from one network to the other.

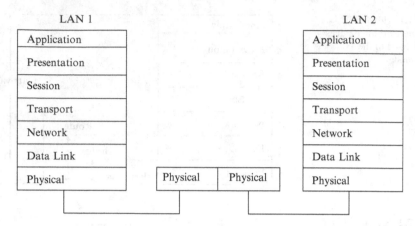

Fig. 7.3 Two LANs interconnected at the physical layer by a repeater

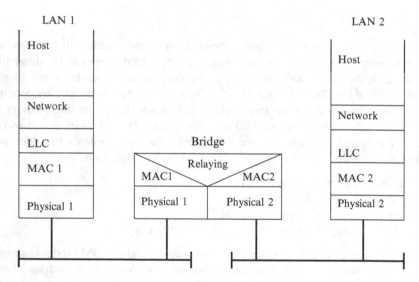

Fig. 7.4 Two LANs interconnected by a bridge

A repeater connects similar LANs at the physical layer, as shown in Fig. 7.3. Repeaters help overcome the electrical limits of a LAN—the limited length and the limited number of stations.

7.2.2   Bridges

A bridge (also known as a data link relay) is a store-and-forward device that operates at the Medium Access Control (MAC) layer, as shown in Fig. 7.4.

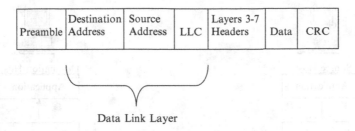

Data Link Layer

Fig. 7.5 A typical frame format that the bridge sees

As a result, it can extend LANs far beyond the distance that repeaters can. It performs the function of a repeater in that it amplifies the signal. In the majority of cases, bridges interconnect homogeneous or similar LANs (i.e. LANs with the same MAC Protocols). For example, a token bus bridge will interconnect two token bus LANs. The main attribute of bridges is transparency—a feature in a distributed system where users can access any local or remote resources just as if they were local. Bridges automatically initialize, configure themselves, and run with no intervention from network management.

A bridge is an intelligent device because it is capable of making decisions. It does this by referring to a table of addresses created for each LAN connected to the bridge. A bridge examines each packet as it passes, checking the source and destination addresses. If a packet coming from Station 2 on LAN A is destined for Station 5 on LAN A, the bridge allows the packet to move on, a process called *filtering*. If the packet is destined for Station 1 on LAN B, the bridges copies the packet onto LAN B, a process known as *forwarding*. Thus, local traffic is kept on the LAN from which it originated, while non-local traffic is forwarded to the appropriate destination. The decision to filter or forward a frame is made after the bridge considers the fields of the MAC frame, as shown typically in Fig. 7.5.

The information concerning which frame to filter or forward is learned by the bridge and stored in the forwarding table. The forwarding table consists of known data link layer or MAC addresses and the associated network segment connected to the bridge. The table is built by the bridge monitoring both incoming and outgoing ports and listening to all transmissions, a process known as *learning*.

Example 7.1 A bridge connects two CSMA/CD networks, each transmitting at the rate of 10 Mbps. Determine how many frames per second the bridge must be capable of forwarding. What would happen if the bridge cannot handle so many frames per second?

Solution

The bridge is receiving data at 20 Mbps. If each frame is 512 bits long plus 64 bits of preamble and 96 bits of interframe gap, the total number of frames that the bridge must handle is

$$\text{No. of frames/s} = \frac{\text{bits/s}}{\text{bits/frame}} = \frac{20 \times 10^6 \text{ bits/s}}{(512 + 64 + 96) \text{ bits/frame}} \cong 29,762$$

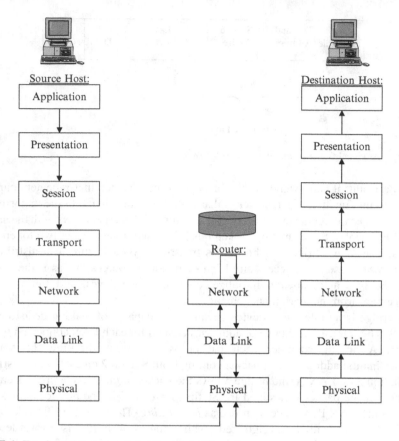

Fig. 7.6 Two hosts interconnected at the network layer by a router

7.2.3 *Routers*

A router is a device that connects dissimilar networks and operates at the network layer in the OSI model, as shown in Fig. 7.6 (The need for connecting dissimilar networks may be due to a corporate merger or acquisition).

All routers possess a number of common characteristics:

- Link networks using different network identities
- Transmit only the data needed by the final destination across the LAN
- Examine and rebuild packets without passing errors on the next LAN
- Store and forward data packets, each with its header containing a destination and source networks from one LAN or WAN to another.

Routers form the core of an internetwork, ranging from LAN to WAN.

A router is protocol-dependent in that it connects logically separate networks operating under identical protocols. In other words, it distinguishes among different

Fig. 7.7 A typical
architecture of a router

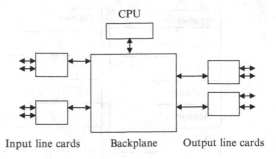

Input line cards   Backplane   Output line cards

protocols and applies the appropriate routing technique to each. It can connect to and
speak the protocols of any communication media such as Ethernet and SONET. Its
operation depends on *internet protocol* (IP), a protocol at OSI layer 3. Consequently,
it does not matter whether underlying networks are ethernet, token ring, or FDDI
(fiber distributed data interface). This implies that routers accommodate a number
of differences among networks. Such differences include different addressing
schemes, routing techniques, maximum packet size, access control, and error
recovery. For example, a router can be used to connect token ring and ethernet.

All router designs follow the same functional architecture, typically shown in
Fig. 7.7. It consists of line cards, a routing processor (or CPU), and a backplane. For
high-speed router, the backplane is replaced by a switch fabric. A switch fabric is
used for interconnection because it offers a much higher aggregate capacity than
that available from the more conventional backplane bus. While a bus typically
offers hundreds of megabits of bandwidth to be shared by all line cards, a switching
fabric provides a high-speed dedicated path from the input port to the output port.

7.2.4 Gateways

When a device performs protocol conversions that enable information exchange
among different types of networks, it is called a *gateway*. A gateway, usually a
computer, PC, or server with special gateway hardware and software, connects
networks with completely different architectures such as an IBM SNA (System
Network Architecture) system and a Macintosh LAN. A TCP/IP-to-SNA gateway,
for example, gives users on a multivendor TCP/IP LAN access to IBM hosts
through the SNA protocols. Gateways are used to connect LANs to other types of
networks, particularly WANs. They act as translators between two inhomogeneous
protocols. A gateway between networks receives messages from one network,
translates them to a form that can be understood in the other network, and routes
them to the appropriate destination. It also translates names and addresses as
necessary when messages are sent from one network to another. Thus, in addition
to routing and flow control (as the bridge does), the gateway implements protocol
conversion all the way up to OSI layer 7, as shown in Fig. 7.8; it reformats the

Application	Gateway	Application
Presentation		Presentation
Session		Session
Transport		Transport
Network		Network
Data Link		Data Link
Physical		Physical

Fig. 7.8 Two LANs interconnected at the equivalent of layer 7

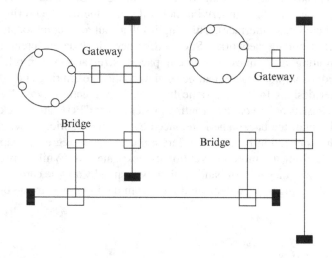

Fig. 7.9 Direct interconnection of LANs using bridges and gateways

packets that go from one type of network to another. The amount and type of protocol conversion done by the gateway vary with the protocols and physical media of the networks involved. In addition to being protocol converters, gateways act as buffers between networks with different transmission rates.

Unlike bridges and routers, a gateway is not used to build a network but to link two or more unrelated networks. A gateway converts a packet from one protocol to another, while a router chooses the best route for the packet but changes only its addressing. Like a router, a gateway performs routing at the network layer. As illustrated in Fig. 7.8, gateways implement the entire protocol suite for each network. Depending on the level of incompatibility, gateways function at the transport through application layers of the OSI model. It is evident that gateways cause more delay than bridges and routers.

A typical example of direct interconnection of three bus and two ring LANs is shown in Fig. 7.9.

7.3 Performance Analysis of Interconnected Token Rings

The purpose of this section is to obtain the performance analysis of interconnected token rings via a backbone ring. A major performance criterion that is used is the mean transfer delay of a message, which is defined as the time from the instant a message becomes available for transmission at a station until the end of its successful reception at the destination. Delay results are useful for designing of communication systems.

A fundamental problem one faces in analyzing interconnected systems is that of characterizing the departure process of the successfully transmitted messages. Description of the process is a difficult task. Therefore, the complexity of the interconnected systems defy exact mathematically tractable solutions. Notwithstanding this, several attempts [9–19] have been made to analyze the performance of interconnected LANs because of the importance of such networks. Such attempts, based on special assumptions, have been carried out through simulation, measurement, approximate analytical solutions, or a combination of these. Only the approximate analysis of interconnected token rings by Ibe and Cheng [10, 11] will be presented here because of its simplicity.

In the interconnected token ring network system, the individual LANs are connected to a backbone ring via a bridge. The backbone ring is a high speed fiber distributed data interface (FDDI), as portrayed in Fig. 7.10.

Each bridge performs a routing and flow control function and is modeled as two independent stations, as shown in Fig. 7.11; one station receives a packet from the backbone ring and transmits it into the local ring, while the other station receives

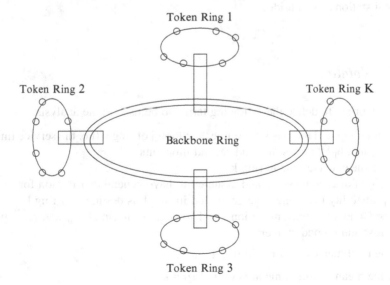

Fig. 7.10 Interconnected token rings

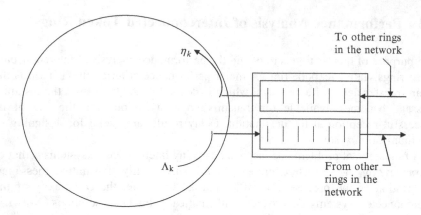

Fig. 7.11 A model of a bridge

from the local ring and transmits into the backbone ring. The packets are buffered in the bridge until they are successfully transmitted into the appropriate ring.

There are two kinds of messages (internetwork and intranetwork messages) and two modes of operation (priority and non-priority) in an interconnected token ring network system. In the non-priority mode, the bridge and all other stations can transmit at most one message each time they receive the token. In the priority mode, on the other hand, the bridge transmits exhaustively while other stations can transmit at most one message upon receiving the token. It is assumed that the network operates in the priority mode in this section.

We consider a system with K token rings network labeled 1, ..., K, connected to a FDDI backbone ring as shown in Fig. 7.10. In each token ring there are $N_k - 1$ identical stations and a bridge.

7.3.1 Notation

It is appropriate to define the following terms to be used in the analysis.

B_{jk} = time required to transmit a frame at station j of ring k (i.e. the service times); b_{jk} and $b_{jk}^{(2)}$ are its first and second moments

C_k = the mean cycle time in ring k

L_k = length of each message and assumed to have general distribution for ring k

q_{kl} = probability that a message generated in ring k is destined for ring l

R_{jk} = switchover time from station j − 1 to station j in ring k; r_{jk} and $r_{jk}^{(2)}$ are its first and second moments

s_k = the total mean walk time in ring k; i.e. $s_k = \sum_{j=1}^{N_k} r_{jk}$

w_{jk} = the mean waiting time at node j of ring k;

η_k = rate at which messages arrive from individual stations in ring k at bridge k for transmission in the backbone ring

λ_k = arrival rate of messages which form a Poisson process for ring k

Λ_k = rate at which messages arrive from other rings at bridge k for transmission in ring k

Note that the switchover time is variably known as the walk time, the polling time, or the token-passing time.

7.3.2 *Distribution of Arrivals*

A stream of messages arrive at each station on ring k at the same average rate of λ_k, which is an independent Poisson process. The number of stations sending messages to bridge k from its own ring has a binomial distribution with parameters $N_k - 1$ and $q = 1 - q_{kk}$. Therefore the probability of n stations sending messages to the bridge is [9]

$$P(n) = \begin{bmatrix} N_k - 1 \\ n \end{bmatrix} q^n (1 - q)^{N_k - 1 - n} \qquad (7.1)$$

Since the stations that communicate with each other are mostly likely on the same ring, the probability q of a station sending messages to stations on other rings is usually small. Also, the number of stations $N_k - 1$ is often large (more than 20). For small q and large N_k, this binomial distribution approximates Poisson distribution. Thus the arrival process to the bridge can be approximated to be Poisson with parameter $(N_k - 1)(1 - q_{kk})$. In an average cycle time C_k, an average of $(N_k - 1)$ $(1 - q_{kk})$ messages arrive at bridge k and hence the arrival rate at the bridge is

$$\eta_k = (N_k - 1)\lambda_k(1 - q_{kk}), \qquad k = 1, \ldots, K \qquad (7.2)$$

Having shown that the arrival of messages to the bridge is Poisson and because the sum of independent Poisson processes is also Poisson, the arrival process of messages from other rings is Poisson distributed with rate

$$\Lambda_k = \sum_{l=1, l \neq k}^{K} (N_l - 1)\lambda_l q_{lk}, \qquad k = 1, \ldots, K \qquad (7.3)$$

7.3.3 *Calculation of Delays*

Our measure of performance is delay. The delay (or transfer time) includes the queuing time (or waiting delay) at the source station, the source bridge delay and destination bridge delay. The mean transfer delay of a message is therefore the sum of the following terms:

D_{ss}^k = the mean message delay at the source station
τ_s^k = the propagation delay from the source station to the source bridge
D_{sb}^k = the mean delay at the source bridge
τ_{sd}^{kl} = the propagation delay between the source bridge and the destination bridge
D_{db}^l = the mean delay at the destination bridge
τ_d^l = the propagation delay between the destination bridge and the destination station

Thus, the total mean delay is defined by

$$D_{remote}^{kl} = D_{ss}^k + D_{sb}^k + D_{db}^l + \tau_s^k + \tau_{sd}^{kl} + \tau_d^l \tag{7.4}$$

In general the propagation delays are negligibly small compared to other delays and can be ignored. Therefore, the total mean delay in Eq. (7.4) becomes

$$D_{remote}^{kl} = D_{ss}^k + D_{sb}^k + D_{db}^l \tag{7.5}$$

For the local message, the mean message delivery time for the message in ring k is

$$D_{local}^k = D_{ss}^k \tag{7.6}$$

For an arbitrary message generated in ring k, the mean message delivery time is given by

$$D_{arb}^k = q_{kk}D_{ss}^k + \sum_{l \neq k} q_{kl}D_{remote}^{kl} \tag{7.7}$$

Arbitrary delay denotes the delay of a message which is generated in a ring but has an arbitrary destination, which could be the ring itself or any other ring. Substituting Eq. (7.5) into Eq. (7.7) gives

$$D_{arb}^k = q_{kk}D_{ss}^k + \sum_{l \neq k} q_{kl}\left(D_{ss}^k + D_{sb}^k + D_{db}^l\right)$$

where $q_{kk} + \sum_{l \neq k} q_{kl} = 1$. Thus,

$$D_{arb}^k = D_{ss}^k + \sum_{l \neq k} q_{kl}\left(D_{sb}^k + D_{db}^l\right) \tag{7.8}$$

Following Ibe and Cheng's mathematical model [10], it is assumed that all the stations in each ring are labeled 2,...,N_k, whereas a bridge is labeled as node 1. Since it is assumed that all the stations are identical in each ring, the local delay and the delay at the destination bridge are given by

$$D_{ss}^k = w_{2k} + b_{2k} \tag{7.9}$$

$$D_{db}^k = w_{1k} + b_{1k} \tag{7.10}$$

where node 2 represents any non-bridge station; w_{1k} and w_{2k} are the waiting delays at the destination bridge and source station, respectively; and b_{1k} and b_{2k} are their respective service times. The traffic intensities at the bridge and each station in ring k are respectively given by

$$\rho_{1k} = \Lambda_k b_{1k} = \sum_{l=1,l\neq k}^{K} (N_l - 1)\lambda_l q_{lk} b_{1k} \tag{7.11}$$

and

$$\rho_{2k} = \lambda_k b_{2k} \tag{7.12}$$

The total traffic intensity of the ring k is the sum of the two traffic intensities and given by

$$\rho_k = \rho_{1k} + (N_k - 1)\rho_{2k} \tag{7.13}$$

The mean cycle time is defined as the mean time between two successive visits of the server to a particular node and it is given by

$$C_k = \frac{s_k}{1 - \rho_k} \tag{7.14}$$

where

$$s_k = \sum_{j=1}^{N_k} r_{jk} \tag{7.15}$$

In terms of these variables, the mean waiting time at the destination bridge is given by [10, 11]:

$$
\begin{aligned}
w_{1k} = {} & \frac{\Lambda_k b_{1k}^{(2)}}{2(1-\rho_{1k})} + \frac{(N_k-1)\lambda_k b_{2k}^{(2)}}{2(1-\rho_k+\rho_{2k})} + \frac{(1-\rho_k)r_{1k}^{(2)} + (N_k-1)(1-\rho_{1k}+\rho_{2k})r_{2k}^{(2)}}{2s_k(1-\rho_{1k})} \\
& + \frac{(N_k-1)\rho_{2k}s_k}{2(1-\rho_{1k})} + \frac{(N_k-1)(N_k-2)\rho_{2k}^2 s_k}{2(1-\rho_{1k})(1-\rho_k+\rho_{2k})} + \frac{(N_k-1)(1-\rho_k)r_{1k}r_{2k}}{s_k(1-\rho_{1k})} \\
& + \frac{(N_k-1)[(N_k-2)(1-\rho_k) - N_k\rho_{2k}]r_{2k}^2}{2s_k(1-\rho_{1k})}
\end{aligned}
\tag{7.16}
$$

The mean waiting time at any non-bridge node in ring k is [19]

$$w_{2k} = \frac{A - 2(1-\rho_k)\rho_{1k}w_{1k}}{2(N_k-1)\rho_{2k}(1-\rho_k-\lambda_k s_k)} \tag{7.17}$$

where

$$
A = \rho_k \left[\Lambda_k b_{1k}^{(2)} + (N_k - 1)\lambda_k b_{2k}^{(2)} \right] + \rho_k(1 - \rho_k)\frac{s_k^{(2)}}{s_k}
$$
$$
+ s_k \left[\rho_k^{(2)} - \rho_{1k}^2 + (N_k - 1)\rho_{2k}^2 \right] \tag{7.18}
$$

To compute the mean delay $D_{sb}{}^k$ at the source bridge, let X_k denote the mean transmission time of a message at bridge k in the backbone ring, where x_k and $x_k{}^2$ are the first and second moments of X_k, respectively. Let

$$
\gamma_k = \eta_k x_k \tag{7.19}
$$

denote the offered load at bridge k, where η_k is the arrival rate at each bridge in the backbone ring. The total traffic intensity γ of the backbone ring is given by

$$
\gamma = \sum_{k=1}^{K} \gamma_k \tag{7.20}
$$

The approximate mean waiting time at bridge k of the backbone ring is given in [20] as

$$
w_{sb}^k = \frac{1 - \gamma_k}{2(1 - \gamma)} \left[s_b + \frac{\gamma \left((1 - \gamma)\Delta_b^2 + s_b \sum_{l=1}^{K} \eta_l x_l^{(2)} \right)}{s_b \sum_{l=1}^{K} \gamma_l (1 - \gamma_l)} \right] \tag{7.21}
$$

where s_b and $\Delta_b{}^2$ are respectively the mean and variance of the total walk time of the backbone ring.

The delay at the source bridge is given by

$$
D_{sb}^k = w_{sb}^k + x_k \tag{7.22}
$$

where x_k is the service time of the backbone ring.

Now the three mean message delivery times given in Eqs. (7.5), (7.6), and (7.7) can be written as

$$
D_{local}^k = w_{2k} + b_{2k} \tag{7.23}
$$

$$
D_{remote}^{kl} = D_{local}^k + w_{sb}^k + x_k + w_{1l} + b_{1l} \tag{7.24}
$$

$$
D_{arb}^k = D_{local}^k + \sum_{l \neq k} q_{kl}\left(w_{sb}^k + x_k + w_{1l} + b_{1l} \right) \tag{7.25}
$$

where w_{1l} and b_{1l} are the waiting delay and service time at the destination bridge, respectively.

Table 7.1 Routing probabilities q_{kl}

| | Destination | | | |
Source	1	2	3	4
1	0.9	0.1	0.0	0.0
2	0.2	0.6	0.1	0.1
3	0.3	0.2	0.4	0.1
4	0.3	0.1	0.1	0.5

Table 7.2 Arrival rates η_k and Λ_k

Arrival from local ring to backbone ring	Arrival from backbone ring to local ring
$\eta_1 = 2\lambda_1$	$\Lambda_1 = 44\lambda_1$
$\eta_2 = 16\lambda_1$	$\Lambda_2 = 20\lambda_1$
$\eta_3 = 36\lambda_1$	$\Lambda_3 = 10\lambda_1$
$\eta_4 = 30\lambda_1$	$\Lambda_4 = 10\lambda_1$

Table 7.3 Traffic intensities ρ_k and γ_k

Traffic intensity for local ring	Traffic intensity for backbone ring
$\rho_1 = 64\lambda_1 b_1$	$\gamma_1 = (0.5/64)\rho_1$
$\rho_2 = (60/64)\rho_1$	$\gamma_2 = (1.6/64)\rho_1$
$\rho_3 = (70/64)\rho_1$	$\gamma_3 = (3.6/64)\rho_1$
$\rho_4 = (70/64)\rho_1$	$\gamma_4 = (3.0/64)\rho_1$

Example 7.2 Consider an interconnected token ring network for which $N_k = 21$ (i.e., 20 stations and 1 bridge), $K = 4$ rings with $\lambda_2 = 2\lambda_1$, $\lambda_3 = 3\lambda_1$, and $\lambda_4 = 3\lambda_1$; i.e. asymmetric traffic conditions. The transmission rates for a local ring and the backbone ring are assumed to be 10 Mbps and 100 Mbps, respectively. It is assumed that the packet length is 6,400 bits and token length is 24 bits. This implies that $b = b_k = 6.4 \times 10^{-4}$ s ($=s_b/R$) and $x_k = 6.4 \times 10^{-5}$ s for all k. The walk time is $r_{jk} = 0.005 \times b_k$ for local ring and $0.0005 \times b_k$ for backbone ring. Throughout the analysis, constant packet length is assumed and all delays are normalized with respect to service time b_k.

The assumed routing probabilities q_{kl} are given in Table 7.1. The arrival rates η_k and Λ_k presented in Table 7.2 are calculated using Eqs. (7.2) and (7.3). The traffic intensities ρ_k and γ_k shown in Table 7.3 are calculated using Eqs. (7.11)–(7.13) and (7.19).

We use both the analytical model discussed in this section and the simulation model in [21] for the interconnected token ring. For the simulation results, the confidence interval is calculated from

$$X = \overline{Y} \pm \frac{S_Y t_{\alpha/2}; N-1}{\sqrt{N}} \tag{7.26}$$

where $t_{\alpha/2}$; $N - 1$ is the percentage point of the Student-t distribution with $N - 1$ degrees of freedom, $\overline{Y}$ is the mean sample value, N (=5 for our case) is the number of simulation runs, S_Y is the sample standard deviation.

Table 7.4 Normalized arbitrary delay D_{arb} for ring 2

Traffic intensity ρ_1	Analytical	Simulation	% Error
0.1	1.6	1.65 ± 0.01	−3.12
0.2	1.7	1.73 ± 0.011	−2.33
0.3	1.83	1.85 ± 0.023	−1.05
0.4	2.01	1.99 ± 0.027	0.84
0.5	2.24	2.21 ± 0.021	1.18
0.6	2.59	2.52 ± 0.053	2.70
0.7	3.15	3.008 ± 0.085	4.51
0.8	4.2	4.026 ± 0.15	4.14
0.9	7.15	6.576 ± 0.43	8.03

Table 7.5 Normalized remote delay D_{remote} for ring 2

Traffic intensity ρ_1	Analytical	Simulation	% Error
0.1	2.32	2.38 ± 0.011	−2.93
0.2	2.46	2.52 ± 0.03	−2.76
0.3	2.64	2.68 ± 0.015	−1.74
0.4	2.86	2.88 ± 0.055	−0.98
0.5	3.16	3.17 ± 0.031	−0.32
0.6	3.59	3.59 ± 0.092	−0.06
0.7	4.23	4.17 ± 0.11	1.42
0.8	5.36	5.44 ± 0.1	−1.53
0.9	7.93	7.93 ± 0.43	0.00

Table 7.6 Normalized local delay D_{local} for ring 2

Traffic intensity ρ_1	Analytical	Simulation	% Error
0.1	1.11	1.15 ± 0.007	−3.96
0.2	1.19	1.2 ± 0.015	−1.34
0.3	1.28	1.28 ± 0.016	−0.08
0.4	1.41	1.37 ± 0.02	2.84
0.5	1.58	1.51 ± 0.1	4.43
0.6	1.84	1.69 ± 0.069	7.72
0.7	2.24	2.07 ± 0.1	7.32
0.8	2.97	2.72 ± 0.11	8.43
0.9	4.64	4.25 ± 0.46	8.62

The results are presented in terms of delay versus traffic intensity of ring 1 (i.e., ρ_1). Tables 7.4, 7.5, and 7.6 show comparison (for ring 2, i.e. $k = 2, l = 1$) between analytical and simulation results for local, remote (or end-to-end), and arbitrary delays. The percent error in each result is also included in the tables, where the percent error is defined as

$$\%Error = 100 \frac{\text{Exact (analytical) Result} - \text{Simulation Result}}{\text{Exact Result}}$$

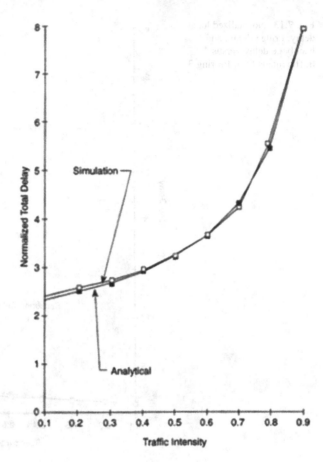

Fig. 7.12 Normalized total delay D_{total} versus traffic intensity ρ_1 for ring 2

It is evident from these tables that analytical results agree fairly well with the simulation results.

Figure 7.12 shows the variation of the normalized mean total delay (D_{total}/b) with traffic intensity for constant packet length. It is evident from the figure that in general the mean delay increases with traffic intensity. This should be expected because as the traffic intensity increases many messages are serviced, thereby compelling the arriving message to wait longer.

Figure 7.13 shows local delay, bridge delay, and backbone delay for ring 3. It is clear from this figure that the backbone delay is very small compared to the bridge and local delays. The reasons for this include: (1) the backbone ring operates at a very high speed, (2) it has very few stations, and (3) it employs an exhaustive service discipline which always has less delays. Figure 7.13 also shows that the bridge and the local delay are almost the same at low traffic intensity. The priority given to the bridge has no effect on the local and bridge delays from low to moderate traffic intensities. However, at high traffic intensities it is observed that

Fig. 7.13 Normalized local
delay, bridge delay, and
backbone delay versus
traffic intensity ρ_1 for ring 3

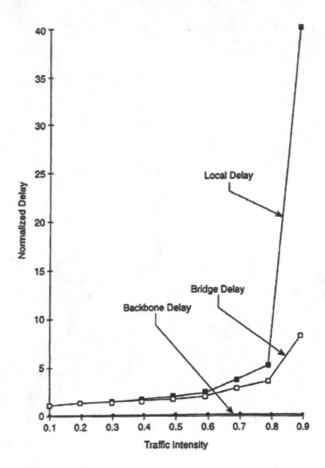

the priority for the messages at the bridge makes the bridge delay much lower than the local delay.

Figure 7.14 shows the arbitrary delay for the four rings.

These figures show the effect of asymmetric traffic conditions (i.e., different arrival rates in each ring) and routing probabilities given in Table 7.1. The arrival rate of ring 1, 2, 3, and 4 are $\lambda_1, 2\lambda_1, 3\lambda_1$, and $3\lambda_1$ respectively. The arbitrary delay for ring 1 is the lowest because it has the lowest routing probability (i.e., $q_{kl} = 0.1$) for the inter-messages. The routing probability for inter-messages of ring 2, 3, and 4 are 0.6, 0.4, and 0.5, respectively. Since the routing probabilities are so close for ring 2, 3, and 4, the arrival rates have the dominating effect on the arbitrary delay. It can be seen from this figure that the higher the arrival rate of the ring the higher the delay.

Fig. 7.14 Normalized
arbitrary delay versus traffic
intensity ρ_1 for the four
rings

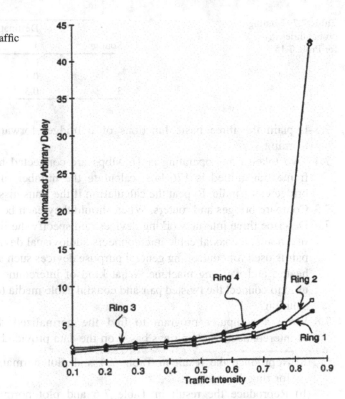

7.4 Summary

1. In this chapter, we have discussed MAN as a composite LAN, i.e., a direct interconnection of LANs via repeaters, routers, bridges, switches, and gateways.
2. The performance evaluation of interconnected token rings is represented as an example. The performance analysis of interconnected token bus or CSMA/CD networks is very difficult, but some attempts have been made in analyzing such networks.

Other attempts on performance analysis of MANs can be found in [22–25].

Problems

7.1 Give two reasons for building MANs using internetworking devices.
7.2 (a) Describe a repeater as an interconnecting device? It is a hardware or software device?
   (b) How is a repeater different from a bridge?

Table 7.7 Routing
probabilities q_{kl}
for Prob. 7.15

Source	Destination		
	1	2	3
1	0.6	0.3	0.1
2	0.1	0.8	0.1
3	0.3	0.2	0.5

7.3 Explain the three basic functions of a bridge: forwarding, filtering, and learning.

7.4 Two token rings operating at 16 Mbps are connected by a bridge. If each frame transmitted is 176 bits, calculate the number of frames/second the bridge can handle. Repeat the calculation if the transmission rate is 4 Mbps.

7.5 Compare bridges and routers. When should they each be used?

7.6 Describe three internetworking devices and specify the limitations of each.

7.7 In a home, a coaxial cable interconnects audiovisual devices, while a twisted pair is used for controlling general purpose devices such as cooking machine, heater, and washing machine. What kind of interconnecting device can be used to connect the twisted pair and coaxial cable media to provide a low cost solution?

7.8 Write a computer program to find the normalized delays in a system of interconnected token rings based on the data provided in Example 7.2.

   (a) Reproduce the result in Table 7.4 and plot normalized D_{arb} versus ρ_1 for ring 2.
   (b) Reproduce the result in Table 7.6 and plot normalized D_{local} versus $\rho_1 = 0.1, 0.2, \ldots, 0.9$.

7.9 (a) Write a computer program to reproduce the result in Table 7.5 and plot normalized D_{remote} versus ρ_1 for ring 2.
   (b) For ring 4, calculate normalized D_{remote} versus $\rho_1 = 0.1, 0.2, \ldots, 0.9$ and plot the data.

7.10 For ring 3, calculate normalized D_{remote} versus $\rho_1 = 0.1, 0.2, \ldots, 0.9$ and plot the data.

7.11 Show that when no station receives service ($N_k = 1$), w_{1k} in Eq. (7.16) becomes

$$w_{1k} = \frac{\Lambda_k b_{1k}^{(2)}}{2(1 - \rho_{1k})} + \frac{r_{1k}^{(2)}}{2r_{1k}}$$

which is the exact solution for the symmetric polling system with exhaustive service.

7.12 For a symmetric single-service polling system, $\rho_{1k} = 0 = r_{1k}$. Obtain the corresponding expression for w_{2k}.

7.13 Reproduce the entries in Table 7.2 using Eqs. (7.2) and (7.3).

7.14 Reproduce the entries in Table 7.3 using Eqs. (7.11)–(7.13) and (7.19).

7.15 Consider an interconnected token ring network with three rings each having 10 stations and 1 bridge. Let $\lambda_1 = \lambda_2 = \lambda_3 = \lambda$. Assuming routing probabilities shown in Table 7.7, obtain η_k and Λ_k, $k = 1, 2, 3$ in terms of λ.

References

1. M. N. O. Sadiku, *Metropolitan Area Networks*. Boca Raton, FL: CRC Press, 1995, p. 3.
2. M. N. O. Sadiku and S. M. Musa, *Computer Communication for Metropolitan and Wide Area Networks*. New York: Nova Science Publishers, 2010, p. 4.
3. J. F. Mollenauer, "Standards for Metropolitan Area Networks," *IEEE Communications Magazine*, vol. 26, no. 4, 1988, pp. 15-19.
4. C. Smythe, *Internetworking: Designing the Right Architectures*. Wokingham, U.K.: Addison-Wesley, 1995, pp. 171-318.
5. E. Taylor, *McGraw-Hill Internetworking*. New York: McGraw-Hill, 2nd ed., 1998, pp. 569-628, 647-673.
6. R. C. Dixon and D. A. Pitt, "Addressing, Bridging, and Source Routing," *IEEE Network*, vol. 2, no. 1, Jan. 1988, pp. 25-32.
7. W. M. Seifert, "Bridges and Routers," *IEEE Network*, vol. 2, no. 1, Jan. 1988, pp. 57-64.
8. M. Gerla and L. Kleinrock, "Congestion Control in Interconnected LANs," *IEEE Network*, vol. 2, no. 1, Jan. 1988, pp. 72-76.
9. R. Kuruppillai and N. Bengtson, "Performance Analysis in Local Area Networks of Interconnected Token Rings," *Computer Communications*, vol. 11, no. 2, April 1988, pp. 59-64.
10. O. C. Ibe and X. Cheng, "Analysis of Interconnected Systems of Token Ring Networks," *Computer Communications*, vol. 13, no. 3, 1990, pp. 136-142.
11. O. C. Ibe and X. Cheng, "Approximate Analysis of Asymmetric Single-Service Token-Passing Systems," *IEEE Transactions on Communications*, vol. 37, no. 6, June 1989, pp. 572-577.
12. W. Bux and D. Gillo, "Flow Control in Local Area Networks of Interconnected Token Rings," *IEEE Transactions on Communications*, vol. 33, no. 10, October 1985, pp. 1058-1066.
13. I. Rubin and J. K. Lee, "Performance Analysis of Interconnected Metropolitan Area Circuit-Switched Telecommunications Networks," *IEEE Transactions on Communications*, vol. 36, no. 2, Feb. 1988, pp. 171-185.
14. I. Stavrakakis and D. Kazakos, "Performance Analysis of a Star Topology of Interconnected Networks Under 2nd-Order Markov Network Output Processes," *IEEE Transactions on Communications*, vol. 38, no. 10, Oct. 1990, pp. 1724-1731.
15. B. Berg and R. H. Deng, "End-to-end Performance of Interconnected LANs," *Computer Communications*, vol. 14, no. 2, March 1991, pp. 105-112.
16. G. S. Poo, "Performance Measurement of Interconnected CSMA/CD LANs," *Computer Communications*, vol. 12, no. 1, Feb. 1989, pp. 3-9.
17. T. Kaneko, S. Hosokawa, and K. Yamashita, "An Interconnection Method for Two CSMA/CD LANs," *Memoirs of the Faculty of Engineering, Osaka City University*, vol. 29, 1988, pp. 81-89.
18. G. M. Exley and L. F. Merakos, "Throughput-Delay Performance of Interconnected CSMA Local Area Networks," *IEEE Journal on Selected Areas in Communications*, vol. 5, no. 9, Dec. 1987, pp. 1380-1390.
19. M. Murata and H. Takagi, "Performance of Token Ring Networks with a Finite Capacity Bridge," *Computer Networks and ISDN Systems*, vol. 24, 1992, pp. 45-64.
20. D. Everitt, "Simple Approximation for token rings," *IEEE Transactions on Communications*, vol. 34, no. 7, July 1986, pp. 719-721.

21. S. Murad, "Performance Analysis of Interconnected LANs," *M.S. The*sis, Department of Electrical Engr., Temple University, Philadelphia, PA, May 1993.
22. P. A. Baziana and I. E. Pountourakis, "An efficient metropolitan WDR ring architecture for a slotted transmission technique," *Journal of Lightwave Technology*, vol. 26, no. 10, Oct. 2008, pp. 3307-3317.
23. Y. Chi, L. Zhengbin, and X. Anshi, "Dual-fiber-link for metropolitan area networks: modeling, analysis and performance evaluation," *Proc. of IEEE GLOBECOM*, 2008.
24. H. Lee et al., "Performance analysis of random access in IEEE 802.16m system," *Proc. of ICTC*, 2010, pp. 185-190.
25. T. Atmaca and T. D. Nguyen, "Delay analysis and queue-length distribution of a slotted metro network using embedded DTMC," *Proc. of IEEE GLOBECOM*, 2010.

Chapter 8
Wide Area Networks

A neurotic is the man who builds a castle in the air.
A psychotic is the man who lives in it. A psychiatrist is
the man who collects the rent.

—Lord Webb-Johnson

A wide area network (WAN) provides long-haul communication services to various points within a large geographical area. A WAN often uses communication facilities provided by common carrier such as telephone companies. The most popular WAN is the global public switched telephone network (PSTN), which is not suitable for data transport because it was originally designed for voice. But it is rare that data networks (such the global X.25) do not interface with the PSTN. Today's WANs are expected to integrate data, voice and video traffic.

The performance analysis of networks covering a large geographical area are discussed in this chapter. Such networks include Internet and broadband integrated services digital network (BISDN).

8.1 Internet

The Internet is a global network of computer systems (or wide area network) that exchange information via telephone, cable television, wireless networks, and satellite communication technologies. It is being used by an increasing number of people worldwide. As a result, the Internet has been growing exponentially with the number of machines connected to the network and the amount of network traffic roughly doubling each year. The Internet today is fundamentally changing our social, political, and economic structures, and in many ways obviating geographic boundaries.

The Internet is a combination of networks, including the Arpanet, NSFnet, regional networks such as NYsernet, local networks at a number of universities

M.N.O. Sadiku and S.M. Musa, *Performance Analysis of Computer Networks*, DOI 10.1007/978-3-319-01646-7_8, © Springer International Publishing Switzerland 2013

Application Layer	TELNET, FTP, Finger, Http, Gopher, SMTP, etc.	DNS, RIP, SNMP, etc.	
Transport Layer	TCP	UDP	
Internet Layer	IP		ARP
Network Layer	Ethernet, Token ring, X.25, FDDI, ISDN, SMDS, DWDM, Frame Relay, ATM, SONET/SDH, Wireless, xDSL, etc		

Fig. 8.1 Abbreviated Internet protocol suite

and research institutions, and a number of military networks. Each network on the Internet contains anywhere from two to thousands of addressable devices or nodes (computers) connected by communication channels. All computers do not speak the same language, but if they are going to be networked they must share a common set of rules known as *protocols*. That is where the two most critical protocols, Transmission Control Protocol/Internet Protocol (TCP/IP), come in. Perhaps the most accurate name for the set of protocols is the *Internet protocol suite*. (TCP and IP are only two of the protocols in this suite.) TCP/IP is an agreed upon standard for computer communication over Internet. The protocols are implemented in software that runs on each node.

8.1.1 Internet Protocol Architecture

The TCP/IP is a layered set of protocols developed to allow computers to share resources across a network. Figure 8.1 shows the Internet protocol architecture. The figure is by no means exhaustive, but shows the major protocols and application components common to most commercial TCP/IP software packages and their relationship.

As a layered set of protocols, Internet applications generally use four layers [1–5]:

- *Application layer*: This is where application programs that use Internet reside. It is the layer with which end users normally interact. Some application-level protocols in most TCP/IP implementations include FTP, TELNET, and SMTP.

For example, FTP (file transfer protocol) allows a user to transfer files to and from computers that are connected to the Internet. Security is handled by requiring the user to specify a user name and password for the other computer. TELNET (network terminal protocol for remote login) allows a user to log on to and use other computers that are connected to the Internet regardless of their location. SMTP (simple mail transfer service; for computer mail) allows a user to send messages to users on other computers. Originally, people tended to use only one or two specific computers. They would maintain "mail files" on those machines. The computer mail system is simply a way for you to add a message to another user's mail file.

- *Transport layer*: This layer controls the movement of data between nodes. The layer provides communication services directly to the application processes running on different hosts. The communication services may include the multiplexing/demultiplexing function. In the Internet, there are two transport protocols: TCP and UDP. TCP (Transmission Control Protocol) is connection-oriented service that provides services needed by many applications. TCP also provides segmentation of long messages and a congestion control mechanism. UDP (User Datagram Protocol) provides connectionless services.
- *Internet Layer*: This handles addressing and routing of the data. It is also responsible for breaking up large messages and reassembling them at the destination. IP (Internet Protocol) provides the basic service of getting datagrams to their destination. ARP (Address resolution protocol) figures out the unique address of devices on the network from their IP addresses. The *Internet Protocol* (IP) can be described as the common thread that holds the entire Internet together. It is responsible for moving datagrams from one host to another, using various techniques (or "routing" algorithms). Prior to transmitting data, the network layer might subdivide or fragment it into smaller packets for ease of transmission. When all the pieces finally reach the destination, they are reassembled by the network layer into the original datagram.
- *Network layer*: This layer is responsible for routing datagrams from one host to another. It contains the IP protocol as well as several routing protocols that determine the routes of the datagrams. The network layer involves every host and router in the network. It also supervises addressing and congestion control. Protocols at this layer are needed to manage a specific physical medium, such as Ethernet or a point-to-point line.

IP provides a *connectionless, unreliable, best-effort* packet delivery service. Information is transferred as a sequence of datagrams. Those datagrams are treated by the network as completely separate. For example, suppose we want to transfer a 15000 octet file. Most networks cannot handle a 15000 octet datagram. So the protocols will break this up into something like 30 500-octet datagrams. Each of these datagrams will be sent to the other end. At that point, they will be put back together into the 15000-octet file. However, while those datagrams are in transit, the network does not know that there is any connection between them. It is perfectly possible that datagram 27 will actually arrive before datagram 19. It is also possible

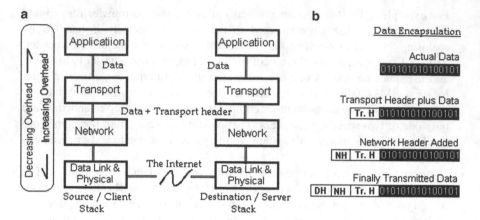

Fig. 8.2 How data travels through the TCP/IP stack

that somewhere in the network, an error will occur, and some datagram would not get through at all. In that case, that datagram has to be sent again.

As shown in Fig. 8.2, each layer of the protocol stack adds a header containing layer-specific information to the data packet. A header for the network layer might include information such as source and destination addresses. The process of appending data with headers is called *encapsulation*. Figure 8.2 shows how data is encapsulated by various headers. The reverse occurs during *decapsulation*: the layers of the receiving stack extract layer-specific information and process the encapsulated data accordingly. It is interesting to note that the process of encapsulation increases the overhead involved in transmitting data. Although each of these layers provides unique and valuable services, the Internet Protocol is perhaps the most important to the overall operation of the Internet in general because it is responsible for getting data from one host to another.

8.1.2 TCP Level

TCP puts a header at the front of each datagram. This header actually contains at least 20 octets, but the most important ones are a source and destination "port number" and a "sequence number." The port numbers are used to keep track of different conversations. Each datagram has a sequence number which is used so that the other end can make sure that it gets the datagrams in the right order, and that no datagrams are missing. Finally, the checksum is a number that is computed by adding up all the octets in the datagram. The result is put in the header. TCP at the other end computes the checksum again. If they disagree, then something bad happened to the datagram in transmission, and it is thrown away. Figure 8.3 shows the datagram format.

Bit 0   **31**

Source Port (16)			Destination Port (16)	
Sequence Number (32)				
Acknowledgement Number (32)				
Data offset(4)	Reserved(6)	Flags(6)	Window (16)	
Checksum (16)			Urgent Pointer (16)	
Options (variable)				Padding (variable)

Fig. 8.3 TCP header format (20 bytes)

Other items in the header are generally involved with managing the connection. In order to make sure the datagram has arrived at its destination, the recipient has to send back an "acknowledgement." This is a datagram whose "Acknowledgement number" field is filled in. For example, sending a packet with an acknowledgement of 1500 indicates that you have received all the data up to octet number 1500. If the sender does not get an acknowledgement within a reasonable amount of time, it sends the data again. The "window" is used to control how much data can be in transit at any one time. Each end indicates how much new data it is currently prepared to absorb by putting the number of octets in its "Window" field. As the computer receives data, the amount of space left in its window decreases. When it goes to zero, the sender has to stop. As the receiver processes the data, it increases its window, indicating that it is ready to accept more data. Often the same datagram can be used to acknowledge receipt of a set of data and to give permission for additional new data (by an updated window). The "Urgent" field allows one end to tell the other to skip ahead in its processing of a particular octet.

8.1.3 IP level

IP (Internet Protocol) is the standard that defines the manner in which the network layers of two hosts interact. All IP packets or datagrams consist of a header part and a text part (payload). The payload has a maximum size limit of 65,536 bytes per packet. The IP header consists of a 20-byte fixed part plus a variable part. Its size is optimized to maximize the packet processing rate without utilizing excessive resources. The header begins with a 4-bit version field that keeps track of the version of the IP protocol to which the datagram belongs. This field helps smoothen the transition from one version of IP to another, which can take months or even years.

IP packet contains a source and a destination address. The source address designates the originating node's interface to the network, and the destination address specifies the interface for an intended recipient or multiple recipients (for multicasting). These addresses are in the form of 32-bit binary strings.

Bit 0   31

Version(4)	IHL(4)	Service type(8)	Total length (16)		
Identification (16)			Flags(3)	Fragment Offset (13)	
Time to live (8)		Protocol (8)	Header Checksum (16)		
Source Address (32)					
Destination Address (32)					
Options (variable)				Padding (variable)	

Fig. 8.4 IP header format (20 bytes)

The header also consists of a *Time to Live* (TTL) that is used to limit the life of the packet on the network. This is to take care of a situation in which an IP packet gets caught in the system and becomes undeliverable. The TTL field maintains a counter that is normally initialized to 30 count and is decremented each time the packet arrives at a routing step. If the counter reaches zero, the packet is discarded.

TCP sends datagrams to IP with the Internet address of the computer at the other end. IP's job is simply to find a route for the datagram and get it to the other end. In order to allow gateways or other intermediate systems to forward the datagram, it adds its own header, as shown in Fig. 8.4. The main things in this header are the source and destination Internet address (32-bit addresses, like 128.6.4.194), the protocol number, and another checksum. The source Internet address is simply the address of your machine. The destination Internet address is the address of the other machine. The protocol number tells IP at the other end to send the datagram to TCP or UDP or some other protocol. Although most IP traffic use TCP, there are other protocols that can use IP, so you have to tell the IP which protocol to send the datagram to. Finally, the checksum allows IP at the other end to verify that the header was not damaged in transit. Note that TCP and IP have separate checksums. IP needs to be able to verify that the header did not get damaged in transit, or it could send a message to the wrong place. After IP has tacked on its header, the message looks like what is in Fig. 8.4.

Conventionally IP addresses are usually written as four integers separated by dots; each integer corresponding to 8 bits. For example, the binary address

10000000 00001011 00000110 00011110

is written in decimal form as

128.11.6.30

Thus, IP addresses are usually written as a sequence of four numbers separated by three dots such as NNN.NNN.HHH.HHH, where N stands for octets that identify network and H denotes octets that specify the host. Each number can be between 0 and 255 except the last number which must be between 1 and 254. Inside your

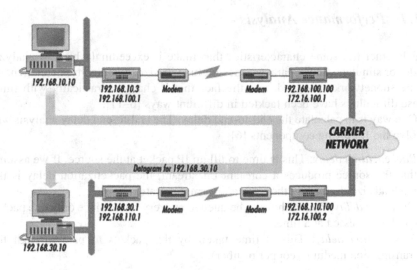

Fig. 8.5 A typical multi-hop network path

computer, an IP address is stored as a 32 bit (4 byte) integer. Dotted decimal notation is just an easy way for humans to write an IP address without having to know the binary numbers that computers work with.

We all know that computers like to work with numbers, and humans prefer *names*. With this in mind, the designers of the internet have set up a system to give names to computers on the internet. A *DNS Server* is a computer somewhere that can change a *hostname* into an *IP address*, and vice versa. It holds a database similar to a telephone book. It also knows the address of other DNS servers it can query if it does not have an entry for address you are looking for. For example, when you ask your web browser to connect to www.yahoo.com, your computer asks a DNS server to look up the IP address of www.yahoo.com. The DNS server will tell your computer that it is *204.71.200.68*. Your computer then uses that IP address to contact yahoo.

IP handles complex networks the same way it handles small networks: one hop at a time. Eventually, the datagrams will get through. This is illustrated in Fig. 8.5, which shows different network segments in between the sending and destination systems.

Most of today's Internet uses Internet Protocol Version 4 (IPv4), which is now nearly 25 years old. Due to the phenomenal growth of the Internet, the rapid increase in palmtop computers, and the profusion of smart cellular phones and PDAs, the demand for IP addresses has outnumbered the limited supply provided by IPv4. In response to this shortcomings of IPv4, the Internet Engineering Task Force (IETF) approved IPv6 in 1997. IPv4 will be replaced by Internet Protocol Version 6 (IPv6), which is sometimes called the Next Generation Internet Protocol (or IPng). IPv6 adds many improvements and fixes a number of problems in IPv4, such as the limited number of available IPv4 addresses.

8.1.4 Performance Analysis

The Internet has some characteristics that make it exceedingly hard to analyze, model or simulate. Such characteristics include its size, complexity, heterogeneity of the subnetworks involved, and the fact that it changes drastically with time. These difficulties have been tackled in different ways [6–11].

One way is to calculate the end-to-end delay. The end-to-end delay analysis will involve the following components [6]:

- *Packetization delay*: This is time to fill an IP packet at the source. If we assume that the source produces a constant bit stream, the packetization delay is the payload size divided by the source information rate.
- *Queueing delay*: Packets have to be queued at every router since only one packet can be processed at a time.
- *Propagation delay*: This is time taken by the packets to pass through the transmission medium (copper or fiber).

Several other factors may contribute to the end-to-end delay but are usually not significant.

Another way is to consider the end-to-end congestion control mechanism. It is conventional to use packet drops as an indication of congestion. A *conformant* TCP connection is one where the TCP sender follows the following two traits. First, the TCP data sender interprets any packet drop in a window of data as an indication of congestion, and responds by reducing the congestion window at least in half. Second, during the congestion avoidance phase in the absence of congestion, the TCP sender increases congestion control by at most one packet per round-trip time. We say a flow is *TCP-friendly* when its arrival rate does not exceed the arrival rate of a conformant TCP connection in the same circumstances. In order to be TCP-friendly, the source's average sending rate must not be higher than that achieved by a TCP connection along the same path. Estimation of the steady state throughput of a long-live TCP connection is given by

$$T = \frac{k^* M}{R^* \sqrt{p}} \qquad (8.1)$$

where k = constant of value 1.22 or 1.31 depending respectively on whether delayed or nondelayed acknowledgement type is used

M = maximum segment (packet) size
R = round trip time experienced by the connection
p = probability of loss during the life time of a connection

This simple formula assumes that the retransmission timeout never happens and that packet loss occurs at random. In view of the current Internet, retransmission timeout occurs as a result of network congestion and packet loss may not occur at random. When the throughput estimation accounts for the retransmission timeout, we obtain [7]

$$T = \frac{M}{R\sqrt{\frac{2bp}{2}} + 3T_o\sqrt{\frac{3bp}{8}}p(1 + 32p^2)} \tag{8.2}$$

where T_o = retransmission timeout and b = 2 (if delayed ACK is used or b = 1 otherwise). From Eqs. (8.1) and (8.2), we notice that the throughput is inversely proportional to the round trip time and the square root of the loss probability.

8.2 Broadband ISDN

The integrated services digital network (ISDN) is a facility which many claim to be the most significant advance in telecommunications since the introduction of the telephone itself. It is a digital end-to-end telecommunication wide area network (WAN) in which voice, video, and data services are integrated. However, the characteristics of narrowband ISDN are inadequate for many applications of interest and in meeting the perceived users' needs for higher speed, broader bandwidth, and more flexibility such as video distribution, HDTV, and HiFi stereo. The needs are accommodated in broadband ISDN (BISDN). Consequently, as far as data networks are concerned, real excitement of ISDN comes about when one considers the capabilities of BISDN [12].

Broadband is the provision of subscriber access at bit rates in excess of 2 Mbps. Broadband applications are those implemented through broadband access and require data rate greater than is generally available in narrowband ISDN. The BISDN concept developed from the fact that a large range of voice, data, and video services can be simultaneously carried on the same optical system. Broadband is the provision of subscriber access at bit rates in the range of 1.5 Mbps up to approximately 150 Mbps. The demand for broadband communication originated from business and residential customers. Residential customers are interested in distribution services such as TV. Business customers require services for video, data, and graphics. The bit rates for these services are in the range of 2–130 Mbps and require broadband communication [13].

BISDN is regarded as an all-purpose digital network in that it will provide an integrated access that will support a wide variety of applications in a flexible and cost-effective manner.

8.3 Summary

1. The TCP/IP has been the foundation of the Internet and virtually all multivendor internetworks. They are the world's most popular open-system (nonproprietary) protocol suite because they can be used to communicate across any set of interconnected networks and are equally suited for LAN, MAN, and WAN communications.

2. BISDN started out as an extension of ISDN and has many concepts similar to ISDN.

More about WAN can be found in [14] and its performance analysis is presented in [15].

Problems

8.1 It is called TCP/IP. Mention three other protocols in the suite and what they are for.
8.2 What is the difference between TCP and UDP if they both operate at the transport layer?
8.3 What are the layers of the TCP/IP model and how are they related to the OSI model?

References

1. J. Crowcroft, "The Internet: a tutorial," *Electronics & Communication Engineering Journal*, June 1996, pp. 113-122.
2. M. R. Arick, *The TCP/IP Companion: a guide for the common user*. Boston, QED Publishing Group, 1993.
3. U. Black, *TCP/IP and Related protocols*. New York: McGraw-Hill, 2nd ed., 1995.
4. J. Martin, *TCP/IP Networking: Architecture, Administration, and Programming*. Englewood Cliffs, NJ: Prentice Hall, 1994.
5. D. M. Peterson, *TCP/IP Networking: a guide to the IBM environment*. New York: McGraw-Hill, 1995.
6. S. Floyd and K. Fall, "Promoting the use of end-to-end congestion control in the Internet," *IEEE/ACM Transactions on Networking*, vol. 7, no. 4, Aug. 1999, pp. 458-472.
7. S. Hassan and M. Kara, "Performance evaluation of end-to-end TCP-friendly video traffic in the Internet," *Proceeding of 9th IEEE International Conference on Networks*, 2001, pp. 56-61.
8. K. Van der Wal et al., "Delay performance analysis of the new Internet services with guaranteed QoS," *Proceedings of the IEEE*, vol. 85, no. 12, Oct. 1997, pp. 1947-1957.
9. S. Floyd and V. Paxson, "Difficulties in simulating the Internet," *IEEE/ACM Transactions on Networking*, vol. 9, no. 4, Aug. 2001, pp. 392-403.
10. J. W. Roberts, "Traffic theory and the Internet," *IEEE Communications Magazine*, Jan. 2001, p. 94-99.
11. J. A. Schormans et al., "Buffer overflow probability for multiplexed on-off VoIP sources," *Electronics Letters*, vol 36, no. 6, March 2000, pp. 523-524.
12. L. Kleinrock, "ISDN – The Path to Broadband Networks," *Proceedings of the IEEE*, vol. 79, no. 2, Feb. 1991, pp. 112-117. Also in [14], pp. 151-156.
13. R. Y. Awdeh, "Why Fast Packet Switching?" *IEEE Potential*, April 1993, pp. 10-12.
14. M. N. O. Sadiku and S. M. Musa, *Computer Communication for Metropolitan and Wide Area Networks*. New York: Nova Science Publishers, 2010.
15. S. V. Subramanian and R. Dutta, "Performance measurements and analysis of M/M/c queuing model based SIP proxy servers in local and wide area networks," *Proc. of 2010 International Conference on Advances in Recent Technologies in Communication and Computing*, 2010, pp. 306-310.

Chapter 9
Wireless Networks

What you do speaks so loudly that I cannot hear what you say.

—Ralph Waldo Emerson

Wireless communications is one of the fastest growing fields in engineering. The last century has witnessed the introduction of many kinds of wireless networks, some of which have become the cornerstone of modern life. Such networks have provided support for nomadic and increasingly mobile users.

Wireless networks evolve around new and old technologies. Such networks include [1]:

- Wireless local area networks (WLANs), which enable communication between stations without cables by means of radio frequency or infrared
- Wireless local loop (WLL) or fixed radio, which provides telephone, fax, and data services
- Wireless private branch exchanges (WPBXs), which facilitate communication with the office environment, allowing workers to roam
- Wireless personal area network (WPAN), which refers to using a near-field electric field to send data across various devices using the human body as a medium
- Wireless personal communications services (PCS), which describe all access technologies used by individuals or subscribers
- Cellular communications, which allows frequency reuse by dividing regions into small cells, each cell with a stationary radio antenna
- Satellite communications, which uses orbiting satellites to relay data between multiple earth-based stations.

The performance analysis of wireless networks is more complicated than that for fixed networks because we must take into account a lot of parameters such as the cell number, buffer size, and user mobility. For this reason, most performance analyses use simulation and very few provide close form solution. In this chapter, we consider ALOHA network, wireless LAN, and wireless MAN.

M.N.O. Sadiku and S.M. Musa, *Performance Analysis of Computer Networks*,
DOI 10.1007/978-3-319-01646-7_9, © Springer International Publishing Switzerland 2013

9.1   ALOHA Networks

ALOHA is the simplest broadcast protocol. The original goal of ALOHA was to investigate the use of radio communications as an alternative to the telephone system for computer networks. At that time, the University of Hawaii was composed of six campuses on different islands all within a radius of 300 km from the main campus near Honolulu. It was envisaged that such a radio data network would connect these campuses and allow sharing of computer resources [2]. Thus, ALOHA networks were proposed to make short delays possible. They are random time-division multiple access networks because stations or terminals make use of the channel at random times. The principles of ALOHA systems are incorporated in both LANs and WANs. For example, ALOHA-based protocols are used in CSMA/CD and token ring, which are LANs. They are also used in VSAT networks, which are WANs [3].

In a pure ALOHA network, all users can initiate transmission at any time, in completely unsynchronized manner. Any station which has a packet to transmit simply transmits the packet regardless of whether other stations are transmitting. If, within some appropriate time-out period, an acknowledgement is received from the destination, the transmission is regarded successful. A transmission is unsuccessful if no acknowledgement is received after a certain time. The station will then assume its packet is lost. Through a random process, the station will determine a certain waiting time and retransmit the packet when that time expires.

A useful performance characteristic for ALOHA network is the relationship between throughput S and offered load G. Assume that the start times of packets in the channel comprise a Poisson point process with parameter λ packets/s so that

$$\text{Prob}[k \text{ arrivals in } \tau \text{ seconds}] = \frac{(\lambda\tau)^k}{k!}e^{-\lambda\tau} \tag{9.1}$$

If each packet lasts τ seconds, we define the normalized channel traffic G as

$$G = \lambda\tau \tag{9.2}$$

We may assume that only those packets which do not overlap with other packets are correctly received. We define the normalized channel throughput S as

$$S = GP_s \tag{9.3}$$

where P_s is the probability that an arbitrary offered packet is successful. The probability that a packet will not overlap a given packet is the probability that no packet starts τ seconds before or τ seconds after the start time of the given packet (i.e. a vulnerable interval of 2τ). Since the start times constitute a Poisson point process, the probability of having no packet overlap is obtained using Eq. (8.1), i.e.

$$P_s = \text{Prob}[0 \text{ arrivals in } 2\tau \text{ seconds}] = e^{-2\lambda\tau} = e^{-2G} \tag{9.4}$$

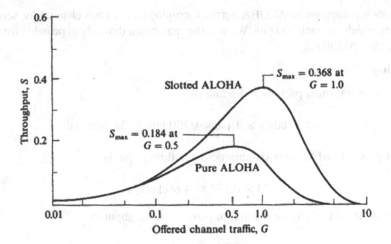

Fig. 9.1 Throughput versus offered load for pure and slotted ALOHA

Thus,

$$S = Ge^{-2G} \qquad (9.5)$$

The pure ALOHA achieves a maximum throughput of $1/(2e) = 0.184$ at $G = 0.5$.

Subsequently, a modified scheme was proposed in which the time axis is segmented into time slots. In this slotted ALOHA, users are still allowed to transmit randomly but a packet needs to be of fixed length and it must fall exactly in one of the time slots. If two packets overlap, they overlap completely rather than partially (i.e. a vulnerable interval of only τ). Hence,

$$S = Ge^{-G} \qquad (9.6)$$

With this simple change, the maximum throughput is increased by a factor of 2 to $1/e = 0.368$ at $G = 1$. This implies that on the average, 36.8 % of the slots are successfully transmitted, 36.8 % are idle, while the rest of the slots contain collisions. The slotted version reduces frequencies of collisions and thereby increases the maximum throughput of the random-access channel.

An example of the slotted ALOHA is in GSM cellular networks. Another application of slotted ALOHA is in very small aperture terminal (VSAT), which a satellite network in which small terminals are geographically widespread. ALOHA is also used in wireline networks [3].

A comparison of both pure and slotted ALOHA is made in Fig. 9.1. It is not possible to have a stable point of operation for $G > 0.5$ for pure ALOHA or $G > 1.0$ for slotted ALOHA [4].

Example 9.1 Suppose an ALOHA network employs a 4.8-kbps channel for sending packets which are each 200 bits. What is the maximum throughput possible for pure and slotted ALOHA?

Solution

The system transmits packets at the rate of

$$4,800 \text{ bits/s} \times 1 \text{ packet/200 bits} = 24 \text{ packets/s}$$

For pure ALOHA, the maximum possible throughput is

$$24 \times 0.184 \approx 4 \text{ packets/s}$$

For slotted ALOHA, the maximum possible throughput is

$$24 \times 0.368 \approx 8 \text{ packets/s}$$

9.2   Wireless LAN

Wireless local area network (WLAN) is a new form of communication system. It is basically a local area network, confined to a geographically small area such as a single building, office, store or campus, that provides high data connectivity to mobile stations. Using electromagnetic airwaves (radio frequency or infrared), WLANs transmit and receive data over the air. A WLAN suggests less expensive, fast, and simple network installation and reconfiguration.

The proliferation of portable computers coupled with the mobile user's need for communication is the major driving force behind WLAN technology. WLAN creates a mobile environment for the PC and LAN user. It may lower LAN maintenance and expansion costs since there are no wires that require reconfiguration. Thus, WLANs offer the following advantages over the conventional wired LANs:

- Installation flexibility: allows the network to go where wire cannot go.
- Mobility: can provide LAN users with access anywhere.
- Scalability: can be configured in a variety of topologies to meet specific needs.

However, WLAN does not perform as well as wired LAN because of the bandwidth limitations and may be susceptible to electromagnetic interference. While the initial investment on WLAN hardware can be higher than the cost of wired LAN hardware, overall installation expenses and life-cycle costs can be significantly lower.

9.2.1 Physical Layer and Topology

WLAN does not compete with wired LAN. Rather, WLANs are used to extend wired LANs for convenience and mobility. Wireless links essentially fill in for wired links using electromagnetic radiation at radio or light frequencies between transceivers. A typical WLAN consists of an access point and the WLAN adapter installed on the portable notebook. The access point is a transmitter/receiver (transceiver) device; it is essentially the wireless equivalent of a regular LAN hub. An access point is typically connected with the wired backbone network at a fixed location through a standard Ethernet cable and communicates with wireless devices by means of an antenna. WLANs operate within the prescribed 900 MHz, 2.4 GHz, and 5.8 GHz frequency bands. Most LANs use 2.4 GHz frequency bands because it is most widely accepted.

A wireless link can provide services in several ways including the following three [5]:

- Replace a point-to-point connection between two nodes or segments on a LAN. A point-to-point link is a connection between two devices for transferring data. A wireless link can be used to bridge two LAN segments. Like a point-to-point link, the link connects two wireless bridges attached to the two LANs. Such an arrangement is useful for linking LANs in two buildings where a highway or river makes direct connection difficult.
- Provide a connection between a wired LAN and one or more WLAN nodes. In this case, a device is attached to the wired LAN to act as a point of contact (called access point) between the wired LAN and the wireless nodes as shown in Fig. 9.2. The device can be a repeater, bridge or router.
- Act as a stand-alone WLAN for a group of wireless nodes. This can be achieved using topologies similar to wired LAN, namely, a star topology can be formed with central hub controlling the wireless nodes, a ring topology with each wireless node receiving or passing information sent to it or a bus topology with each wireless capable of hearing everything said by all the other nodes.

9.2.2 Technologies

When designing WLANs, manufacturers have to choose from two main technologies that are used for wireless communications today: radio frequency (RF) and infra red (IR). Each technologies has its own merits and demerits.

RF is used for applications where communications are over long distances and are not line-of-sight. In order to operate in the license free portion of the frequency spectrum known as the ISM band (Industrial, Scientific, and Medical), the RF system must use a modulation technique called *spread spectrum* (SS). (SS was used in IEEE 802.11b.) Spread spectrum is wideband radio frequency technology developed by the military during World War II for use in reliable, secure, mission-critical

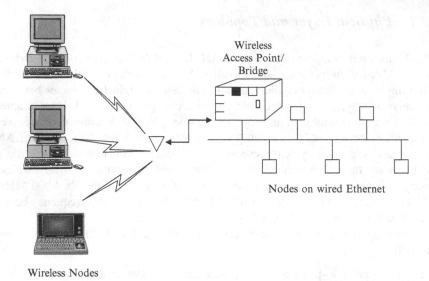

Wireless Nodes

Fig. 9.2   Connection of a wired LAN to wireless nodes

communications systems. SS system is one in which the transmitted signal is spread over frequency much wider than the minimum bandwidth required to send the signal. Using spread spectrum, a radio is supposed to distribute the signal across the entire spectrum. This way, no single user can dominate the band and collectively all users look like noise. The fact that such signals appear like noise in the band makes them difficult to find and jam, thereby increasing security against unauthorized listeners. There are two types of spread spectrum technology: frequency hopping and direct sequence.

Frequency hopping spread spectrum (FHSS) offers a current maximum data rate of 3 Mbps. It uses a narrowband carrier that changes frequency in a pattern known to both transmitter and receiver. It is based on the use of a signal at a given frequency that is constant for a small amount of time and then moves to a new frequency. The sequence of different channels for the hopping pattern is determined in pseudorandom fashion. This means that a very long sequence code is used before it is repeated, over 65,000 hops, making it appear random. Thus it is very difficult to predict the next frequency at which such a system will stop and transmit/receive data as the system appears to be a noise source to an unauthorized listener. This makes FHSS system very secure against interference and interception.

Direct sequence spread spectrum (DSSS) takes a signal at a given frequency and spreads it across a band of frequencies where the center frequency is the original signal. The spreading algorithm, which is the key to the relationship of the spread range of frequencies, changes with time in a pseudorandom sequence. When the ratio between the original signal bandwidth and the spread signal bandwidth is very large, the system offers great immunity to interference. For example, if 10 kbps signal is spread across 1 GHz of spectrum, the spreading ratio is 100,000 times or

50 dB. However, in the ISM band used in WLAN, the available bandwidth critically limits the ratio of spreading and so the advantages of DSSS scheme against interference is greatly limited. It has been shown that for the WLAN system using DSSS, the spreading ratio is at best ten times. DSSS is characterized by high cost, high power consumption, and more range than FHSS and infrared physical layers. FHSS is characterized by low cost, low power consumption, and less range than DSSS but greater range than infrared. Most WLAN systems use FHSS.

The second technology used in WLAN is Infra Red (IR), where the communication is carried by light in the invisible part of the spectrum. It is primarily used for very short distance communications (less than 1 m), where there is a line-of-sight connection. Since IR light does not penetrate solid materials (it is even attenuated greatly by window glass), it is not really useful in comparison to RF in WLAN system. However, IR is used in applications where the power is extremely limited such as a pager.

9.2.3 Standards

Although a number of proprietary, non-standard wireless LANs exist, standards have now been developed. Two international organizations have contributed to the development of standards for WLANs: the Institute of Electronics and Electrical Engineers (IEEE) and the European Telecommunications Standards Institute (ETSI). Mainly it is IEEE for 902.11; ETSI is involved in cellular.

In 1997, the IEEE 802.11 committee (http://ieee802.org/11) issued a standard for wireless LANs. The standard addresses the physical and MAC layers of the OSI model and includes the following [5, 6]:

- A transmission rate of up to 2 Mbps
- Two different media for transmission over wireless LAN: infrared (IR) and radio frequency (RF)
- The media access control (MAC) protocol as carrier sense multiple access with collision avoidance (CSMA/CA), i.e. devices can interoperate with wired LANs via a bridge
- MAC protocol provides two service types: asynchronous and synchronous (or contention-free). The asynchronous type of service is mandatory while the synchronous type is optional
- MAC layer protocol is tied to the IEEE 802.2 logical link control (LLC) layer making it easier to integrate with other LANs
- Three different physical layers: an optical-based physical-layer implementation that uses IR light to transmit, two RF based physical-layer choices: direct sequence spread spectrum (DSSS) and frequency hopping spread spectrum (FHSS) both operating at 2.4 GHz industrial, scientific, and medical (ISM)

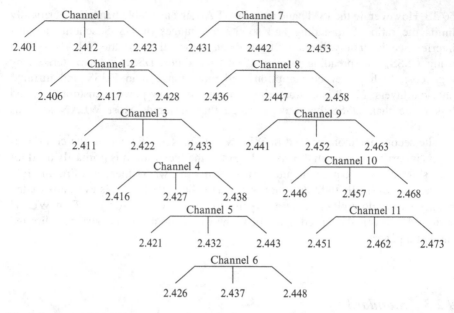

Fig. 9.3 Eleven 22-MHz-wide channels for DSSS wireless LANs

frequency bands. (The ISM bands 902–928 MHz, 2,400–2,483.5 MHz, and 5,725–5,850 MHz do not require a license to operate.) The IEEE 802.11 specifications for DSSS wireless LAN is shown in Fig. 9.3.

- Added features to the MAC that can maximize battery life in portable clients via power-management schemes.
- Data security through which the wireless LANs can achieve wired equivalent privacy.

The standard basically defines the media and configuration issues, transmission procedures, throughput requirements, and range characteristics for WLAN technology. It avoids rigid requirements and gives room for vendors in the following areas: multiple physical media, common MAC layer irrespective of the physical layer, common frame format, power limit, and multiple on-air data rates [7].

There are three major problems encountered by an RF LAN [8]. First, frequency allocation is limited for LANs. But since LANs operate with low power, frequency reuse is possible. Second, interference from other wireless LANs controlled by different organization and other wireless sources is a problem. This problem can be controlled by using spread spectrum techniques. Third, security is at stake because RF signal can penetrate through the wall and hostile operators can intercept RF LAN communications. Encryption can be used to lessen this problem. IR LAN uses both laser diodes and light-emitting diodes as emitters. It is useful in high electromagnetic interference (EMI) environments. It is also secure since IR signal cannot penetrate the wall.

CSMA/CA is slightly different from carrier sense multiple access with collision detection (CSMA/CD), which is the MAC protocol used in Ethernet wired LAN. In CSMA/CA, when a node has something to transmit, it waits for silence on the network. When no other nodes are heard, it transmits and waits to receive an acknowledgement from the recipient node. If it fails to receive an acknowledgement within a time period, it assumes that collision has occurred and follows a process similar to CSMA/CD. Each node then waits for silence and only transmits after a random amount of waiting. While CSMA/CA protocol is slower that CSMA/CD due to the need for waiting for acknowledgement, it works well for wireless LANs. Also, WLANs operate in strong multipath fading channel where channel characteristics can change resulting in unreliable communication.

The ETSI devoted its attention to RF wireless LANs. The ETSI is close to finalizing its standard, which is based on the 2.4 GHz range used for spread-spectrum LANs in several European countries. European standard WLAN, called HiperLAN, will allow speeds of 24 Mbps [9].

Besides IEEE and ETSI, there are organizations that are more interested in the implementation and interoperability of WLAN products. Such organizations include Wireless LAN Alliance (WLANA at www.wlana.com) and Wireless Ethernet Compatibility Alliance (WECA at www.wi-fi.org or www.wirelessethernet. com). WLANA was formed in 1996 with 12 members as a trade association for wireless LAN vendors. WECA is a nonprofit manufacturing consortium with over 60 companies as members; it was formed in 1999 to certify interoperability of IEEE 802.11 products. Research groups are working hard to shrink radios into a chip that can be mass produced cheaply. If they succeed, the demand for radio LANs may follow the same trend as cellular phones in recent years.

9.2.4 Performance Analysis

We now present an accurate but simple analytical evaluation of the wireless networks using gated and exhaustive polling protocols combined with the stop-and-wait or go-back-N automatic repeat request (ARQ) techniques. In gated access policy, upon receiving a polling message, a station is permitted to transmit all packets stored in its buffer until that time. For the exhaustive policy, a station upon receiving a polling message is permitted to transmit all packets in its buffer as well as packets arriving while transmitting.

Assuming that the transmission system is completely symmetric, the average packet waiting time for gated policy is (in slots)

$$\overline{W}^g = \frac{1}{2}\left(\frac{N\lambda\overline{t^2}}{1 - N\lambda\overline{t}} + \frac{(1 + \lambda\overline{t})N\overline{R}}{1 - N\lambda\overline{t}} + \frac{\overline{R^2}}{\overline{R}} - \overline{R} - 1 \right) + \overline{t} - 1 \qquad (9.7)$$

where λ is the arrival rate; N is the number of stations; t is the packet transmission time with first moment $\bar{t}$ and second moment $\overline{t^2}$; R is the walk time with first moment $\bar{R}$ and second moment $\overline{R^2}$. For exhaustive policy, the corresponding equation is

$$\overline{W}^e = \frac{1}{2}\left(\frac{N\lambda\overline{t^2}}{1 - N\lambda\overline{t^2}} + \frac{(1 - \lambda\bar{t})N\bar{R}}{1 - N\lambda\bar{t}} + \frac{\overline{R^2}}{\bar{R}} - \bar{R} - 1 \right) + \bar{t} - 1 \qquad (9.8)$$

The above analysis has been presented in a summarized form. For more details, the interested reader is referred to [10, 11].

The above model is on a general WLAN. We now consider an IEEE 802.11 based WLAN, where the nodes use Distributed Coordination Function (DCF) mode of the MAC protocol. We recall that DCF is governed by a "listen-before-talk" protocol known as CSMA. Every station that wants to transmit first senses the channel for at least a duration of DIFS (Distributed Inter Frame Spacing). If the channel is idle for the entire DIFS, the station transmits the packet. Otherwise, it avoids collision by selecting a random back-off time uniformly distributed in the range [0, CW], where CW is the Contention Window. Under saturation conditions, the CSMA/CA process can be modeled as a two dimensional Markov chain.

We now can express the probability τ that a station transmits in a randomly selected slot time. Let p be the probability that its transmission will collide with at least one other node. In [12–14], the access probability τ is related to the collision probability of each packet p as

$$\tau = \frac{2(1 - 2p)}{(1 - 2p)(W + 1) + pW[1 - (2p)^m]} \qquad (9.9)$$

where W is the minimum backoff window in terms of backoff slots, and m is the maximum backoff stage. Notice from Eq. (9.9) that when m = 0, i.e. no exponential backoff is considered,

$$\tau = \frac{2}{W + 1} \qquad (9.10)$$

i.e. τ is independent of p. However, τ generally depends on the collision probability p, which is yet to be found. To find p. we note that p is the probability that, in a time slot, at least one the n − 1 remaining stations transmits

$$p = 1 - (1 - \tau)^{n-1} \qquad (9.11)$$

Equations (9.9) and (9.11) together form a system of nonlinear system and need to solved using numerical techniques (e.g. Newton's method). Once τ is known, we can calculate the throughput.

Let S be the normalized system throughput, defined as the fraction of time the channel is used to successfully transmit. Let P_{tr} be the probability that there is at least one transmission in the considered slot time. Since n stations contend for transmission and each transmit with probability τ:

$$P_{tr} = 1 - (1 - \tau)^n \tag{9.12}$$

The probability P_s that a transmission is successful is

$$P_s = \frac{n\tau(1-\tau)^{n-1}}{P_{tr}} = \frac{n\tau(1-\tau)^{n-1}}{1-(1-r)^n} \tag{9.13}$$

We now express the throughput S as the ratio

$$S = \frac{E[\text{payload information transmitted in one slot time}]}{E[\text{length of a slot time}]} \tag{9.14}$$

If E[P] is the average packet payload size, the average amount of payload information successfully transmitted in a slot time is $P_{tr}P_s E[P]$, since a successful transmission occurs in a slot time with probability $P_{tr}P_s$. Hence, Eq. (9.14) becomes

$$S = \frac{P_s P_{tr} E[P]}{(1-P_{tr})\sigma + P_{tr}P_s T_s + P_{tr}(1-P_s)T_c} \tag{9.15}$$

Where σ is the duration on an empty slot time, T_s is the average time the channel is senses busy because of a successful transmission, and T_c is the average time the channel is sensed busy by each node during a collision.

Other models on performance analysis of WLAN and WMAN can be found in [15–17].

9.3 Multiple Access Techniques

Since spectrum is a scarce and limited resource, multiple access schemes are designed to share the resource among a large number of wireless users. There are three popular multiple-access techniques for sharing the available bandwidth in a wireless communication system:

- The frequency division multiple access (FDMA) serves users with different frequency channels. Signals are transmitted in nonoverlapping frequency bands that can be separated using bandpass filters.
- The time division multiple access (TDMA) serves users with different time slots. Signals are transmitted in nonoverlapping time slots in a round-robin fashion. In each slot only one user is allowed to either transmit or receive.

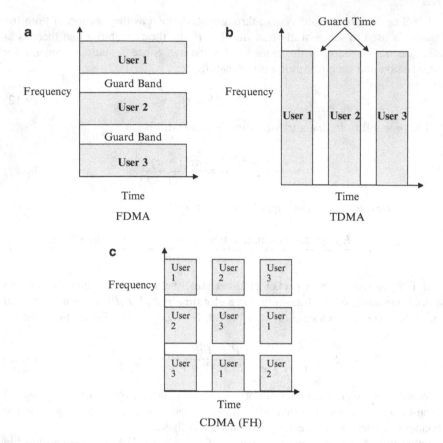

Fig. 9.4 Multiple access techniques for wireless systems

• The code division multiple access (CDMA) serves users with different code sequences. Different users employ signals that have small cross-correlation.

The three access methods are portrayed in Fig. 9.4. In addition to FDMA, TDMA, and CDMA, there are other two multiple access schemes—polarization division multiple access (PDMA) which serves users with different polarization and space division multiple access (SDMA) which controls the radiated energy for users in space by using spot beam antenna [18].

9.3.1 FDMA, TDMA, and CDMA

FDMA requires that the total bandwidth be divided into a number of disjoint frequency subchannels. Each subchannel is assigned on demand to individual users who request service. As shown in Fig. 9.4, guard bands are maintained

Fig. 9.5 TDMA frame structure

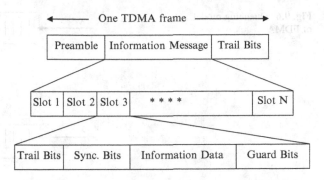

between adjacent spectra to minimize cross talk between channels. The present FM radio subdivides the spectrum into 30-kHz channels so that each channel is assigned to one user. In FDMA, the 30-kHz channel can be split into three 10-kHz channels. This band-splitting, however, incurs costs. For reasons of spectral efficiency, the transmission rate on a single FDMA channel is usually close to the maximum rate required by the user. Consequently, FDMA is suitable for users with nonbursty and predictable traffic. Cellular networks do not use FDMA by itself anymore. That passed with first generation networks. TDMA, at least in cellular, is used with FDMA. TDMA and CDMA can support more users in the space spectrum region. The GSM air interface uses a mixture of FDMA and TDMA.

TDMA is a channelization scheme that triples the capacity of the available channels without requiring additional RF spectrum. A frame consists of a number of time intervals called slots. As shown in Fig. 9.5, each TDMA frame consists of a preamble, information message, and trail bits. The preamble has the address and synchronization information that both the base station and the subscribers will use to identify each other. Guard times are used between slots to minimize cross talk. One downside of TDMA is that the high rate switching/multiplexing of the time-domain transmission signals places stringent requirements on the analog components following the modulator.

CDMA is a spread spectrum technique in which the narrowband signal from each user is spread out in frequency using a unique spreading code. Several signals may occupy the same frequency band and still be individually recovered by the receiver with the knowledge of the spreading code. Each user operates independently of other users. Each user is assigned a unique code sequence that he uses to encode his information signal. The receiver, fully aware of the code sequence of the user, decodes the received signal after reception and recovers the original data.

9.3.2 Performance Analysis

In this section, we develop some analytical models to provide insights into the characteristics of FDMA and TDMA systems [19]. Suppose N users, each with infinite buffer size, transmit packets of constant length L bits. The packet arriving

Fig. 9.6 Queueing model
of FDMA

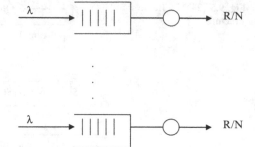

rate is λ packets/s. For TDMA, packets are transmitted using the full channel
bandwidth of NR bps, while FDMA systems transmit at R bps.

9.3.2.1   Frequency Division Multiple Access

The queueing model is shown in Fig. 9.6.

Using the result of M/G/1 queueing model, the waiting time is

$$E(W) = \frac{\lambda E^2(S)}{2(1 - \rho)} = \frac{\lambda \left(\frac{L}{R/N}\right)^2}{2(1 - \rho)} = \frac{\lambda N^2 L^2}{2R^2(1 - \rho)} \tag{9.16}$$

The overall delay is

$$\begin{aligned} E(D) &= E(W) + E(S) \\ &= \frac{\lambda N^2 L^2}{2R^2(1 - \rho)} + \frac{NL}{R} \end{aligned} \tag{9.17}$$

For the queue to be stable with finite delay,

$$\rho = \lambda E(S) = \frac{\lambda NL}{R} < 1 \tag{9.18}$$

9.3.2.2   Time Division Multiple Access

The delay in TDMA comprises of two components: (a) waiting time for the start of
the time slot, (b) waiting time for packets that arrived earlier in the same queue to be
transmitted. Using the result of M/G/1 queue,

$$E(W) = \frac{\lambda E^2(S)}{2(1-\rho)} + \frac{E(S^2)}{2E(S)}$$

$$= \frac{\lambda \left(\dfrac{L}{R/N}\right)^2}{2(1-\rho)} + \frac{\left(\dfrac{L}{R/N}\right)^2}{2\left(\dfrac{L}{R/N}\right)} \qquad (9.19)$$

$$= \frac{\lambda N^2 L^2}{2R^2(1-\rho)} + \frac{NL}{2R}$$

The second term represents the fact that on the average, an arriving packet has to wait half the frame length (NL/R) before it is transmitted in its own time slot. The overall delay is

$$E(D) = E(W) + \frac{L}{R}$$

$$= \frac{\lambda N^2 L^2}{2R^2(1-\rho)} + \frac{NL}{2R} + \frac{L}{R} \qquad (9.20)$$

Note that

$$E(W)_{TDMA} = E(W)_{FDMA} + \frac{NL}{2R} > E(W)_{FDMA} \qquad (9.21)$$

$$E(D)_{TDMA} = E(D)_{FDMA} + \frac{L}{R} - \frac{NL}{2R} \qquad (9.22)$$

i.e.

$$E(D)_{FDMA} > E(D)_{TDMA} \rightarrow \frac{NL}{2R} - \frac{L}{R} > 0 \rightarrow N > 2 \qquad (9.23)$$

This indicates that in terms of performance TDMA is superior to FDMA because the packet delay in FDMA is typically larger than TDMA. For three or more users, the overall delay in FDMA is greater than TDMA.

9.4 Cellular Communications

Perhaps no single development has done more for wireless technologies than has cellular communications. It is one of the fastest growing and most demanding telecommunication applications. It has been predicted that cellular will be the universal method of personal communication.

Fig. 9.7 A typical wireless seven-cell patterns; cells overlap to provide greater coverage

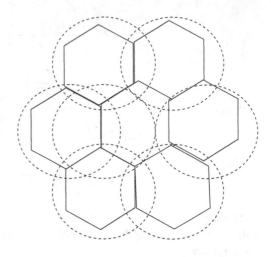

9.4.1   The Cellular Concept

The cellular concept is not so much a new technology as it is a new idea of organizing old technology. It was developed in 1947 at Bell Laboratories; the first cellular system began operation in Japan in 1979, and the first cellular system in the U.S. began in October, 1983 in Chicago. The first generation of cellular systems was based on analog FM radio technology. The second-generation cellular systems are based on digital radio technology and conform to at least three standards: GSM for Europe and international applications, AMPS for the U.S., and JDC for Japan. Third-generation cellular systems use TDMA, CDMA, CSMA, and FDMA.

The conventional approach to mobile radio involved setting up a high-power transmitter on top of the highest point in a coverage area. The mobile telephone had to have a line-of-sight to the base station for proper coverage. Line-of-sight transmission is limited to as much as 40–50 miles on the horizon. Also, if a mobile travels too far from the base station, the quality of the communications link becomes unacceptable. These and other limitations of conventional mobile telephone systems are overcome by cellular technology.

Areas of coverage are divided into small hexagonal radio coverage units known as *cells*. (The hexagonal shape is only for the sake of illustration; the shapes of real cells are irregular.) A cell is the basic geographical unit of a cellular system. A cellular communications system employs a large number of low-power wireless transmitter, as shown in Fig. 9.7.

Cells are base stations transmitting over small geographical areas that are represented as hexagons. Cell size varies depending on the landscape and tele-density. Each side typically covers a maximum area of 15 miles across, depending on the local terrain. Urban cells are smaller for reuse. The cell sites are spaced over the area to provide a slightly overlapping blanket of coverage. Like the early mobile

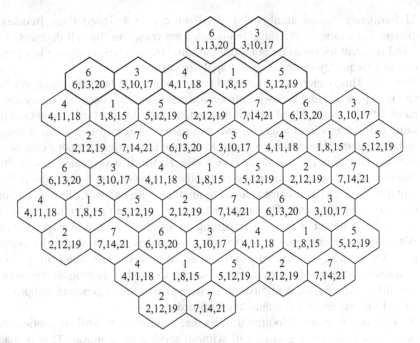

Fig. 9.8 Frequency reuse in a seven-cell pattern cellular system

systems, the base station communicates with mobiles via a channel. The channel is made of two frequencies: the *forward link* for transmitting information to the base station and the *reverse link* to receive from the base station.

9.4.2   Fundamental Features

Besides the idea of cells, the essential principles of cellular systems include cell splitting, frequency reuse, hand-off, capacity, spectral efficiency, mobility, and roaming [1, 20].

- *Cell splitting*: As a service area becomes full of users, the area is split into small ones. Consequently, urban regions with heavy traffic can be split into as many areas as necessary to provide acceptable service, while a large cell can be used to cover remote rural regions. Cell splitting increases the capacity of the system.
- *Frequency reuse*: This is the core concept that defines the cellular system. The cellular-telephone industry is faced with a dilemma: services are growing rapidly and users are demanding more sophisticated call-handling features, but the amount of the electromagnetic spectrum allocation for cellular service is fixed. This dilemma is overcome by the ability to reuse the same frequency (channel) many times. Several frequency reuse patterns are in use. A typical example is shown in Fig. 9.8, where all available channels are divided into

21 frequency groups numbered 1–21. Each cell is assigned three frequency groups. For example, the same frequencies are reused in the cell designated as 1 and adjacent locations do not reuse the same frequencies. A cluster is a group of cells; frequency reused does not apply to clusters.

- *Hand-off*: This is another fundamental feature of the cellular technology. When a call is in progress and the switch from one cell to another becomes necessary, a hand-off takes place. Hand-off is important, because adjacent cells do not use the same radio channels as a mobile user travels from one cell to another during a call, the call must be either dropped (blocked) or transferred from one channel to another. Dropping the call is not acceptable. Hand-off was created to solve the problem. Handing off from cell to cell is the process of transferring the mobile unit that has a call on a voice channel to another voice channel, all done without interfering with the call. The need for hand-off is determined by the quality of the signal, whether it is weak or strong. A hand-off threshold is predefined. When the received signal level is weak and reaches the threshold, the system provides a stronger channel from an adjacent cell. The hand-off process continues as the mobile moves from one cell to another as long as the mobile is in the coverage area. A number of algorithms are used to generate and process a hand-off request and eventual hand-off order.
- *Mobility and roaming*: Mobility implies that a mobile user while in motion will be able to maintain the same call without service interruption. This is made possible by the built-in hand-off mechanism that assigns a new channel when the mobile moves to another cell. Because several cellular operators within the same region use different equipment, and a subscriber is registered with only one operator, some form of agreement is necessary to provide services to subscribers. Roaming is the process whereby a mobile moves out of its own territory and establishes a call from another territory.
- *Capacity*: This is the number of subscribers that can use the cellular system. For a circuit-switched system, the capacity is determined by the loading (number of calls and the average time per call). Capacity expansion is required because cellular system must serve more subscribers. It takes place through frequency reuse, cell splitting, planning, and redesigning of the system.
- *Spectral efficiency*: This is a performance measure of the efficient use of the frequency spectrum. It is the most desirable feature of a mobile communication system. It produces a measure of how efficiently space, frequency, and time are utilized. Expressed in channels/MHz/km^2, channel efficiency is given by

$$\eta = \frac{\text{Total no. of channels available in the system}}{\text{Bandwidth} \times \text{Total coverage area}} \qquad (9.24)$$

$$\eta = \frac{\frac{B_w}{B_c} \times \frac{N_c}{N}}{B_w \times N_c \times A_c} = \frac{1}{B_c N A_c} \qquad (9.25)$$

where B_w is bandwidth of the system in MHz, B_c is the channel spacing in MHz, N_c is the number of cells in a cluster, N is the frequency reuse factor of the system, and A_c is the area covered by a cell in km^2.

9.4.3   Performance Analysis

There are two common performance indices used in designing cellular systems [21, 22]. The first index is the *call blocking probability*, which is the probability that a new, originating call is denied due to the unavailability of free channels. The second index is the *call dropping probability* of hand-off call, which is the probability that an ongoing call is ended while a hand-off attempt is being made, again due to the unavailability of free channels. These two metrics are used with different traffic load to show the performance of a proposed system. A major goal is to keep these probabilities as low as possible by effectively utilizing the bandwidth.

To determine the two metrics, let λ_i be the hand-off request rate for traffic type $i \in \{0,1, \cdots, n\}$, which follows a Poisson process and $1/\mu_i$ be the mean holding time of a channel for traffic type i within an exponential distribution. When j channels are busy, handoff calls depart at rate $j\mu_i$. When the number of requested channels reaches the total number of available channels s_i, i.e. $j = s_i$, then all channels are in use and the channel exchange rate is $s_i\mu_i$. In this case, any new arriving hand-off call is blocked.

Let P_j be the probability that j channels exchanges are requested for traffic type i. Then P_0 is the probability that no channel exchange is requested for traffic type i. The balance equations are [23]:

$$\begin{aligned} \lambda_i P_0 &= \mu_i P_1 \quad \text{for } j = 0 \\ \lambda_i P_{j-1} &= j\mu_i P_j \quad \text{for } 0 < j < s_i \end{aligned} \tag{9.26}$$

It then follows that

$$\begin{aligned} P_1 &= \rho_1 P_0 \\ P_j &= \frac{\rho_i P_{j-1}}{j} = \frac{\rho_i^j P_0}{j!} \end{aligned} \tag{9.27}$$

where $\rho_i = \frac{\lambda_i}{\mu_i}$ is the offered load. Since the sum of the probabilities must be 1,

$$P_0 = \frac{1}{\displaystyle\sum_{j=0}^{s_i} \frac{\rho_i^j}{j!}} \tag{9.28}$$

Thus, from Eqs. (9.27) and (9.28), we obtain

$$P_j = \frac{\rho_i^j}{j! \sum\limits_{j=0}^{s_i} \frac{\rho_i^j}{j!}} \tag{9.29}$$

When $j = s_i$, all the available channels are busy and any handoff call gets blocked. Thus, the handoff dropping probability is given by

$$P_{s_i} = \frac{\rho_i^{s_i}}{s_i! \sum\limits_{j=0}^{s_i} \frac{\rho_i^j}{j!}} \tag{9.30}$$

It is evident from Eq. (9.30) that the dropping probability P_{s_i} is directly proportional to the mean channel exchange time. Also, the dropping probability decreases when the number of available channels increases. This means that the more bandwidth is available in a cell, the less chance a handoff call is blocked.

9.5 Summary

1. The ALOHA systems are random time-division multiple access systems. They are used as a basis of comparing various random access methods. It is found that slotted ALOHA performs better than pure ALOHA
2. Wireless LAN allows laptop PC and LAN users to link through radio waves or infrared links, eliminating the need for restrictive cables and opening a wider range of possible applications.
3. The IEEE 802.16 standard addresses the "first-mile/last-mile" connection in wireless MANs. Such wireless MANs allow thousands of users share capacity for data, voice, and video.
4. Multiple access techniques include TDMA, FDMA, and CDMA. In TDMA protocol, the transmission time is divided into frames and each user is assigned a fixed part of each frame, not overlapping with parts assigned to other users. In FDMA protocol, the channel bandwidth is divided into nonoverlapping frequency bands and each user is assigned a fixed band. CDMA protocols constitute a class of protocols in which multiple-access capability is primarily achieved by means of coding.
5. Cellular systems operate on the principles of cell, frequency reuse, and hand-off.

Problems

9.1 Show that the maximum value of the throughput is 0.184 for pure ALOHA and 0.368 for slotted ALOHA.

9.2 A computer network uses a pure ALOHA access method. Let the channel bit rate be 100 kbps and packet length be 20 bytes. If each node generates 20 packets/min on the average, how many stations can the network support?

9.3 A random access network uses the ALOHA access scheme. It consists of two stations which are 800 m apart. Assume each station generates frames at an average rate of 600 packets/s and that the data rate is 2 Mbps. Let the packet length be 12 bytes and the propagation velocity be 2×10^8 m/s. (a) Calculate the probability of collision for pure ALOHA protocol. (b) Repeat for slotted ALOHA.

9.4 Compare and contrast CSMA/CD and CSMA/CA.

9.5 Compare and contrast RF LAN and IR LAN.

9.6 Consider a system with ten stations and deterministic values of walking times with $\overline{R} = 0.4\mu s$. Assume message lengths are exponentially distributed with mean message length of 1,000 bits and gated service. Plot the mean message delay as a function of the total traffic load $\rho = \lambda\overline{\tau} = 0.1$, 0.2, ... 0.8. Take the bit rate to be 1 Mbps.

9.7 Repeat the previous problem for exhaustive service.

9.8 Describe the requirements for the PHY, MAC, and DLC layers of a wireless ATM network.

9.9 Describe FDMA and CDMA.

9.10 An FDMA system has the following parameters:

λ/station $= 100$ bps
$R = 10^6$ bps
$N = 50$
$L = 1,000$ bits

Plot the mean delay versus offered load ρ.

References

1. M. N. O. Sadiku, *Optical and Wireless Communications*. Boca Raton: CRC Press, 2002.
2. N. Abramson, "Development of the ALOHANET," *IEEE Transactions on Information Theory*, vol. 31, no. 2, March 1985, pp. 119-123.
3. A. Kumar et al., *Wireless Networking*. New York: Morgan Kaufman Publishers, 2008, pp. 194, 195.
4. G. Keiser, *Local Area Networks*. New York: McGraw-Hill, 2nd ed., 2002, pp.108-112.
5. P. T. Davis and C. R. McGuffin, *Wireless Local Area Networks*. New York: McGraw-Hill, 1995, pp. 41-117.
6. N. J. Muller, *Mobile Telecommunications Factbook*. New York: McGraw-Hill, 1998, pp. 219-270.

7. V. K. Garg, K. Smolik, and J. E. Wilkes, *Applications of CDMA in Wireless/Personal Communications*. Upper Saddle River, NJ: Prentice Hall, 1997, pp. 233-272.
8. F. J. Ricci, *Personal Communications Systems Applications*. Upper Saddle River, NJ: Prentice Hall, 1997, pp. 109-118.
9. G. Anastasi et al, "MAC Protocols for Wideband Wireless Local Access: Evolution Toward Wireless ATM," *IEEE Personal Communications*, Oct. 1998, pp. 53-64.
10. S. Nannicini and T. Pecorella, "Performance evaluation of polling protocols for data transmission on wireless communication networks," *Proceedings of IEEE 1998 International Conference on Universal Personal Communications,* 1998, vol. 2, pp. 1241-1245.
11. R. Fantacci and L. Zoppi, "Performance Evaluation of Polling Systems for Wireless Local Communication Networks," *IEEE Transactions on Vehicular Technology*, vol. 49, no. 6, Nov. 2000, pp. 2148-2157.
12. B. P. Tsankov, R. A. Pachamanov, and D. A. Pachamanova, "Modified Brady voice traffic model for WLAN and WMAN," *Electronics Letters,* vol. 43, no. 23, Nov. 2007.
13. Z. Changping et al., "Performance analysis of a wireless local area networks (WLAN) in a coal-mine tunnel environment," *Mining Science and Technology*, vol. 20, 2010, pp. 0629-0634.
14. Z. Yang et al., "Performance analysis of rate-adaptive cooperative MAC based on wireless local area networks," *The Journal of China Universities of Posts and Telecommunications,* vol. 16, no. 5, 2009, pp. 78-85.
15. B. P. Tsankov, R. A. Pachamanov, and D. A. Pachamanova, "Modified Brady voice traffic model for WLAN and WMAN," *Electronics Letters,* vol. 43, no. 23, Nov. 2007.
16. Z. Changping et al., "Performance analysis of a wireless local area networks (WLAN) in a coal-mine tunnel environment," *Mining Science and Technology*, vol. 20, 2010, pp. 0629-0634.
17. Z. Yang et al., "Performance analysis of rate-adaptive cooperative MAC based on wireless local area networks," *The Journal of China Universities of Posts and Telecommunications,* vol. 16, no. 5, 2009, pp. 78-85.
18. T. S. Rappaport, *Wireless Communications: Principles and Practice*. Upper Saddle River, NJ: Prentice-Hall, 2001, pp. 324-327.
19. B. Bing, *Broadband Wireless Access.* Boston, MA: Kluwer Academic Publishers, 2000, pp. 65-68.
20. C. M. Akujuobi and M. N. O. Sadiku, *Introduction to Broadband Communication Systems.* Boca Raton, FL: CRC Press, 2008.
21. P. V. Krishna et al., "An efficient approach for distributed dynamic channel allocation with queues for real-time and non-real-time traffic in cellular networks," *The Journal of Systems and Software*, vol. 28, 2009, pp. 1112-1124.
22. A. Hamad, E. Morsy, and S. Adel, "Performance analysis of a handoff scheme for two-tier cellular CDMA networks." *Egyptian Informatics Journal*, vol. 12, 2011, pp. 139-149.
23. S. M. Musa and N. F. Mir, "An analytical approach for mobility load balancing in wireless networks," *Journal of Computation and Information Technology*, vol. 19, no. 3, 2011, pp. 169-176.

Chapter 10
Self-Similarity of Network Traffic

Everybody wants to live longer but nobody wants to grow old.

—Jules Rostand

In 1993, it was found out that there are modeling problems with using Markovian statistics to describe data traffic. A series of experiments on Ethernet traffic revealed that the traffic behavior was fractal-like in nature and exhibit self-similarity, i.e. the statistical behavior was similar across many different time scales (seconds, hours, etc.) [1, 3]. Also, several research studies on traffic on wireless networks revealed that the existence of self-similar or fractal properties at a range of time scale from seconds to weeks. This scale-invariant property of data or video traffic means that the traditional Markovian traffic models used in most performance studies do not capture the fratal nature of computer network traffic. This has implications in buffer and network design. For example, the buffer requirements in multiplexers and switches will be incorrectly predicted. Thus, self-similar models, which can capture burstiness (see Fig. 10.1) over several time scales, may be more appropriate.

In fact, it has been suggested that many theoretical models based on Markovian statistics should be reevaluated under self-similar traffic before practical implementation potentially show their faults.

Self-similarity is the property of an object which "looks the same" when viewed at different scales [4].

Self-similarity describes the phenomenon where a certain property of an object is preserved with respect to scaling in space and/or time. That is, as one zooms in or

M.N.O. Sadiku and S.M. Musa, *Performance Analysis of Computer Networks*,
DOI 10.1007/978-3-319-01646-7_10, © Springer International Publishing Switzerland 2013

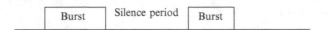

Fig. 10.1 An example of a burst traffic

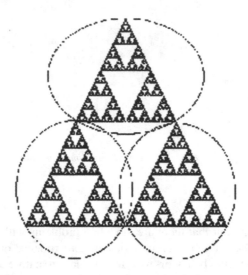

Fig. 10.2 The Sierpinski triangle

out the object has a similar (sometimes exact) appearance. For example, if an object is self-similar or fractal, its parts, when magnified resemble the shape of the whole. This idea is easily illustrated using the Sierpinski triangle (also known as Sierpinski gasket named after the Polish mathematician) shown in Fig. 10.2. The triangle S consists of three self-similar copies of itself, each with magnification of 2. We can look further and find more copies of S. The triangle S also consists of nine self-similar copies of itself, each with magnification of 4. Or we may cut S into 27 self-similar pieces, each with magnification factor 8. This kind of self-similarity at all scales is a hallmark of the images known as fractals.

Another example is the well known Koch snowflake curve shown in Fig. 10.3. As one successively zooms in the resulting shape is exactly the same no matter how far in the zoom is applied. A far more common type of self similarity is an approximate one, i.e. as one looks at the object at different scales one sees structures that are recognizably similar but not exactly so.

This chapter attempts to account for the self-similar traffic. We begin by first introducing the mathematics of self-similar process. We then present Pareto distribution as a typical example of a heavy-tailed distribution. We investigate the behavior of single queueing system with interarrival times having a large variance. We finally consider wireless networks with self-similar input traffic.

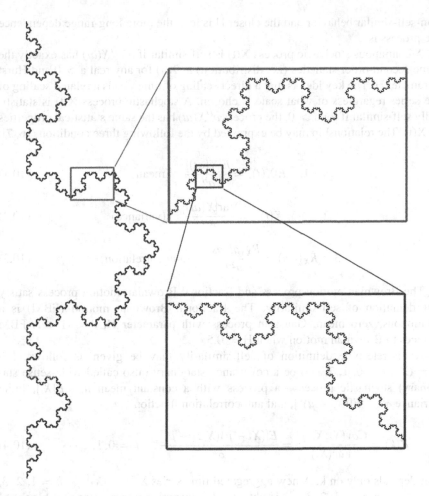

Fig. 10.3 Koch snowflake curve

10.1 Self-Similar Processes

Self-similar processes are stochastic processes, which can be described mathematically. They can be described by their characteristic of being scale-invariant. They are also characterized by fractal (i.e. fractional) dimensions, of which a number have been defined. One of these dimensions is the correlation dimension. A perfectly self-similar process on the average looks exactly the same regardless of the time scale observed.

Self-similarity manifests itself in a variety of ways: traffic appearing fractal-like, a spectral density obeying a power-law behavior, long-range dependence, slowly decaying variance, etc. [5]. The degree of self-similarity of a process is typically specified by the Hurst parameter H, where $0.5 < H < 1.0$. 0.5 represents non-self-similar behavior and the closer H is to 1, the more long-range dependence the process is.

A continuous stochastic process X(t) is self-similar if $a^{-H}X(at)$ has exactly the same second-order statistics (i.e. distribution) as X(t) for any real a > 0 and Hurst parameter H. The key idea is that a direct scaling of time yields a related scaling of the series regardless of what scale is chosen. A stochastic process X(t) is statistically self-similar if for a > 0, the process $a^H X(at)$ has the same statistical properties as X(t). The relationship may be expressed by the following three conditions [6, 7]:

$$1. \quad E[X(t)] = \frac{E[X(at)]}{a^H} \quad \text{(mean)} \tag{10.1}$$

$$2. \quad \text{Var}[X(t)] = \frac{\text{Var}[X(at)]}{a^{2H}} \quad \text{(variance)} \tag{10.2}$$

$$3. \quad R_X(t,s) = \frac{R_X(at, as)}{a^{2H}} \quad \text{(autocorrelation)} \tag{10.3}$$

The Brownian motion process and fractional Brownian motion process satisfy our definition of self-similarity. The fractional Brownian motion (FBM) is a continuous, zero mean, Gaussian process with parameter H, $0 < H < 1$. FBM reduces to Brownian motion when H $= 0.5$.

A discrete-time definition of self-similarity may be given as follows. Let $X = (X_t : t = 0, 1, 2, \cdots)$ be a covariance stationary (also called wide-sense stationary) stochastic process—a process with a constant mean $\mu = E[X_t]$, finite variance $\sigma^2 = E[(X_t - \mu)^2]$, and autocorrelation function

$$R(k) = \frac{Cov(X_t, X_{t+k})}{Var(X_t)} = \frac{E[(X_t - \mu)(X_{t+k} - \mu)]}{\sigma^2}, \quad k = 0, 1, 2, \cdots \tag{10.4}$$

that depends only on k. A new aggregated time series $X^{(m)} = (X_k^{(m)} : k = 1, 2, 3, \ldots)$ for each m $= 1, 2, 3, \ldots$ is obtained by averaging non-overlapping blocks of size m from the original series X. In other words,

$$X_k^{(m)} = \frac{(X_{km-m+1} + \ldots + X_{km})}{m}$$

For example,

$$X_k^{(3)} = \frac{X_{3k-2} + X_{3k-1} + X_{3k}}{3}$$

A process X is self-similar with parameter β $(0 < β < 1)$ if

$$\text{Var}\left[X^{(m)}\right] = \frac{\text{Var}[X]}{m^β} \quad \text{(variance)} \tag{10.5a}$$

$$R_{X(m)}(k) = R_X(k) \quad \text{(autocorrelation)} \tag{10.5b}$$

We also assume that X has autocorrelation function of the form

$$R(k) \sim L(t)k^{-\beta} \quad \text{as} \quad k \to \infty \tag{10.6}$$

where $0 < \beta < 1$, the symbol $\sim$ means "behaves asymptotically as," and $L(t)$ is "slowly varying" at infinity, i.e.

$$\lim_{t \to \infty} \frac{L(tx)}{L(t)} = 1 \tag{10.7}$$

This self-similar process has self-similarity Hurst parameter

$$H = 1 - \beta/2 \tag{10.8}$$

There are two important characteristics of self-similar processes [6–10]. The first feature has to do with the their *long-range dependence* (LRD), i.e. their autocorrelation function decays hyperbolically (less than exponentially fast). Equation (10.5a) implies this. In spite of the serious effects of this characteristic on queueing behavior, it cannot be accounted for in Markovian traffic models. For short range dependent (SRD) processes, such as the traditional traffic models, their functions show a fast exponential decay. The two concepts of self-similarity and long-range dependence are often used interchangeably to mean the same thing.

The second feature of self-similar process is the *slowly decaying variance* (SDV). The variance of the sample mean decays more slowing than the reciprocal of the sample size:

$$\text{Var}\left[X^{(m)}\right] \approx a_1 m^{-\beta}, \quad m \to \infty \tag{10.9}$$

a_1 is a positive constant and $H = 1 - \beta/2$. This result indicates that the process has infinite variance. However, this result differs from traditional Markovian models where the variance is given by

$$\text{Var}\left[X^{(m)}\right] \approx a_1 m^{-1} \tag{10.10}$$

10.2   Pareto Distribution

Another issue related to self-similarity is that of heavy-tailed distribution. In fact, to produce self-similar behavior, the traffic model should employ heavy-tailed distribution with infinite variance. A distribution is heavy-tailed if [11]

$$\text{Prob}[X > x] = 1 - F(x) \approx \frac{1}{x^\alpha} \tag{10.11}$$

where $1 < \alpha < 2$. One of the distributions that are heavy-tailed is the Pareto distribution, which is defined as

$$\text{Prob}[X > x] = \left(\frac{\delta}{x}\right)^{\alpha} \tag{10.12}$$

where δ is a parameter which indicates the minimum value that the distribution can take, i.e. $x \geq \delta$ and α is the shape parameter ($1 \leq \alpha \leq 2$), which describes the intensity of self-similarity. α also determines the mean and variance of X. Thus, the cumulative distribution function is

$$F(x) = 1 - \left(\frac{\delta}{x}\right)^{\alpha} \tag{10.13a}$$

while the probability density function is

$$f(x) = \frac{\alpha}{\delta}\left(\frac{\delta}{x}\right)^{\alpha+1} \tag{10.13b}$$

The mean value of the Pareto distribution is

$$E(X) = \delta\frac{\alpha}{1-\alpha} \tag{10.14}$$

For our purposes, it is convenient to set $\delta = 1$.

It is common in simulating self-similar traffic to assume that the packet interarrival times are independent, identically distributed according to a Pareto distribution [12, 13]. The Pareto distribution is a distribution with memory, heavy tail, and strong burstiness. It can have finite mean and infinite variance depending on the value of one of its parameters. It has been shown that the ON/OFF source model with heavy-tailed distribution reproduces the self-similar traffic [14]. The lengths of the ON-periods are identically distributed and so are the lengths of the OFF-periods. Traffic obtained through infinite radix multiplexing of ON/OFF source traffic so that the ON interval or the OFF period follows a Pareto distribution is not as Fractional Gaussian Noise (FGN).

Example 10.1 Let there be a queue with time-slotted arrival process of packets. The load is 0.5 and there is a batch arriving according to Bernoulli process such that

$$\text{Prob}[\text{there is a batch in a time slot}] = 0.25$$

so that the mean number of arrivals in any batch is 2. Calculate the probability of having more than x arrivals in any time slot if the batch size is: (a) exponentially distributed, (b) Pareto-distributed.

Solution

(a) $\text{Prob}[\text{batch size} > x] = e^{-x/2}$

so that

$$\text{Prob}[> 10 \text{ arrivals in a time slot}] = \text{Prob}[\text{batch size} > 10]$$
$$\times \text{Prob}[\text{there is a batch in a time slot}]$$
$$= e^{-10/2} \times 0.25 = 0.001684$$

(b) In this case, assuming $\delta = 1$,

$$E[X] = 1\frac{\alpha}{\alpha - 1} = 2$$

or

$$\alpha = \frac{E[X]}{E[X] - 1} = 2$$

Thus,

$$\text{Prob}[\text{batch size} > x] = \left(\frac{1}{x}\right)^2$$

$$\text{Prob}[> 10 \text{ arrivals in a time slot}] = \text{Prob}[\text{batch size} > 10]$$
$$\times \text{Prob}[\text{there is a batch in a time slot}]$$
$$= \left(\frac{1}{10}\right)^2 \times 0.25 = 0.0025$$

For the two distributions, the probability is of the same order of magnitude. This indicates that for a batch size of greater than 10 arrivals, there is not much difference between the two distributions. However, there would be significant difference is we try more than 100 arrivals. For exponential case,

$$\text{Prob}[> 100 \text{ arrivals in a time slot}] = e^{-100/2} \times 0.25 = 4.822 \times 10^{-23}$$

and for Pareto case

$$\text{Prob}[> 100 \text{ arrivals in a time slot}] = \left(\frac{1}{100}\right)^2 \times 0.25 = 2.5 \times 10^{-5}$$

10.3 Generating and Testing Self-Similar Traffic

A proper way of modeling network traffic is a prerequisite for an adequate design of networks. Several approaches have been developed for modeling self-similar traffic. These include the random midpoint displacement algorithm, on-off model, and wavelet transformation [15].

10.3.1   Random Midpoint Displacement Algorithm

This algorithm is used for generating Fractional Brownian Motion (FBM) with Hurst parameter $H \in (0.5,1)$ in a given time interval. If the trajectory of FBM $Z(t)$ is to be computed in the interval $[0,T]$, we start by setting $Z(0) = 0$ and $Z(T)$ from a Gaussian distribution with mean 0 and variance T^{2H}. Next $Z(T/2)$ is calculated as the average of $Z(0)$ and $Z(T)$ plus an offset δ_1, i.e.

$$Z(T/2) = \frac{1}{2}[Z(0) + Z(T)] + \delta_1 \qquad (10.15)$$

where δ_1 is a Gaussian random variable with zero mean and a standard deviation given by T^{2H} times the initial scaling factor s_1, i.e.

$$\Delta_1 = T^{2H}.s_1 = \frac{T^{2H}}{2^H}\sqrt{1 - 2^{2H-2}} \qquad (10.16)$$

The two intervals from 0 to T/2 and from T/2 to T are further subdivided and we reduce the scaling factor by $\frac{1}{2^H}$ and so on. At the nth stage, a random Gaussian variable δ_n is added to the midpoint of the stage $n - 1$ with a variance.

$$\Delta_n = \frac{T^{2H}}{(2^n)^H}\sqrt{1 - 2^{2H-2}} \qquad (10.17)$$

Once a given point has been determined, its value remains unchanged in all later stages. As H goes to 1, Δ_n goes to 0 and $Z(t)$ remains a collection of smooth line segment connecting the starting points.

10.3.2   On-Off Model

This traffic model is aggregated by multiple single ON/OFF traffic source. In other words, traffic is generated by a large number of independent ON/OFF sources such as workstations in a large computer network. An ON/OFF source is a burst traffic source which alternates active (ON) with silent (OFF) periods. During an active period (that is, a burst), data is generated at a fixed peak rate, while during silent periods no data is generated. Every individual ON/OFF source generates an ON/OFF process consisting of alternating ON- and OFF-periods. The lengths of the ON-periods are identically distributed and so are the lengths of OFF-periods. The ON/OFF source model with the "heavy-tailed" (Pareto-like) distribution reproduces the self-similar traffic. In other words, the superposition of many independent and identically distributed (i.i.d.) ON/OFF sources results in self-similar aggregate traffic.

Suppose there are N traffic sources, let the ON time of the ith traffic by $\tau^{(i)}$ and OFF time be $\theta^{(i)}$. The random variables $\tau^{(i)}$ and $\theta^{(i)}$ are i.i.d.; they satisfy

$$P(X > t) \sim at^{-\alpha}, \quad \text{with } t \to \infty, 1 < \alpha < 2 \tag{10.18}$$

where X is the length of the ON or OFF period. Since Pareto distribution is the simplest example of a heavy-tailed distribution, we may say that X follows Pareto distribution with finite mean and infinite variance.

There are several statistical methods that can be used for testing the time scale of self-similarity in traffic generation. These methods are used in the estimation of the Hurst parameter. They include R-S (Rescaled adjusted Range statistic) analysis and Variance-Time analysis.

Variance-Time Analysis

The method applies the following fact. The process X is said to be exactly *second-order self-similar* with Hurst parameter

$$H = 1 - \frac{\beta}{2} \quad (0 < \beta < 2) \tag{10.19}$$

if, for any m = 1, 2, 3, ...,

$$Var\left(X^{(m)}\right) \propto m^{-\beta} \tag{10.20}$$

We take advantage of this equation. Taking the logarithm of both sides results in

$$\log\left[Var\left(X^{(m)}\right)\right] = c_1 - \beta\log(m) \tag{10.21}$$

for some constant c_1. Plotting $\log[Var(X^{(m)})]$ versus $\log(m)$ (i.e. a log-log graph) for many values of m of a self-similar process will result in a linear series of points with slope $-\beta$ or $2H - 2$. This plot is known as a *variance-time plot*.

R-S Analysis

This is rescaled-adjusted range method. It obtains H based on overlapped data windows. Define a sequence $X_i (i = 1, 2, 3, ..., M)$. Let $\overline{X}_M$ and $S(M)$ be the sample mean and the sample variance of the sequence respectively. We evaluate

$$W_0, W_m = \sum_{i=1}^{m} X_i - m\overline{X}(m), \quad m = 1, 2, 3, ..., M \tag{10.22}$$

The adjusted range is defined as

$$R(M) = Max(W_m) - Min(W_m), \quad 0 \le m \le M \tag{10.23}$$

The ratio R(M)/S(M) is called the rescaled adjusted range or R/S statistic. The log of R/S statistics (for several values of M) plotted against log(M) will have an asymptotic slope, which is the approximation of H.

10.4 Single Queue

Classical modeling techniques of queues assume Poisson arrival rates. However, several different types of input processes have been found to exhibit self-similar or fractal-like behavior. In this section, we consider the performance of a single server queue with interarrival times having a large variance [16, 17].

Let X be the random variable denoting the interarrival time of packets. X is assumed to have a Gamma distribution, i.e. the packet interarrival times are assumed to have a Gamma distribution.

$$f_X(t) = \frac{r\lambda(r\lambda t)^{r-1}}{\Gamma(r)} e^{-r\lambda t}, \quad \lambda, t > 0, 0 < r < 1 \tag{10.24}$$

Packet interarrival times which have a Gamma distribution with a specific range of parameter values give large values of variances. The service time is assumed to be exponentially distributed with parameter μ. The results of the G/M/1 queue can be readily used. Let p_n be the probability that k packets are in the queue at the arrival moment. Then

$$p_n = (1 - \sigma)\sigma^k \tag{10.25}$$

where σ is the unique root of

$$\sigma = F_X(\mu - \mu\sigma), \quad 0 < \sigma < 1 \tag{10.26}$$

$F_X(s)$ is the Laplace transform of $f_X(t)$.

$$F_X(s) = \int_0^\infty f_X(t)e^{-st}dt = \left(\frac{r\lambda}{s + r\lambda}\right)^r \tag{10.27}$$

If W_q is the random variable which denotes the waiting time of a packet in the queue, the mean and variance of W_q are respectively

$$E(W_q) = \frac{\sigma}{\mu(1-\sigma)} \tag{10.28}$$

$$\text{Var}(W_q) = \sigma_{W_q}^2 = \frac{1-(1-\sigma)^2}{\mu^2(1-\sigma)^2} \tag{10.29}$$

The complimentary queue waiting time distribution is

$$\text{Prob}(W_q > t) = \sigma e^{-\mu(1-\sigma)t}, \quad t \geq 0 \tag{10.30}$$

It remains to solve for σ. The value of σ is evaluated as follows. Using Eqs. (10.26) and (10.27),

$$\sigma = \left(\frac{r\rho}{1-\sigma+r\rho}\right)^r \tag{10.31}$$

where $\rho = \lambda/\mu$. If we define

$$z = \frac{r\rho}{1-\sigma+r\rho} \tag{10.32}$$

then

$$\sigma = 1 + r\rho - \frac{r\rho}{z} \tag{10.33}$$

From Eqs. (10.31) to (10.33), we obtain

$$z = \frac{r\rho}{(1+r\rho)} + \frac{z^{r+1}}{(1+r\rho)} \tag{10.34}$$

which can be evaluated using Lagrange series. Now we let

$$z = a + \xi\phi(z), \quad a = r\rho/(1+r\rho), \quad \xi = 1/(1+r\rho), \quad \text{and} \quad \phi(z) = z^{r+1} \tag{10.35}$$

in the Lagrange series expansion, we get

$$z = \sum_{n=0}^{\infty} \frac{\xi^n \Gamma(nr+n+1)}{n!\Gamma(nr+2)} a^{nr+1} \tag{10.36}$$

This series can be summed by letting

$$z = \sum_{n=0}^{\infty} d_n \tag{10.37}$$

where

$$d_n = \frac{\xi^n}{n!} \frac{\Gamma(nr + n + 1)}{\Gamma(nr + 2)} a^{nr+1} \tag{10.38}$$

The values of d_n can be evaluated recursively as follows.

$$d_0 = a$$

$$d_1 = \xi a^r d_0 \tag{10.39}$$

$$d_2 = \xi a^r (r + 1) d_1$$

$$d_n = b_n d_{n-1}, \quad n \geq 3$$

where

$$b_n = \xi a^r (r + 1) \prod_{k=1}^{n-2} \frac{(nr + k + 1)}{(nr - r + k + 1)}, \quad n \geq 3 \tag{10.40}$$

Only a finite number of terms in Eq. (10.37) is needed in practice. Once we calculate z using Eq. (10.38), we use Eq. (10.33) to obtain σ.

One should keep in mind that the application of self-similar traffic model does not mean that traditional queueing analysis is now irrelevant. It only means that under certain conditions, performance analysis critically depend on taking self-similarity into account.

10.5   Wireless Networks

Although self-similarity was originally found for Ethernet traffic [1, 2, 18], research has shown that the same holds for wireless networks [19]. This implies that simulating a wireless network with Poisson distributed input traffic will give wrong results.

A logistic function or logistic curve can be described by the following differential equation.

$$\frac{dP}{dt} = rP\left(1 - \frac{P}{K}\right) \tag{10.41}$$

where P is population size, K is capacity, and t is time. Setting $x = P/K$ in Eq. (10.41) gives

$$\frac{dx}{dt} = rx(1 - x) \tag{10.42}$$

Logistic map is a discrete representation of Eq. (10.42) and is written as recurrence relation as follows:

$$x_{n+1} = rx_n(1 - x_n) \tag{10.43}$$

This equation has been used to obtain self-similar time sequence which could be used for traffic generation for wireless network systems [19]. Values of r in the range $3.50 < r < 3.88$ and $0 < x_0 < 0.5$ have been used.

10.6 Summary

1. Studies of both Ethernet traffic and variable bit rate (VBR) video have demonstrated that these traffics exhibit self-similarity. A self-similar phenomenon displays the same or similar statistical properties when viewed at different times scales.
2. Pareto distribution is a heavy-tailed distribution with infinite variance and is used in modeling self-similar traffic.
3. The most common method of generating self-similar traffic is to simulate several sources that generate constant traffic and then multiplex then with ON/OFF method using heavy-tailed distribution such as Pareto.
4. We analytically modeled the performance of a single server queue with almost self-similar input traffic and exponentially distributed service times.
5. Logistic map for self-similar traffic generation is used for wireless network.
6. OPNET can be used to simulate the network traffic's self-similarity [20].

Problems

10.1 (a) Explain the concept of self-similarity.
  (b) What is a self-similar process?
10.2 Show that the Brownian motion process B(t) with parameter $H = 1/2$ is self-similar. Hint: Prove that B(t) satisfy conditions in Eqs. (10.1) to (10.3).
10.3 Show that the Eq. (10.14) is valid and that the variance of Pareto distribution is infinite.

10.4 If X is a random variable with a Pareto distribution with parameters α and δ, then show that the random variable $Y = \ln (X/\delta)$ has an exponential distribution with parameter α.

10.5 Evaluate and plot σ in Eq. (10.24) for $0 < \rho < 0.2$ with $r = 0.01$.

References

1. W. E. Leland et al., "On the self-similar nature of Ethernet traffic," *Computer Communications Review*, vol. 23, Oct. 1993, pp. 183-193.
2. –, "On the self-similar nature of Ethernet traffic (extended version)," *IEEE/ACM Transactions on Networking*, vol. 5, no. 6, Dec. 1997, pp. 835-846.
3. M. E. Crovella and A. Bestavros, "Self-similarity in World Wide Web traffic: Evidence and possible causes," *IEEE/ACM Transactions on Networking*, vol. 5, no. 6, Dec. 1997, pp. 835-846.
4. C. D. Cairano-Gilfedder and R. G. Cleggg, "A decade of internet research—advances in models and practices," *BT Technology Journal*, vol. 23, no. 4, Oct. 2005, pp. 115-128.
5. B. Tsybakov and N. D. Georganas, "On self-similar traffic in ATM queues: definitions, overflow probability bound, and cell delay distribution," *IEEE/ACM Transactions on Networking*, vol. 5, no. 3, June 1997, pp. 397-409.
6. W. Stallings, *High-Speed Networks and Internets: Performance and Quality of Service*. Upper Saddle, NJ: Prentice Hall, 2nd ed., 2002, pp. 219-247.
7. W. Jiangto and Y. Geng, "An intelligent method for real-time detection of DDOS attack based on fuzzy logic," Journal of Electronics (China), vol. 25, no. 4, July 2008, pp. 511-518.
8. D. Kouvatsos (ed.), *Performance Evaluation and Applications of ATM Networks*. Boston, MA: Kluwer Academic Publishers, 2000, pp. 355-386.
9. A. Ost, *Performance of Communication Systems*. New York: Springer Verlag, 2001, pp. 171-177.
10. K. Park and W. Willinger (eds.), *Self-similar Network Traffic and Performance Evaluation*. New York: John Wiley & Sons, 2000.
11. J.M. Pitts and J. A. Schormans, *Introduction to IP and ATM Design and Performance*. Chichester, UK: John Wiley & Sons, 2000, pp. 287-298.
12. Z. Harpantidou and M. Paterakis, "Random multiple access of broadcast channels with Pareto distributed packet interarrival times," *IEEE Personal Communications*, vol. 5, no. 2, April 1998, pp. 48-55.
13. Z. Hadzi-Velkov and L. Gavrilovska, "Performance of the IEEE 802.11 wireless LANs under influence of hidden terminals and Pareto distributed packet traffic," *Proceedings of IEEE International Conference on Personal Wireless Communication*, 1999, pp. 221-225.
14. W. Willinger et al., "Self-similarity through high-variability: statistical analysis of Ethernet LAN traffic at the source level," *IEEE/ACM Transactions on Networking*, vol. 5, no. 1, 1997, pp. 71-86.
15. A. R. Prasad, B. Stavrov, and F. C. Schoute, "Generation and testing of self-similar traffic in ATM networks," IEEE International Conference on Personal Wireless Communications, 1996, pp. 200-205.
16. N. Bhatnagar, "Model of a queue with almost self-similar or fractal-like traffic," *Proc. IEEE GLOBECOM '97*, 1997, pp. 1424-1428.
17. E. Y. Peterson and P. M. Ulanov, "Methods for simulation of self-similar traffic in computer networks," *Automatic Control and Computer Science*, vol. 36, no. 6, 2002, pp. 62-69.
18. M. S. Taqqu, "The modeling of Ethernet data and of signals that are heavy-tailed with infinite variance." *Scandinavian Journal of Statistics*, vol. 29, 2002, pp. 273-295.

19. R. Yeryomin and E. Petersons, "Generating self-similar traffic for wireless network simulation," *Proc. of Baltic Congress of Future Internet and Communications*, 2011, pp. 218-220.
20. Y. Fei et al., "An intrusion alarming system based on self-similarity of network traffic," *Wuhan University Journal of Natural Sciences* (WUJNS), vol. 10, no. 1, 2005, pp. 169-173.

Appendix A: Derivation for M/G/1 Queue

In this appendix, we apply the *method of z-transform* or generating functions to find the waiting time of the M/G/1 model.

The probability of having k arrivals during the service time t is

$$p_k = \int_0^\infty p(k)dH(t) = \int_0^\infty \frac{(\lambda t)^k}{k!} e^{-\lambda t} dH(t) \tag{A.1}$$

where H(t) is the service time distribution.

Let N be the number of customers present in the system and Q be the number of customers in the queue. Let the probability that an arriving customer finds j other customers present be

$$\Pi_j = \text{Prob}(N = j), \quad j = 0, 1, 2, \cdots \tag{A.2}$$

It can be shown using the theorem of total probability and the equilibrium imbedded-Markov-chain that

$$\Pi_j = p_j \Pi_0 + \sum_{i=1}^{j+1} p_{j-i+1} \Pi_i, \quad j = 0, 1, 2, \cdots \tag{A.3}$$

We define the probability-generating functions

$$g(z) = \sum_{j=0}^\infty \Pi_j z^j \tag{A.4a}$$

$$h(z) = \sum_{j=0}^\infty p_j z^j \tag{A.4b}$$

M.N.O. Sadiku and S.M. Musa, *Performance Analysis of Computer Networks*,
DOI 10.1007/978-3-319-01646-7, © Springer International Publishing Switzerland 2013

Substituting (Eq. A.4a) into (Eq. A.3) results in

$$g(z) = \frac{(z-1)h(z)}{z - h(z)}\Pi_0 \qquad\qquad (A.5)$$

The normalization equation

$$\sum_{j=0}^{\infty} \Pi_j = 1 \qquad\qquad (A.6)$$

implies that g(1) = 1. With a single application of L'Hopital's rule, we find

$$\Pi_0 = 1 - \rho \qquad\qquad (A.7)$$

where $\rho = \lambda/\mu = \lambda\tau$. If we define $\eta(s)$ as the Laplace-Stieltjes transform of the service-time distribution function H(t),

$$\eta(s) = \int_0^{\infty} e^{-st} dH(t) \qquad\qquad (A.8)$$

Substitution of (Eq. A.1) into (Eq. A.4b) yields

$$h(z) = \eta(\lambda - \lambda z) \qquad\qquad (A.9)$$

and substitution of (Eq. A.7) and (Eq. A.9) into (Eq. A.5) leads to

$$g(z) = \frac{(z-1)\eta(\lambda - \lambda z)}{z - \eta(\lambda - \lambda z)}(1 - \rho) \qquad\qquad (A.10)$$

Differentiating this and applying L'Hopital rule twice, we obtain

$$g'(1) = \frac{\rho^2}{2(1-\rho)}\left(1 + \frac{\sigma^2}{\tau^2}\right) + \rho \qquad\qquad (A.11)$$

The mean values of the number of customers in the system and queue are respectively given by

$$E(N) = \sum_{j=0}^{\infty} j\Pi_j = g'(1) \qquad\qquad (A.12a)$$

$$E(Q) = E(N) - \rho \qquad\qquad (A.12b)$$

By applying Little's theorem, the mean value of the response time is

$$E(T) = \frac{E(N)}{\lambda} = \frac{\rho\tau}{2(1-\rho)}\left(1 + \frac{\sigma^2}{\tau^2}\right) + \tau$$

$$= E(W) + \tau$$

(A.13)

Thus we obtain the mean waiting time as

$$E(W) = \frac{E(Q)}{\lambda} = \frac{\rho\tau}{2(1-\rho)}\left(1 + \frac{\sigma^2}{\tau^2}\right)$$

which is *Pollaczek-Khintchine formula*.

Appendix B: Useful Formulas

$$\sum_{i=1}^{n} i = \frac{n}{2}(n+1)$$

$$\sum_{i=1}^{n} i^2 = \frac{n}{6}(n+1)(2n+1)$$

$$\sum_{i=1}^{n} i^3 = \left[\sum_{i=1}^{n} i\right]^2 = \frac{n^2}{4}(n+1)^2$$

$$\sum_{n=1}^{\infty} x^n = \frac{1}{1-x}, \quad |x| < 1$$

$$\sum_{n=k}^{\infty} x^n = \frac{x^k}{1-x}, \quad |x| < 1$$

$$\sum_{n=1}^{k} x^n = \frac{x - x^{k+1}}{1-x}, \quad x \neq 1$$

$$\sum_{n=0}^{k} x^n = \frac{1 - x^{k+1}}{1-x}, \quad x \neq 1$$

$$\sum_{n=1}^{\infty} n x^n = \frac{x}{(1-x)^2}, \quad |x| < 1$$

$$\sum_{n=1}^{k} n x^n = x \frac{(1 - x^k) - k x^k (1-x)}{(1-x)^2}, \quad x \neq 1$$

M.N.O. Sadiku and S.M. Musa, *Performance Analysis of Computer Networks*,
DOI 10.1007/978-3-319-01646-7, © Springer International Publishing Switzerland 2013

$$\sum_{n=1}^{\infty} n^2 x^n = \frac{x(1+x)}{(1-x)^3}, \quad |x| < 1$$

$$\sum_{n=1}^{\infty} n(n+1)x^n = \frac{2x}{(1-x)^3}, \quad |x| < 1$$

$$\sum_{n=0}^{\infty} \frac{(n+k)!}{n!} x^n = \frac{k!}{(1-x)^{k+1}}, \quad |x| < 1, k \geq 0$$

$$\sum_{n=0}^{\infty} \frac{x^n}{n!} = e^x, \qquad -\infty < x < \infty$$

$$\sum_{n=0}^{\infty} \frac{x^n}{(n+1)!} = \frac{e^x - 1}{x}, \qquad -\infty < x < \infty$$

$$\sum_{n=1}^{\infty} \frac{x^n}{n} = \ln\left(\frac{1}{1-x}\right), \qquad |x| < 1$$

$$\sum_{n=1}^{\infty} \frac{x^{(2n-1)}}{(2n-1)!} = \frac{e^x - e^{-x}}{2}, \qquad -\infty < x < \infty$$

$$\sum_{n=0}^{\infty} \binom{N+n-1}{n} x^{-n} = \left(\frac{x}{x-1}\right)^N, \quad |x| < 1$$

$$\sum_{k=1}^{n} \binom{n}{k} x^k = (1+x)^n$$

Bibliography

1. C. M. Akujuobi and M. N. O. Sadiku, *Introduction to Broadband Communication Systems.* Boca Raton, FL: CRC Press, 2008.
2. D. Bertsekas and R. Gallaher, *Data Networks.* Englewood Cliffs, NJ: Prentice-Hall, 1987.
3. G. C. Cassandras, *Discrete Event Systems.* Boston, MA: Irwin, 1993.
4. W. C. Chan, *Performance Analysis of Telecommunications and Local Area Networks.* Boston, MA: Kluwer Academic Publishers, 2000.
5. J. D. Claiborne, *Mathematical Preliminaries for Computer Networking.* New York: John Wiley, 1990.
6. R. B. Cooper, *Introduction to Queueing Theory.* New York: North-Holland, 2nd ed., 1981.
7. G. R. Dattatreya, *Performance Analysis of Queuing and Computer Networks.* Boca Raton, FL: CRC Press, 2008.
8. E. Gelembe (ed.), *Computer System Performance Modeling in Perspective.* London, UK: Imperial College Press, 2006.
9. E. Gelenbe and G. Pujolle, *Introduction to Queueing Networks.* Chichester, UK: John Wiley & Sons, 1987.
10. D. Gross and C. M. Harris, *Fundamentals of Queueing Theory.* New York: John Wiley, 3rd ed., 1998.
11. A. M. Haghighi and D. P. Mishev, *Queueing Models in Industry and Business.* New York: Nova Science Publishers, 2008.
12. P. G. Harrison and N. M. Patel, *Performance Modelling of Communication Networks and Computer Architecture.* Wokingham, UK: Addison-Wesley, 1993.
13. D. P. Heyman (ed.), *Handbook in Operations Research and Management Science.* New York: North-Holland, 1990.
14. G. M. Higginbottom, Performance Evaluation of Communication Networks. Boston, MA: Artech House, 1998.
15. A. Holt, *Network Performance Analysis Using the J Programming Language.* London, UK: Springer-Verlag, 2008.
16. N. C. Hock, *Queueing Modelling Fundamentals.* Chichester, UK: John Wiley & Sons, 1996.
17. O. C. Ibe, *Fundamentals of Applied Probability and Random Processes.* Burlington, MA: Elsevier Academic Press, 2005.
18. O. C. Ibe, *Markov Processes for Stochastic Modeling.* Burlington, MA: Elsevier Academic Press, 2009.
19. R. Jain, *The Art of Computer Systems Performance Analysis.* New York: John Wiley, 1991.
20. K. Kant, Introduction to Computer System Performance Evaluation. New York: McGraw-Hill, 1992.
21. P. J. B. King, *Computer and Communication System Performance Modelling.* New York: Prentice Hall, 1989.

M.N.O. Sadiku and S.M. Musa, *Performance Analysis of Computer Networks,*
DOI 10.1007/978-3-319-01646-7, © Springer International Publishing Switzerland 2013

22. L. Kleinrock, *Queueing Systems*. New York: John Wiley, 1975, vol. I.
23. S. S. Lavenberg (ed.), *Computer Performance Modeling Handbook*. New York: Academic Press, 1983.
24. D. Maki and M. Thompson, *Mathematical modeling and Computer Simulation*. Belmont, CA: Thomson Brooks/Cole, 2006, pp. 153-211.
25. J. Medhi, *Stochastic Models in Queueing Theory*. San Diego, CA: Academic Press, 1991.
26. M. K. Molloy, *Fundamentals of Performance Modeling*. New York: MacMillan, 1989.
27. R. Nelson, *Probability, Stochastic Processes, and Queueing Theory*. New York: Springer-Verlag, 1995.
28. M. S. Obaidat and N. A. Boudriga, *Fundamentals of Performance Evaluation of Computer and Telecommunication Systems*. Hoboken, NJ: John Wiley & Sons, 2010.
29. T. G. Robertazzi, *Computer Networks and Systems: Queueing Theory and Performance Evaluation*. New York: Springer-Verlag, 1990.
30. S.M. Ross, Simulation. San Diego, CA: Academic Press, 3rd ed., 2002.
31. M. N. O. Sadiku and M. Ilyas, *Simulation of Local Area Networks*. Boca Raton, FL: CRC Press, 1995.
32. M. Schartz, *Telecommunication Networks*. Reading, MA: Addison-Wesley, 1987.

Index